Cognitive Behavioural
Counselling in Action

SAGE Counselling in Action
Series Editor: WINDY DRYDEN

SAGE Counselling in Action is a bestselling series of short, practical introductions designed for students and trainees. Covering theory and practice, the books are core texts for many courses, both in counselling and other professions such as nursing, social work and teaching. To celebrate its 20th Anniversary, SAGE has redesigned the series with a fresh, contemporary look to re-launch it into its next 20 years of widespread readership and success. Books in the series include:

Michael Jacobs
Psychodynamic Counselling in Action, Fourth Edition

Tim Bond
Standards and Ethics for Counselling in Action, Third Edition

Windy Dryden and Andrew Reeves
Key Issues for Counselling in Action, Second Edition

Dave Mearns and Brian Thorne
Person-Centred Counselling in Action, Third Edition

Ian Stewart
Transactional Analysis Counselling in Action, Third Edition

Sue Culley and Tim Bond
Integrative Counselling Skills in Action, Second Edition

Windy Dryden
Rational Emotive Behavioural Counselling in Action, Third Edition

Petrūska Clarkson
Gestalt Counselling in Action, Third Edition

Patricia D'Ardenne and Aruna Mahtini
Transcultural Counselling in Action, Second Edition

Cognitive Behavioural Counselling in Action

Second Edition

Peter Trower, Jason Jones, Windy Dryden and Andrew Casey

> ## SAGE Counselling in Action
> ### Series Editor Windy Dryden

Los Angeles | London | New Delhi
Singapore | Washington DC

First edition published 1988
Reprinted 1990, 1991, 1992, 1993, 1995, 1996, 1998, 1999,
2000, 2002, 2003, 2004 (twice), 2005, 2006, 2007
This second edition published 2011

SAGE Publications Ltd
1 Oliver's Yard
55 City Road
London EC1Y 1SP

SAGE Publications Inc.
2455 Teller Road
Thousand Oaks, California 91320

SAGE Publications India Pvt Ltd
B 1/I 1 Mohan Cooperative Industrial Area
Mathura Road
New Delhi 110 044

SAGE Publications Asia-Pacific Pte Ltd
33 Pekin Street #02-01
Far East Square
Singapore 048763

Library of Congress Control Number available

British Library Cataloguing in Publication data

A catalogue record for this book is available from the British Library

ISBN 978-1-84920-193-3
ISBN 978-1-84920-194-0 (pbk)

Typeset by C&M Digitals (P) Ltd, Chennai, India
Printed by CPI Antony Rowe, Chippenham, Wiltshire
Printed on paper from sustainable resources

Contents

1

What is Cognitive Behavioural Counselling?

Since the first edition of *Cognitive Behavioural Counselling in Action* (Trower, Casey and Dryden) was published in 1988, there has been an almost exponential growth in the development and applications of cognitive behavioural therapy (CBT). Within the UK, it is now government policy to make CBT widely available for a number of common emotional disorders. As part of this rapid growth, there are now many introductory texts, academic papers and case studies available. In fact, one would be forgiven for arguing that a second edition of *Cognitive Behavioural Counselling in Action* was unnecessary. However, the task facing counsellors and therapists has become more rather than less difficult because of this growth. New and rival theories and therapies have created the potential for confusion, and CBT arguably lacks theoretical clarity as a therapeutic system (Mansell, 2008a,b; Trower, in press). In our experience trainee counsellors and therapists often raise questions and problems while developing their competence in CBT that remain unanswered and unresolved, despite the proliferation of introductory texts and training courses. Our intention is to address these issues in this second edition. We do so by retaining what is helpful in the first edition, but also by addressing the difficulties that counsellors and therapists often have in developing their effectiveness in CBT.

In this edition we have therefore updated the CBC model and practice from the first edition, to include many of the key later developments in

CBT, and to address some of the basic principles of psychology that we consider either omitted or insufficiently addressed elsewhere. It is again designed for a wide range of problems but the less severe and complex of these problems.

There are two parts to this edition. The first is the Basic Guide, which aims to provide a clear and up-to-date evidence-based guide to CBC which takes the practitioner step-by-step through the actual process when face to face with the client, from initial contact to termination. The second part addresses how CBC can be applied to specific emotional problems.

Introduction to Cognitive Behavioural Counselling

An Integrated Approach

We have explicitly drawn our main inspiration for the second edition from the cognitive models of the two 'founding fathers' of CBT – the late Albert Ellis (Rational Emotive Behaviour Therapy or REBT) and Aaron T. Beck (Cognitive Therapy or CT) who continues to have a profound influence on the field. These models are similar in major respects; indeed Beck acknowledges Ellis's influence on his early formulation of CT (Beck, 1976, 2005). However, there are also important differences and the two models have different strengths.

Both the Beck and Ellis models can be summed up at the most general level by the proposal that people are not disturbed by events themselves directly but by the way they interpret those events – the famous principle attributed to the ancient Greek Stoic philosopher Epictetus.

In various of his many writings Beck proposed that emotional disorders are characterised at the 'surface' level by negative automatic thoughts (NATs) which intrude into clients' conscious minds often involuntarily, and negatively distort their perceptions and memories, leading to emotional and behavioural disturbances. A NAT might, for example, be a negative prediction that 'I will fail the test'.

Then clients have certain 'dysfunctional assumptions' at the second or intermediate and less conscious level, which are conditional propositions, for example 'If I fail at something, then I am a failure'.

At the third or deepest and least consciously accessible level are negative 'core beliefs' which are unconditional and accepted as truths about the self, the world and the future, such as 'I am a failure'.

The dysfunctional assumptions and core beliefs are components of cognitive schemas often established early in life which are activated by certain internal or external triggers, like a 'key in a lock' as Beck puts it. Once activated the schemas can lead to the cognitive distortions, and self-maintaining vicious cycles can then ensue. So in the above example, an exam will trigger a schema that contains the core belief 'I am a failure' and the dysfunctional assumption 'If I fail I will be a failure', the schema giving rise to NATs such as 'I will fail the test'.

Ellis's model similarly proposes that emotional disturbances are the consequence (C) of Beliefs (B) about adverse events (A), but differs from Beck in how he identifies beliefs. Ellis identified two types of Belief, namely inferences, which are if . . . then propositions which could be true or false, and evaluations, which are good–bad judgements. Ellis asserted that it is only certain specific rigid and extreme evaluations that he specified in his theory that can generate emotional disturbances.

We have drawn on the conceptual and empirically grounded strengths of both models in CBC. One of the strengths of Beck's CT that we have drawn on is the focus on NATs. Capturing NATs in ordinary everyday thinking is a task most clients can usually identify with, and helping them learn how to capture or 'catch' the NATs enables them to get a handle on the otherwise extremely elusive disturbance-inducing thoughts, and also to begin the process of decentring from them – both functions being essential for cognitive change. Another strength is the therapeutic process Beck originated in accessing the toxic beliefs and images embedded in the schemas out of which the NATs arise, and the methods by which these beliefs are restructured in cognitive therapy.

On the other hand, we have also drawn on some of Ellis's unique contributions, particularly the distinction between inferences and evaluations, between the specific irrational and rational beliefs and between healthy and unhealthy, qualitatively distinct, negative emotions. Lack of clarity in these two areas can, we believe, translate into confusion in assessment, formulation and intervention for both counsellor and client.

In brief, NATs can be thoughts or images, can be dysfunctional assumptions or core beliefs in Beck's terminology, or can be inferences or evaluations in Ellis's. Dysfunctional assumptions can be inferences or evaluations. Some core beliefs in Beck's system are one type of evaluation – those that are equivalent to self, other, life or future 'downing' in Ellis' system. In each of these cases, we believe it is important to be clear whether the client's NAT or dysfunctional assumption is an inference or an evaluation, and we give guidance on this in the relevant tasks in the Basic Guide.

How do you Feel?

This is probably one of the most important questions the counsellor will ask her client, so we think it may be helpful to invite you, as a counsellor, to answer the same question as part of our introduction to the CBC journey.

Just before you answer this question, stop and observe what you are doing. Be aware of the senses and processes you are using to determine your response. Normally, we spend most of our time oblivious to our emotional experiences or at least not consciously aware of them. Behind the scenes our emotions tend to power us along, enabling us to overcome obstacles we face and helping us to recognise when something we like or dislike happens. We typically only become aware of our emotions when they are particularly intense or problematic. Otherwise they are functional, beneficial and consistent with our experiences. Distress tells us that something is wrong, and we become aware of the discomfort or the behaviour associated with our emotional response to an experience. So, how do you feel?

If you started to consider your response to this question, you may have drawn on information from a range of sources. You may have considered what has been going on in your recent experiences or perhaps turning your attention to something that is due to happen to you in the near future. You may have heightened your awareness of your physical sensations, checking whether you are tense, relaxed, alert, or perhaps tired. You may have thought about what you are doing and what this tells you about your emotional experiences. You may have immediately started to think about what you are feeling, trying to locate some capsule of here and now experience. If you are currently having problems in life, you may have already been more acutely aware of your emotional experiences. You might feel anxious or concerned about some event in your short- or mid-term future. You might feel depressed or sad about something that has happened recently. Perhaps you feel hurt, shame, anger, envy or a range of other emotions. You might even be feeling more than one, right now. The answer to the question is in our view the key to understanding the cognitive behavioural approach to counselling and psychotherapy. If you can answer this specific question accurately, we think you are more than halfway towards understanding how you can use this knowledge to help the clients you work with.

When you first read the question 'How do you feel?', you might have responded in a habitual manner. Consider how many times you have asked this question within your everyday life. There might be variations, such as

'How are you?', 'Are you well?', but most of the time when we ask such questions we are not usually expecting others to reveal their physical well-being, offering you a specification of every ache or pain. No, usually we are enquiring about the other person's general well-being. Most people respond to this question in a habitual manner. Responses such as 'Fine', 'OK' or 'Good' are commonplace. However, when you as a counsellor ask this question of a client, you are not typically doing this as a standard aspect of a greeting. You are also not expecting the client to respond habitually, in their usual manner. Usually when a counsellor asks this question of a client, the counsellor expects the client to reveal something of their internal world, their current status or perhaps the problem they are experiencing. As a counsellor it might be necessary to place some context around the question, such as 'And how do you feel about that?' But when you ask this question in this context you are expecting the client to undertake the same process that we asked of you. We wanted you to reflect on and respond with your current emotional experience.

We are asking this question 'How are you feeling?' not only to stimulate thought, but also to show you just how difficult this question can be to answer. In the remainder of this chapter, step-by-step we will introduce the cognitive behavioural model of human emotions used in CBC. We feel strongly that this model can help you to understand how all of us, clients included, experience problems in a manner which we believe will enable you to facilitate real change for your clients.

One reason why the 'How are you feeling?' question is difficult to answer is because human emotion is complex. It is not just 'feeling', which is only one component of emotion. Emotion can be construed as a broad theoretical construct which encompasses an activating stimulus event of some kind, an appraisal process and a response, which is both the feeling and the closely associated actions tendencies (see Scherer, 2009 for a detailed account of the component process model of emotion). For the purposes of CBC, emotions can be viewed as capsules of experience, where the capsule is the ABC model used in CBC.

Formulating Emotions – the ABC Model of CBC

At the heart of CBC is the use of an ABC formulation of here and now emotional problems. Using an ABC structure is nothing new; it has featured in nearly all forms of the cognitive therapies in one form or another, and was first developed by Albert Ellis. Our core model is an integrated approach, using the fundamental principles of both Beck and Ellis, as we feel this is the most straightforward method that is both comprehensive and easily understood by counsellors and clients alike. The model is also in keeping with the understanding of emotions across the therapeutic and cognitive science literature (see Figure 1.1).

FIGURE 1.1   *A basic model of the relationships between events, cognition and emotion*

In the ABC model, the event is represented by A, which stands for Activating Event; and serendipitously also for Adverse Event or adversity; cognition is represented by B, or Beliefs; and emotion is represented by C, Consequences. Therefore, the central tenet is that Activating Events (A) lead to Beliefs (B) that in turn produce emotional and behavioural Consequences (C). It is important to note, that people do not experience As, Bs and Cs in an apparent temporal sequence. Rather, the ABC is an emotional episode which is experienced as a whole. However, for change to occur, it is important to identify the components and understand the relationships between them in order to carry out the necessary cognitive restructuring that is the raison d'être of all forms of CBT.

Let us consider the example of anxiety at the idea of having to give a presentation, a not infrequent anxiety, and the main problem in our illustrative Case Example in the Basic Guide. In the ABC model it is not the event of having to give a presentation at some point in the future (at A) that causes the emotion of anxiety (at C). Rather the inferences and evaluations made by the individual (at B) create the specific emotion and its associated Action Tendencies. The As can be past, present or future, Bs can comprise inferences (or memories, images or predictions) and evaluations (dysfunctional and functional), negative emotions can be functional (or healthy) or dysfunctional (unhealthy) and are closely associated with action tendencies (urges to act) and actual actions. As noted above, the client who feels anxious at the idea of having to give a presentation is unlikely to experience first a reminder of the event of giving a talk, then an inference and evaluation, and then the emotion in a temporal sequence like this. If this were within our everyday awareness we would already know how to help ourselves and question our beliefs. The problem is these experiences happen so quickly that our emotions usually seem to occur automatically and simultaneously when the A occurs, particularly in anxiety and anger. The ABC offers a memorable method of enabling your client to formulate their problems and so be prepared to commit to working to change.

A summary of the ABC model in CBC is presented in Figure 1.2. The basic premise is that as humans we encounter adversities (Activating Events at A), about which we infer beyond the available data and then evaluate those inferences (Beliefs at B), which in turn leads to our experience of emotion and our urges to act (Consequences at C). Also evident in Figure 1.2 is the connection from C to A (this is depicted as a dotted line because it is not always the case a C leads to an A). Many problems do feature this cyclical relationship (see Beck and Emery, 1985, for an explanation of the vicious cycle effect in anxiety disorders and phobias, and Chapter 6. For example, for many people with anxiety problems, anxiety would occur at C in the ABC model. This C then becomes a new A, so people then go on to make further inferences and evaluations about their experience of anxiety, which might lead to more anxiety or depression or anger, depending on the nature of the inferences and evaluations. In CBC this is a meta-emotional experience, a feeling about a feeling, and this can often have a debilitating impact on the individual, and be one of the factors that maintain a problem for very long periods of time. Meta-emotional experiences (to be distinguished from metacognitive

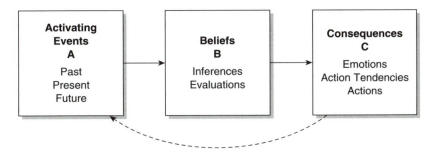

FIGURE 1.2 *The ABC model in CBC*

beliefs, which are beliefs about beliefs) are common across the emotional problems and in subsequent chapters we will show you how to consider this in your assessment process. Of course, meta-emotional problems can continue for many levels. For example, it is possible to feel anger, then shame, then anxiety and each of these can be understood in terms of interconnected ABCs, which can become self-maintaining vicious cycles. Examples of how this may manifest clinically are presented in Chapters 12 to 17.

An Emotional Life – or the C in the ABC Model

Developing understanding and knowledge about emotions has been a central theme in psychology, philosophy, cognitive science, counselling and psychological therapy. Some 20 years before Sigmund Freud established what we now know as psychotherapy, the psychologist William James was interested in why human beings experience emotion and how. He developed a theory that humans know what they feel when they are acting in accordance with their emotional experiences. In his often quoted example, he described how we would know we are scared of a bear because we may find ourselves running from the bear. The act of flight tells us that we are afraid. James (1890) had developed a behavioural-cognitive model of emotion. However, his thesis was limited by failing to address everyday emotional experience and our ability as humans to change what we feel. The difficulty lies in that James failed to explain why we ran from the bear in the first place. Therefore, this is an A–C model, where the emotion was caused by the adversity faced at A. This is all too common in clients, who often arrive at counselling holding an A–C model of their problems, such as how somebody acted made them angry, depressed, ashamed and so on.

Let us modernise James's example. Replace the bear with poverty, the behaviour with resignation and the feeling with depression. Now we have a common dilemma. So common, that in the UK, the Department of Health has recently invested heavily in its Improving Access to Psychological Therapies (IAPT) programme (Department of Health, 2007) to help people who are depressed or anxious. If we apply James's theory, then people living in poverty would know they are depressed if they noticed their behaviour – that that they had given up, withdrawn, resigned themselves to their lot. This behaviour is unlikely to address the key problem of being poor. Withdrawal and resignation rarely generate income or motivate us in any way. In fact this is as good as seeing the bear and just lying down. In that case we would just have to hope that the bear gets bored and walks away, not giving in to its hunger. People all over the world live in poverty or conflict and most are not depressed or resigned. Certainly they have negative feelings about it but still face up to their problems as best they can. A minority will feel depression and give in, rendering themselves stuck, unable to escape their very own bear. Poverty rarely stops being a problem of its own accord. So, if our behaviour or environment determines our emotions, how come people feel and behave differently when presented with the same problem? The answer to this lies in understanding how you feel.

Healthy vs. Unhealthy Emotions

The primary aim of CBC is to help our clients overcome *unhealthy* negative emotions such as anxiety and depression, and the associated self-defeating and dysfunctional behaviours, in their reaction to genuine adversities, and instead to respond with *healthy* negative emotions like concern or sadness, and functional behaviours that help to solve rather than exacerbate problems. We will show in the Basic Guide that ascertaining the client's emotional problem and their corresponding goal is one of the key tasks undertaken in CBC. There is a clear rationale for this focus.

The two founding fathers of CBT, Beck and Ellis, agree on the core aspects of human nature. They assume that human beings share common goals in life. As Ellis put it, beyond basic survival, adaptation and reproduction, all individuals are motivated to pursue every day goals such as relating, working and achieving – and having fun. Simple though it is, this paradigm provides the necessary starting point to begin an understanding of human distress and misery. With these goals in mind, we set about life, striving to achieve our basic aims through forming relationships, gaining knowledge and skills, and learning how to maximise our happiness. However, life does not always facilitate our goals. We encounter events that are adverse and challenging. In the vast majority of cases our 'healthy' negative emotional reaction to such adversities actually motivates us to strive to overcome adversity in order to achieve our goals. However, from time to time we turn our healthy negative emotions into unhealthy disturbance about such events, and this disturbance forms the basis of what Albert Ellis referred to as Unhealthy Negative Emotions and Aaron T Beck considered to be symptoms of mental disorder. Either way, they are emotional experiences that lead to dysfunctional behaviour that serves to further block our basic goals or paralyse us in the face of an event.

Following this reasoning, we propose that the *problems* for CBC are these unhealthy negative emotions and dysfunctional behaviours (rather than the adversities *per se*) and the *goals* for CBC are to develop healthy negative emotions and associated functional behaviours. Examples of healthy negative emotions that facilitate our efforts to overcome difficult experiences have been clearly described in Rational Emotive Behaviour Therapy (REBT). Some of the adaptations of the original Cognitive Therapy (CT) (Beck, 1976) typically follow a diagnostic or quasi-medical model, and conceptualise problematic emotions and behaviours as symptoms of a mental disorder. Emotions are considered to be symptoms that manifest as a consequence of some underlying disorder. In CBC we depart from this conceptualisation, as it does not readily permit the fundamentally important distinction between healthy and unhealthy negative emotions.

We have found that by not helping clients distinguish between healthy and unhealthy negative emotions, we may be leaving them at a disadvantage when faced with adverse experiences. For example, suppose we help a client with an anger problem. In the diagnostic system, the client is suffering from an anger *disorder*, and the anger is a symptom to be eradicated or reduced. So our goal is to help the client to feel less angry, more relaxed and less explosive in response to their trigger stimuli. On occasion this approach might be acceptable and appropriate. However, what if the reduction of arousal renders the client vulnerable to future transgression or even abuse and does not aid them to act functionally to address their current challenge in life? If you have ever been in a relationship, you may have had the experience of feeling angry towards that individual on occasion. Imagine if that person frequently treated you badly, ignored your requests for leniency and sought to dominate you. You seek help for your anger and learn methods to reduce your physiological arousal so that you do not experience the same, often overwhelming, level of emotion. Then in an ideal state completely free of all traces of anger, you might then develop skills in assertion. But what then gives you the courage to address the problem? In this instance, we would encourage the client to develop a feeling of healthy anger (Chapter 14), that gives them the courage to face the transgressor but in a safe and controlled manner. This approach helps clarify the emotional goal from the beginning and is the rubric used in CBC in action.

We think there is a qualitative as well as a quantitative difference in emotions. So in CBC the aim is to change the quality (or nature of the emotion) rather than simply the quantity (intensity). All emotions have a purpose, and the purpose of negative emotions is to alert us to problems, prepare us to deal with the problems and directly motivate our behaviours (Frijda, 1986). However, while healthy/functional negative emotions are adaptive, indeed essential to our well-being, unhealthy/ dysfunctional negative emotions tend to be maladaptive and can maintain or even worsen problems. To aim to reduce dysfunctional negative emotions while neglecting to facilitate healthy, functional emotions can only be with the aim of helping clients to feel less, which may not be adaptive. In CBC the goal is different, we want clients to feel and be more adaptive, not return them to a state of non-arousal, or at its worst a state of under-arousal, but to feel *differently*. Box 1.1 contains an example that illustrates this point.

Box 1.1   Reflecting on Anxiety

Take a Moment to Reflect

Try to recall the last time you felt anxious about some upcoming experience in which you wanted the outcome to be good for you. This might have been a job interview, a presentation, an exam, a trip to the dentist, a date, etc. Once you can recall such an event and the feeling associated, recall what you did or wanted to do. You may have wanted to cancel the interview or date, you may have sought reassurance that things would turn out just fine, you may have tried really hard to distract yourself or reduce your arousal to make the idea of the event more manageable. In the run up to the event do you over- or under-prepare? How did your anxiety help you? Probably, not a lot and might have made itself even worse. Now think about how you felt just before the event actually started. You might have been sitting in the waiting

(Continued)

(Continued)

room, waiting for the audience to go silent, or waiting for the date to show up. Had the reassurance or relaxation strategy worked? Or were you still feeling anxious about the imminence of the event? Now recall how you felt as the event actually took place. Did you immediately start to enjoy the experience, or were you preoccupied with your performance or thoughts about what other people might think of you or what might happen next? And after the event, did it go as well as you had wanted it to, or could you have performed better?

Now try to recall a time when you felt profound concern about an upcoming event. This might have been an interview, the health of a loved one, a task at work, a date, etc. You probably really wanted the outcome to be good for you or those you care about. The experience of profound concern probably was not comfortable, but did you even think about avoiding the event or the problem, or were you motivated to try to deal with the problem? Probably this motivation was intrinsic – you did not even have to think, just act.

Now contrast the two. Would you rather approach a potential threat (to your self or your image of yourself) feeling anxious and wanting to avoid, preoccupied with exaggerated thoughts about the potential negative outcomes, or would you rather be concerned and cautiously propelled towards facing up to the threat? You decide.

Emotions that are functional (healthy) tend to implicitly motivate us to act in a way that is adaptive to the problem we face. Dysfunctional (unhealthy) emotions, on the other hand, are inherently counter-adaptive or self-defeating; no matter how compelling they might feel at the point of experience. It is these dysfunctional emotions that form the first part of the model used within CBC. They are the Consequences (C) that define the nature of the problem experienced by the client. Distinguishing dysfunctional and functional emotions is not difficult to do intuitively but not so easy to put into words. We provide a guide in Table 1.1 (a more in-depth treatment of the distinctions is provided in Dryden, 2008). Within CBC we use these distinctions to help and encourage clients to identify and replace a dysfunctional emotion with the more functional alternative. This might involve a reduction in arousal, but rarely would the client be helped to feel nothing about an

TABLE 1.1   *Dysfunctional and functional emotions*

Dysfunctional	Action tendency	Functional	Action tendency
Anxiety	Avoidance of the threat	Concern	Approaching the threat
Depression	Withdrawal into self	Sadness	Communicative of feelings
Dysfunctional anger	Seek vengeance or hold it in (thereby not addressing the problem)	Functional anger	Assert self about the transgression
Hurt	Sulk and wait for the other to approach	Sorrow	Openly communicate feeling
Shame	Hide or shrink away from others	Disappointment	Face up to others
Guilt	Begging for forgiveness or denial of wrongdoing	Remorse	Asking for forgiveness or taking a penalty
Invidious envy	Seek to obtain the desired thing, no matter what	Benign envy	Working hard to obtain that which is desired

adversity they face as, put simply, it is almost never to their benefit to do so. Consider the experience you reflected on earlier (see Box 1.1). How would you have actually benefited from feeling almost nothing about the experience? You might have failed to prepare for the experience or, even worse, not cared about the outcome. The counsellor is best advised to be mindful of this when discussing problems and goals with their client. The notion of dysfunctional (or unhealthy or disordered) and functional (or healthy or ordered) emotions is not unique to REBT, but is also a paradigm adopted in cognitive science (Power and Dalgleish, 1997).

Functional vs. Dysfunctional Action Tendencies

When we feel an emotion we invariably experience an urge to act or may spontaneously act. In CBC the urge to act is called an Action Tendency. Each of the unhealthy and healthy feelings has an associated action tendency. Broadly speaking, the unhealthy feelings lead to dysfunctional (such as avoidance) Action Tendencies and the healthy feelings lead to functional (such as approach) Action Tendencies. Let us consider the experience of shame to illustrate. When we experience shame we simultaneously experience an Action Tendency to shrink away, to jump into some hole, to avoid the gaze or scrutiny of others, we want more than anything to escape. When we experience disappointment our Action Tendency is different, we tolerate the scrutiny and make use of what was learned for self-improvement. The counsellor uses this information in a number of ways. The Action Tendency can be understood so that the client is encouraged to act differently, become more self-enhancing than self-defeating. The counsellor might also use the Action Tendency to help the client describe their feeling where they might otherwise find it difficult to describe the feeling in words.

Life is a Challenge – or the A in the ABC Model

In trying to achieve our basic human goals, we encounter the challenges of life. These challenges are adverse to us and are often the events that commence the activation of our emotional experiences. Such adversities may take the form of setbacks, transgressions, hardships and opportunities. They may emanate from ourselves, other people, the world around us or the future. No matter how privileged, virtually all humans will encounter adversities. Within the CBC model, challenges and adversities are Activating Events (A).

Activating events can trigger different types of emotional response, and though never directly cause the response; experience can mislead us – and our clients – into believing that they do. Indeed, some As seem to be the direct cause of the individual's emotional experience. Consider the arachnaphobe who sees a spider crawling towards them. Their panic and extreme behavioural response might seem almost automatic. But the spider does not cause the response. Similarly other people cannot make us angry, though they can certainly act in ways that we can make ourselves angry about. Unfortunately, when all of us experience emotional problems we rarely jump to the conclusion that we are distressing ourselves. Therefore, when many clients first enter the therapeutic relationship they rarely immediately report emotional responsibility, an awareness that they are creating their emotional problem. Rather, they typically attribute their emotional response to the activating event. It follows therefore that the client has not been able to work their way out of their problem, as with this account in mind, their emotions can change only if the event alters or disappears.

The presentation of the model of CBC does not explicitly focus on the history and genesis of the problems for the client at this stage – the As of the past. Rather, to begin with we will present an episodic, cross-sectional (or horizontal) model for formulation, and focus on the As of the present. We are not discounting a consideration of history, rather we prefer at first to concentrate on the here and now experiences of the client. This is not because an individual's history is unimportant, but because the cognitive model does not hypothesise that the answers to a client's problems lie in resolving the issues of their past. Therefore, within the CBC model, historical events that continue to present as problematic for the client are conceptualised as a form of activating event at A which the client is carrying with them in their memories into the present. We will of course demonstrate in later chapters how to make use of the CBC model within longitudinal (or vertical) formulations that incorporate the individual's experiences and learning histories.

It is not possible to produce a list of the typical activating events for all clients, though themes do emerge in the literature. For example, depression is usually associated with loss or failure (Beck, 1976; Beck et al., 1979), anxiety with threat (e.g. Wells, 1997), and anger with transgression (DiGiuseppe and Tafrate, 2007).

Making Sense of Life – or the B in the ABC Model

Men are disturbed not by things but by the views which they take of them

This statement by the second-century Greek philosopher Epictetus is often quoted in books on CBT because the phrase neatly presents the key conceptual element of cognitive theory. By views, Epictetus is referring to the thoughts and beliefs we have about our experiences. It is these thoughts and beliefs that put the B into the ABC model.

In CBC beliefs at B are separated out into inferences and evaluations. Both are important in mediating the experience of emotion and they have a particular relationship. Put simply, inferences about the activating event establish the cognitive frame and the evaluations provide the emotional heat. However, the relationship is not unidirectional, as having evaluated an inference we might then go on to make further inferences.

Inferences

Thoughts that are inferences and images tend to be fleeting in our minds, though they can also become persistent and habitual. Beck (1976) refers to these experiences as Negative Automatic Thoughts. However, inferences are not necessarily negative until they have been evaluated. In CBC an inference is a judgement about an event (real or imagined) that goes beyond the available data. Images may be associated with inferences or may exist separately and may take the form of visual or other sensory memory episodes or imagined scenes about the future. For example, if a client is anxious about presenting their work to an audience, their anxiety is likely to be amplified when they are reminded of the upcoming event, such as a programme of presentations arriving through their letterbox. At such a moment the individual may infer that their presentation will go badly (despite them being keen for it to go well). They might infer 'people will find out that I do not know what I'm talking about!' This is an inference because the event at the moment the inference is made about the future and by definition goes beyond the available data in the present as there is no way of knowing what judgements the audience will arrive at until after the event has occurred (and even then the task to identify their genuine reactions would be a significant challenge). Thus, a future-oriented inference is often a prediction or forecast about the event. Similarly, the client might receive the programme of the day and experience an image of themselves standing in front of a disinterested or critical audience, a room full of derision and frown. Such an experience, whether inference or image, may seem automatic in response to the trigger stimulus of the activating event, because they are sudden and often intrusive. However, the inference might also be deliberate. In the example of depression, an individual may spend considerable time dwelling on a particular loss or failure, inferring the reasons that might lie behind that experience.

Inferences, in mainstream cognitive-behavioural therapy, tend to be the focus of considerable therapeutic attention. Because inferences go beyond the evidence available, their truth can be questioned. For example, if a client infers that nobody likes them, the counsellor could ask them to consider any examples of times when people have liked them. In so doing the counsellor is gently encouraging the client to challenge the truth of or evidence for the inference. Inferences also tend to generate further inferences, as we seek to understand our experience of an adversity. Taking the client who infers that nobody likes them, it is likely that this will have stemmed from a previous inference about a significant other not liking them, which in turn may have been generated after an inference that the significant other has acted badly towards them and so on. In the Basic Guide we will demonstrate techniques to uncover inference chains. For now, consider the following example from a clinical session, where the client was angry at the way the receptionist had spoken to them:

Counsellor: So, when you first approached the receptionist he did not immediately acknowledge you, rather he was looking at the computer screen?

Client: Yeah. They couldn't even be bothered to look me in the eye (inference)!

Counsellor: And then what happened?

Client: I said 'Hello, I've got an appointment at 10 o'clock' and they ignored me again (inference). They just think I'm not important (inference), just like how everyone else treats me (inference), nobody respects me (inference).

As we can see from the above example, inferences are often experienced assertions or statements of fact. However, it is important for the counsellor to help the client recognise that inferences are assumptions, as they infer (or assume) beyond that which is actually known.

In CBC inferences (or images) are necessary but not sufficient for an emotional experience. In order for an emotional problem to occur the inferential thought has to be evaluated further. We will come to evaluative beliefs shortly. However, it might be helpful to offer a metaphorical example to illustrate our point. If you are baking a sponge cake, you will require a set of ingredients, which usually you mix together, often adding one after the other. At the end of mixing, however, you do not yet have a cake, but you are getting there. What you need in order to produce a sponge cake is heat, and this comes from placing the mixed together ingredients in an oven. The ingredients may vary dramatically, as there are many types of sponge cake, but heat is required before it becomes a cake. Here we would argue that the ingredients are akin to inferences and the evaluations are the heat.

The following transcript from a supervision session is used to further illustrate this point.

Trainer (or supervisor):	Supposing you have a client who expresses the phrase 'Nobody loves me', how do you think this person would feel?
Trainee (supervisee):	(Answering instinctively, perhaps biased by their own judgements) I think they would feel depressed.
Trainer (or supervisor):	How did you come to that conclusion?
Trainee (supervisee):	Well, it's not very nice is it? You know, believing that nobody loves you, especially if you carry on thinking like that, it would really get you down.
Trainer (or supervisor):	OK, and how do you think that client might act?
Trainee (supervisee):	Give up, mope about, maybe just withdraw from interpersonal relationships.
Trainer (or supervisor):	And would that behaviour help them discover any evidence to contradict their judgement that nobody likes them?
Trainee (supervisee):	No, not at all. They might become like an emotional hermit. That might make it hard for other people to get to know the client and then decide that whether they like that person or not. Though I have to say, it would be kind of hard to genuinely like someone who adamantly believes that nobody likes them.
Trainer (or supervisor):	And I guess it would be easy to see how that goes full circle. But I'm interested in why you quite easily came up with the notion that the *idea* of having nobody like you, even if the reality were true, that nobody did, would *make* you feel depressed.
Trainee (supervisee):	So let me see if I get your point. Are you saying that even if nobody likes the client (which is unlikely, but remains possible), then they might feel something other than depression?
Trainer (or supervisor):	Well, not quite so fast. First let's think about how your client, or anyone for that matter, might depress themselves about the idea that nobody likes them. Is it automatic, so that whenever any human thinks 'nobody likes me' they feel depressed?

Trainee (supervisee):	I don't think so. I guess it's an unpleasant thought, and we are all social animals. It would make life very hard for us and so we might just give up, overwhelmed with depressed affect.
Trainer (supervisor):	Let me help you. Having concluded that 'nobody likes them' your client might make themself feel depressed, but I think it is possible that they might also make themself feel other emotions about the same thought. Can you think of how else they might feel?
Trainee (supervisee):	Sure. They might feel ashamed of themself for being unlikeable. They might be angry with other people for not treating them better. They might be anxious about some social event that they have to attend. They might feel guilty about something that they might have done that led other people to not be as friendly towards them.
Trainer (supervisor):	OK, now that sounds more like your average human being! So what determines how they feel if the same thought, or more accurately, the same inference, can lead to all sorts of different emotions and corresponding behaviours?
Trainee (supervisee):	Well I guess their past experiences, both in the distant and proximal history of the client.
Trainer (supervisor):	I'm interested to understand why you think this.
Trainee (supervisee):	Well, it's quite obvious really. Most of the models make reference to early life experiences in the formation of beliefs. So I guess, if the client had bad experiences as a child, perhaps received criticism from a parent, then they might become sensitised to people not liking them and might conclude that nobody does, distorting their perception of reality.
Trainer (supervisor):	Let's try and think about all that guesswork and speculation. You are right that many formulations often refer to the impact of early learning experiences on the formation of beliefs. You pointed out, as many do, that the experience of negative feedback or criticism might have occurred.

Trainee (supervisee):	Well yeah, of course.
Trainer (supervisor):	If someone else had experienced exactly the same feedback and criticism during their life (both in terms of distant and proximal events), would it be possible for that individual to depress themself even more about their judgement that nobody likes them than your client?
Trainee (supervisee):	I guess so, I can't think of why not.
Trainer (supervisor):	So how might they do that?
Trainee (supervisee):	Well it can't be just their early experiences, because you are asking me to think that these are the same for both people. I guess, you could depress yourself more if you added more kind of emotional weight to the observation or inference.
Trainer (supervisor):	And how would you do that?
Trainee (supervisee):	Well by making a different evaluation of the inference that nobody likes me. So one person might think that's really bad and another might think it's bad but not the worst thing that could happen. I guess this would then distort, or magnify, the inference.
Trainer (supervisor):	OK, good!

Inferences, as judgements that go beyond the available data, can be either true or false. When counselling clients, you will invariably encounter inferences that are obviously false. For example, if a client infers that their wife 'absolutely hates everything about me', then it is possible to establish that this cannot be entirely true, hence is false. However, for some inferences the case is less clear, especially where predictions of the future are involved (such as in anxiety-related problems). Take, for example, an inference that a woman might reject a romantic advance. These inferences are therefore difficult to challenge effectively. Hence in CBC we propose focusing attention at least as much, if not more, on the evaluations drawn by the client.

Evaluations

As the transcript above demonstrates, the CBC model asserts the importance of the beliefs that evaluate the inferences about the event. It is these evaluations that create the emotional distress in the here and now, not the inferences alone. The inferences only assert what is true or false. Evaluations assert our likes and dislikes, loves and hates; in other words our preferences. The experience of evaluations is just as rapid as that of inferences. Humans seem to intuitively accept the evaluations they make such that they are experienced as real or true.

To illustrate the importance of evaluations, let us return to the anxiety felt about giving a presentation. The event, inference, evaluation, emotion and action tendency can be considered in two forms:

1 Receiving a programme through the letterbox, Jill infers 'people will find out that I do not know what I'm talking about', and this inference is evaluated 'which will be true and that will be terrible', leaving Jill anxious and with an impulse to pretend to be ill so that she does not have to endure the experience.
2 Receiving a programme through the letterbox, Jill infers 'people will find out that I do not know what I'm talking about', and this inference is evaluated 'and even if that does happen it will be bad, but not the end of the world!', leaving Jill concerned (having challenged both evaluations and has conviction in the truth of the second) and with an impulse to adequately prepare for the experience.

So, what was the difference between the two forms? In the first, Jill evaluates the inference as being terrible, while in the second, Jill evaluates the inference as being bad but not terrible. Changing the evaluation of the inference produces a different emotional and behavioural outcome.

Evaluations are defined as cognitions that assert a value judgement that an event or experience is good or bad, in contrast to inferences, which assert a proposition that could be true or false, though clearly evaluations can be true or false as well. Most of the time we are not aware of the evaluations that occur frequently in life that are not associated with emotional distress. Think about your favourite food. Imagine the smell, texture and taste. Do you like what you imagine? Of course, the answer is yes, as we asked you to think about your favourite food, but because of this we knew that this would be associated with an implicit evaluation of the food being good. As humans, we just know. Similarly, when we distress ourselves and our evaluations are exaggerations of the badness (as opposed to an appraisal that is more consistent with reality) we remain equally convinced that we are right. Therefore the primary task in CBC is to help the client challenge their evaluations on various grounds and in various ways.

Evaluations can take many forms. In REBT there are four types of dysfunctional or 'irrational' negative evaluations: demands, awfulising, low frustration tolerance and self/other/life downing. All of these implicitly or explicitly take the prefix 'absolutely', making them both rigid and extreme, for example, absolutely must or must not, absolutely awful, absolutely intolerable and absolutely worthless. For each of these there are four functional or 'rational' alternatives, namely strong preferences, relative badness, high frustration tolerance and self, other, life acceptance. In CBT a number of the common cognitive distortions are also evaluative rather than inferential in nature: shoulds/oughts/musts, over-generalising, magnifying (and minimising) and labelling. Evidently, there is a similarity between the two approaches, and we make use of all them in CBC. The types of evaluations and goals for intervention are defined in Table 1.2.

TABLE 1.2   *Types of evaluation and targets for intervention*

Evaluations leading to disturbance	Target for intervention
Demands: absolute shoulds, oughts, musts, needs	Flexible preference/desire
These can be focused on how a person (self or other) must behave/think/feel or how life must be	Evaluating according to what one desires or wants rather than on what must be
Extreme Magnification	Badness-rating
Evaluating an experience or inference as so bad/negative/terrifying that it is truly awful or a catastrophe	Evaluating the experience of inference on a continuum rather than at one end of the continuum
Global Labelling	Acceptance
Self/other/life downing evaluations that rate a person or conditions in their entirety based on one aspect of the person or situation	Evaluating self/other/life as un-definable, incapable of having their entirety described in one way
Frustration Intolerance	Frustration Tolerance
Evaluating an experience or inference as unbearable such that the individual has no way of coping with that experience	Evaluating an experience of inference as uncomfortable but bearable and worthy of the struggle

This chapter has introduced the rationale and overview of our integrated ABC model for use in formulating client problems. There is far more to this model, such as vicious cycles and complex chains that help the counsellor attend to more longitudinal factors in the client's presentation, which we will come to in the Basic Guide section that follows. The Basic Guide section also presents the tasks of CBC.

PART 1

A Basic Guide to Cognitive Behavioural Counselling

2

Structure and Outline of the Basic Guide

In this second edition of our Basic Guide to cognitive behavioural counselling (CBC) we offer to take you, as a cognitive behavioural counsellor, through the basic principles and practice of CBC, based on the integrative model outlined in Chapter 1. We follow the counselling process in an intuitive way, from initial preparation right through all the stages of CBC to the final session and follow-up.

The Four Stages

We view CBC as a process that has four stages – preparation, beginning, middle and ending. The preparation stage starts with the receipt of the referral but before the first meeting, with the initial screening of suitability of the referral. Then there is the crucial first meeting, establishing a bond, gaining a general overview of the main problems, explaining the cognitive model and helping the client get a clear idea of how it might help, and all this before obtaining informed consent.

Then the real assessment work of CBC can commence in the next, beginning stage, where counsellor and client collaborate on the detailed work of cognitive assessment and conceptualisation, in a spirit of guided discovery, designed to help the client learn the 'cognitive' framework essential for the work of therapeutic change.

In the middle stage, counsellor and client collaborate closely together within and between sessions on the work that is needed to best overcome the emotional and behavioural problems, and achieve the goals through cognitive change.

Finally, in the ending stage the counsellor prepares for termination by helping the client 'take over' and become his own counsellor, so as to maximise his potential to independently maintain his or her gains and overcome further problems.

We have organised the guide according to this four-stage structure, into which we have also incorporated the concept of the working alliance, used the ABC framework described in Chapter 1 for analysing problems, and specified some of the key counsellor tasks and client steps that flow from this approach.

The Working Alliance

The core components of CBC – clarifying the problems and goals, agreeing the tasks to achieve the goals, and establishing the client–counsellor bond – form the basis of the working alliance, first clearly defined by Bordin (1979) in terms of the three components: bonds, goals and tasks.

It is the cognitive behavioural counsellor's job to set up and maintain the working alliance. She has to develop a strong and enduring bond with her client, to guide her client to identify the problems and goals and to discover a cognitive conceptualisation of them, and to facilitate the actual tasks the client will need to undertake. We have operationalised these components of the working alliance into a series of tasks for the counsellor and steps for the client.

The ABC Framework

In designing the counsellor tasks and client steps that comprise the working alliance, we have drawn on the integrated model of cognitive behaviour therapy described in Chapter 1. As with the first edition we have used a generic version of the *ABC* organising framework, where *A* represents external or internal adverse events, *B* represents cognitions, including evaluative beliefs, dysfunctional assumptions and other inferences, and *C* represents the emotional, behavioural and further cognitive consequences of the beliefs, given the adverse events. This *ABC* organising framework is shown graphically in Figure 1.2.

The ABC framework provides the counsellor, and in due course the client, with a clear guide throughout the counselling process, including cognitive assessment, conceptualisation and intervention. From our teaching and clinical experience we believe it to be the most easily understood of the cross-sectional descriptive and explanatory frameworks for the majority of mental-health problems. We suggest its use in this guide for the less complex problems, and show how the counsellor can use it to capture most of the client's relevant current experience.

We will later introduce a further aspect of the ABC model that can occur in more complex cases. This is that ABC episodes can go round in vicious circles that maintain or worsen the problem. A further aspect of more complex cases is that some beliefs have their origins in early learning but can be activated again and again by current negative events. The ABC framework accommodates current manifestations of imagery and beliefs that may have had early origins.

Finally, the ABC framework has been adapted, and can be further adapted, for more severe problems that we do not cover in this Basic Guide, in particular psychosis (e.g. Chadwick et al., 1996; Harrop and Trower, 2003; Byrne et al., 2006; Chadwick, 2006).

Counsellor Tasks

The counsellor tasks and client steps fall naturally into the preparation, beginning, middle and ending stages, and this is how we structure this guide. Each stage has a rationale and aim, and the tasks and steps are designed to meet the aims of that stage. We first give an overview of the rationale and aim of the stage, and then describe the tasks. We present the tasks in a recommended sequence, a suggested order in which the task at hand should usually, though not invariably, be completed before moving on to the next one. However, this is a guide and not an instruction manual – a distinction we discuss later, but briefly means that we are not recommending a rigid adherence to our suggested order, but providing a sequence of choice points – the counsellor needs to be ever mindful of the client's unique needs and to respond flexibly.

Each identified task has, where appropriate, three components. The first is a Briefing on the aims of the task and the qualities and skills the counsellor will need to deploy in order to carry out the task in practice. The second is an Action Summary of the steps that the task comprises. The third is a Case Example, an illustrative dialogue between our counsellor Joan White and our client Brian Dell whom we introduce shortly.

Client Steps

CBC is a collaborative undertaking, so that alongside the counsellor's tasks the client also has his tasks. We refer to them as Client Steps to avoid confusing them with the counsellor tasks. It is the counsellor's responsibility to help the client to identify, consider, choose and then to follow these steps in the pursuit of therapeutic goals. To assist with this, we provide client guides, each with a suggested sequence of client steps. These steps are designed to guide the client methodically through the CBC process, from initially considering and preparing for CBC, assessment, conceptualisation and cognitive change methods during CBC, and finally methods to help the client become his own counsellor after the end of CBC. So that the counsellor knows which steps to use and when to use them, we have introduced and described them at the relevant places in each of the counsellor tasks, and also presented them in graphic form in the Appendices.

Chapter Structure of the Guide

The guide is divided into the four stages in seven chapters – preparation (two chapters), beginning (two chapters), middle (four chapters) and ending (one chapter), as summarised in Box 2.1.

Box 2.1   Chapter Structure of the Basic Guide Section (Part 1)

Chapter 3: Preparation Stage I – Breaking the Ice: Initial Screening, First Meeting, Establishing a Bond

This chapter introduces the preparation stage, which starts with the receipt of the referral and the initial screening, the first meeting and introducing the CBC method of working, and guidance on the essential counselling skills for establishing and maintaining a therapeutic bond.

Chapter 4: Preparation Stage II – Will this Help? Clarifying Problems and Goals, Introducing the Cognitive Approach, Making an Informed Commitment

This chapter includes guidance on clarifying and prioritising the client's problems and goals, drawing up a problem list, introducing the cognitive perspective and reaching an informed decision and commitment to the cognitive behavioural counselling process.

Chapter 5: Beginning Stage I – What's the Problem Specifically? Cognitive Assessment of a Specific Example

This chapter introduces the beginning stage and starts the CBC process 'proper' with an assessment of a specific example of the problem, including the detailed analysis of the critical aspects of the problem, namely the adverse event, the dysfunctional emotions and behaviours, and the mediating beliefs.

Chapter 6: Beginning Stage II – What Are We Aiming For? Conceptualising the Problem, New Thinking, Feeling and Action Goals

This chapter provides guidance on conceptualising the problem and constructing alternative functional emotions, behaviours and beliefs.

Chapter 7: Middle Stage I – Getting Realistic: Challenging and Changing Inferences

This chapter introduces the middle stage which shifts from assessment to intervention, starting with a check that the client has insight into the cognitive perspective. The chapter then provides guidance on techniques for testing the validity of inferences by weighing the evidence and by carrying out real world behavioural experiments.

Chapter 8: Middle Stage II – Changing Hot Thoughts: Challenging and Changing Evaluations

This chapter focuses on challenging and changing core beliefs and other evaluative beliefs, by disputation, by means of imagery and by behavioural exposure in 'shame attacking' exercises.

Chapter 9: Middle Stage III – Imagery Rescripting: Changing Distressing Memories

This chapter focuses on changing distressing memories by imagery rescripting.

(Continued)

> *(Continued)*
>
> **Chapter 10: Middle Stage IV – Working Through: Agenda Setting and Homework**
>
> This chapter provides general guidance on the routine structuring of sessions and monitoring of progress.
>
> **Chapter 11: Ending Stage – Coaching the Client To Become His Own Counsellor**
>
> This chapter focuses on coaching the client to become his own counsellor, jointly anticipating specific and more general problems and ensuring he has the knowledge and skills to address them after termination.

List of Counsellor Tasks

The guide consists of a total of 21 counsellor tasks, grouped into the four stages across the seven chapters as follows:

Preparation Stages I and II

1 Initial Screening and Preparation before Meeting the Client
2 First Meeting and Introducing the CBC Method of Working
3 Establishing a Therapeutic Bond
4 Clarifying the First Problem from the Client's Perspective
5 Clarifying the Client's Goals for the First Problem
6 Clarifying any Further Problems and Goals and Drawing Up a Problem List
7 Introducing the Cognitive Perspective as One Approach

Beginning Stages I and II

8 Reaching an Informed Joint Decision and Commitment to the Method of Working
9 Eliciting a Specific Example of the Problem
10 Assessing the Dysfunctional Emotions, Behaviours and Beliefs
11 Conceptualising the Problem: the B–C Connection and Vicious Circles
12 Constructing Alternative Functional Emotions, Behaviours and Beliefs

Middle Stages I to IV

Ending Stage

3

Preparation Stage I – Breaking the Ice: Screening, First Meeting, Estabilishing a Bond

How is the cognitive behavioural counsellor to know how to begin? What necessary steps might there be? How can she be certain she is doing the right thing? These and other questions often lead the novice to either a manual or a guide, in the hope of finding out 'how to do it'. A manual is highly prescriptive, providing precise, step-by-step instructions, which may be helpful for the counsellor but often not for the client, since each client is unique and a manualised approach can be too rigid, insensitive and unproductive (see also Kuyken et al., 2009).

In this chapter we have sought to provide the counsellor with guidance in which the uniqueness of clients (and counsellors!) is recognised, that problems are unpredictable in many ways and will always be a challenge for any counsellor or therapist, but at the same time to provide suggestions about how to proceed, the options, and how to go about choosing between them.

Client Expectations

Despite the uniqueness of each client, there are also common factors: the client is almost certainly unhappy and demoralised, believing he is helpless to find a solution to his difficulties, wanting help and yet maybe hating to ask, pessimistic about anyone being able to help, even if he does ask. The client may have ruminated for months, perhaps years about his difficulties, and will have many ideas about the problem but will still be profoundly confused, ending up in ever more vicious circles of negative rumination. He may have some vague – or even clear – notions about what will help him – perhaps about what kind of 'treatment' or what kind of 'doctor'. He will expect to be asked – and will usually want to talk – about his difficulties, but may find it very difficult, shaming, even harrowing, to do so. He will want the counsellor to have expertise and experience, and be someone who will treat him with respect, give him time to tell his story, and to understand. Yet he may harbour anxieties that the counsellor is very busy with more 'important' things and will judge his problem as trivial and the interview as a waste of her time, or he may be suspicious that he has been delegated to someone junior and inexperienced. On the other hand, he may think the counsellor is going to simply 'give' him treatment that will 'cure' him, as might be expected in a doctor–patient relationship, and be unaware of and unprepared for the work he will have to undertake during CBC and even after discharge.

These are important issues, since it is at this early stage of CBC that the counsellor is most likely to lose her client. Our aim in these two preparation stage chapters, therefore, is to provide guidance for the counsellor to successfully engage most clients with less complex problems despite these negative expectations. Some clients with more complex problems will present with greater challenges and obstacles to engagement.

Counsellor Preparation

Success in engaging the client depends to a significant degree on various aspects of preparation before the first meeting. It goes without saying that a fundamental aspect of preparation is to have been trained in counselling skills, particularly those based on Rogerian client-centred counselling (see Mearns and Thorne, 2007, in this series). Although we have assumed the practitioner–reader has these skills, we nonetheless review some of the basic skills as one of the tasks in this chapter. Another aspect of preparation is familiarisation with the cognitive behavioural therapy model in general, and for those following our guide, familiarisation with the integrated CBC model presented in Chapter 1, particularly the ABC framework. We have in mind that the counsellor will bring to the case the CBC/ABC framework, and will try to understand the client's problem within that framework. But she also has to understand the client's problem from his perspective, to listen with a completely open mind, adhering to the true spirit of client-centredness, and to be open to the fact that he or she will almost certainly have a different set of assumptions, including some dysfunctional assumptions, negative automatic thoughts and unhealthy beliefs including core beliefs. She has to accommodate these two 'world views', that of the cognitive behavioural counsellor with the ABC model, and that of the client with his problematic perspective. She also has to look ahead to the end of counselling, and prepare the client for this even from the first session, since he himself will eventually need to become his own counsellor, with all that this implies about acquiring the counselling perspective.

Summary of the Preparation Stage

In this preparation stage then, the counsellor's goal will be to present the client with an alternative and more 'healthy' perspective from his own current dysfunctional perspective of his current difficulties. Once she has gained an initial insight into the client's understanding of his problems, she will attempt the difficult task of introducing her client to the alternative cognitive perspective as a potential way of overcoming his problems.

With these and other goals in mind, the preparation stage contains a sequence of counsellor tasks with accompanying client steps which may take most of the first two or three sessions, and with complex cases, probably more. These tasks occupy the current and the next chapter (Chapters 3 and 4). The counsellor should also familiarise herself with the end stage at this early point (Chapter 11) as part of the preparation process.

The tasks included in this chapter are:

1   Initial Screening and Preparation before Meeting the Client
2   First Meeting and Introducing the CBC Method of Working
3   Establishing a Therapeutic Bond

The chapter consists of a Briefing, an Action Summary and Case Example for each of the listed tasks. Suggestions on how to use the client guides will be covered in the tasks.

Task 1. Initial Screening and Preparation before Meeting the Client

Briefing

Initial Screening

The CBC process starts, of course, with a referral, either from the client directly (or client's relative), or from a health professional, such as a GP, specialist physician or another mental-health professional. The first question for the counsellor then, either alone or with her multidisciplinary team if she works within one, is the initial screening question: is this an appropriate referral for CBC? This answer will be influenced to some degree by whether the counsellor is working in an NHS setting or in private practice. In the NHS it may be the counsellor's responsibility to ensure that the client has a problem sufficiently serious to warrant counselling, given the limited resources. In private practice the counsellor does not have this constraint, though it is still the counsellor's responsibility to tell the client whether, in her view, it is relevant and needed, and she can, of course, decide not to take on a private-practice referral.

A decision not to accept a referral can be made at this initial screening point. However, a decision to accept a referral for CBC involves not only this initial screening but also further evaluation by counsellor and client in a face-to-face assessment interview.

So how does the counsellor decide? In this section we will provide some guidelines for making such a decision, which can be resolved at the initial screening stage, but may take one or more sessions. The background to this decision process is the ABC framework outlined in Chapter 1, and with this in mind, we will look at four criteria for initial screening, with the proviso that these criteria are dimensional rather than categorical, and a clinical judgement has to be made in each case as to whether to include or exclude (also see Chapter 4 for broader consideration regarding exclusion).

First Criterion

The first criterion is that the client is disturbed and/or behaving in a way that is dysfunctional to a degree that their quality of life (or in some circumstances, that of closely associated others) is seriously affected. This criterion refers to the *C* in the *ABC* framework.

Second Criterion

The second criterion is that the emotional and/or behavioural problem is triggered by external psychosocial adversities or internal, physiological symptoms – the A in the ABC framework – rather than being the direct consequence of a physical illness or injury, such as dementia (although the counsellor will want to keep in mind that clients have psychological reactions to physical/medical events). So a pattern of emotional and behavioural disturbance (C) triggered by adverse life events like rejection or failure (A) may be appropriate for CBC, whereas if C is the direct consequence and symptom of, say, organic impairment like dementia, they may not be. Clients complaints can be presented as As (adversities) or Cs (distress or dysfunctional behaviours) or both. The counsellor will want both.

Information for these criteria may be provided with the referral. If not, a questionnaire can be sent as suggested below. A useful and quick rating of overall psychological functioning on a 0–100 severity index can also be estimated with the Global Assessment of Functioning (GAF) Scale (APA, 1994). On this scale, anyone above a rating of 71 (symptoms, if present, are transient and expectable reactions to psychosocial stressors) would probably not be considered appropriate for CBC or indeed any formal psychiatric intervention. A rating of 70 (mild symptoms and difficulties but generally functioning pretty well) right through to 100 (persistent danger of severely hurting self or others, including suicidal threat) would warrant further assessment, but to be suitable for CBC we emphasise that the core problem needs to be specifically an emotional and/or behavioural disturbance – the C in the ABC framework.

Third Criterion

The third criterion is whether the client is likely to be able to benefit from CBC, even if they meet the first two criteria of having an emotional/behavioural problem and a psychosocial trigger. For example someone with severe learning disabilities may have had adverse life circumstances and be quite disturbed, but lacks the ability to achieve cognitive insights that would help them to identify and change their thoughts and beliefs that mediate between the events and their reaction – the B in the ABC model. We emphasise nonetheless that excellent progress has been made with cognitive behaviour therapy for people with mild learning disabilities (Jahoda et al., 2009).

Fourth Criterion

The fourth criterion is whether the client is ready for CBC. A client, who may well have a problem suitable for CBC but does not accept this fact, is clearly not ready for any such intervention. The counsellor might want to explore this issue if the client has been referred by a relative or other third party, or the client has been pressured into referring himself. A useful and evidence-based theory of stages of change is recommended (Prochaska and diClemente, 1984) as this can help the counsellor decide whether the client accepts there is a problem and is prepared to undergo the difficult work to change.

Other Criteria

A related problem is where clients have other agendas other than the problem presented. A client may have a motive not to get better, such as if there is an outstanding litigation claim for psychological trauma, or the client has a motive to 'punish' a significant other by remaining unwell. In these cases the client might have a motive to show that CBC was ineffective, and this may (though not necessarily will) thwart progress in counselling.

In addition to these criteria, the counsellor may be working in a service that itself has criteria which the counsellor is bound by, or in the case of those trained in the IAPT initiative, low-intensity workers would work with low-intensity problems but be required to assess but refer on clients with moderate or severe and enduring mental-health problems to high-intensity workers or to specialist services designed for long-term psycho-therapy or rehabilitation. Clearly the counsellor needs to be familiar with their service criteria.

Questionnaires and Biographical Information

The cognitive behavioural counsellor will assess all referrals in terms of these criteria, and will sometimes be able to make a decision (or in discussion with their multidisciplinary team) that the referral is not appropriate, at this initial screening stage, and without interviewing the client. If she decides the referral is not appropriate, the counsellor explains to both client and referrer why CBC is unlikely to be suitable and if possible offers a suggestion as to whom and where to refer.

If the counsellor cannot make a decision at this stage because of lack of information, she can ask for the additional information to be sent, or she can decide to actually interview the client and obtain the information that way, or both. She can send an appointment and include a problem and biographical information questionnaire (see Scott, 2009 for a brief screening inventory, or Kuyken et al., 2009, for a more comprehensive Aid to History Taking Form), that should at a minimum ask for basic information on the client, his family and his educational and occupational background, asks about any subsidiary problems and their onset, factors which might have a bearing on the problems (for example, relationships), any kind of previous or present help, medication, etc., and any additional information they might think relevant.

The counsellor could also send a copy of the Preparation Guide (Appendix 1) which asks the client to describe the main problem, the type and intensity of emotional disturbance and/or behavioural dysfunction they are experiencing (C information in terms of the ABC framework), an account of adverse circumstances triggering this disturbance (A information), how he would like to respond to these adverse circumstances, and if possible some indication of the client's negative thoughts and attitudes towards his situation (B information). The client can be asked to bring these forms with them to the first appointment.

Once the counsellor is satisfied that the referral meets the initial screening criteria, she will invite the client for an assessment interview. The next task is for both counsellor and client to decide whether to commit to a CBC intervention, and this can only be done through at least one face-to-face assessment interview. The counsellor will want to make it clear in the acceptance letter to both the client and referrer that the first, and maybe second, interviews will be only assessment interviews, with no commitment on either side that therapy will be offered or accepted until both client and counsellor have made an informed decision.

A final point is that the client will want to know what to expect in CBC. This can be done prior to the first interview, either by sending the client a brief handout on CBC and an idea of recommended client and counsellor roles, or by a more elaborate induction procedure, with videotape demonstrations of CBC. However, such client induction can also be carried out during the opening interviews, as we shall indicate.

Action Summary

1 On receiving the referral letter, consider its appropriateness, and if not appropriate inform the referrer and client and if possible suggest an alternative, such as a specialist service.
2 If uncertain about the appropriateness at this stage, accept the referral for an assessment only interview, and inform the client and referrer of this.
3 Send client a problem and biographical data questionnaire and handout on CBC.

Case Example

The following 'client' is fictitious but is based upon genuine case material. The client is a 23-year-old university student, Mr Brian Dell, referred by his GP at the University Medical Practice, Dr Smith, to our cognitive behavioural counsellor, Mrs Joan White. In a referral letter, Dr Smith said Brian was diagnosed with depression and social phobia, and had been prescribed with the anti-depressant venlafaxine but he did not feel this had helped.

Brian was studying for a BA in African Studies but had dropped out for a year because he had developed such intense anxiety about giving presentations, which were part of his assessed work that he felt he couldn't face it for the time being. Brian was also quite a shy person, at times bordering on social phobia in ordinary social situations.

The problem with giving presentations had become so serious that it had also led to depression, social withdrawal and low self-esteem, and he had felt hopeless and helpless about ever returning to university again and would have to get a job in a shop or something similar but felt even that would be too much for him, having to face the public.

He felt he was a terrible disappointment to his parents, who had been so proud of him obtaining a place at a prestigious university, and humiliated with his friends, many of whom had gone on to university and were doing well. He felt they had lost respect for him.

Brian was at a critical point, having with great difficulty just returned to university to attempt to repeat his second year, but with just as much anxiety about his presentations as previously. Dr Smith thought he was insightful and highly motivated to work with a cognitive behavioural counselling approach and was very well able to do so.

Joan felt Brian satisfied all the referral criteria. He was seriously disturbed (depressed, socially phobic) and behaving in a way that was affecting his quality of life (first criterion), and there was a clear psychosocial trigger (second criterion). It was not considered necessary to assess further with, for example, the GAF. On the strength of Dr Smith's opinion, Joan thought he probably satisfied the third and fourth criteria – he was insightful, well motivated and accepted there was a psychological problem. There were no other criteria issues so Joan accepted the referral for assessment and invited Brian for his first interview, enclosing a simple screening question-naire (Scott, 2009, Appendix B, pp. 144–5) and leaflet on the cognitive behavioural counselling approach to problems.

Task 2. First Meeting and Introducing the CBC Method of Working

Briefing

Two-way Assessment
At the start of this first face-to-face contact with the client, the counsellor will want to make it clear that this initial meeting is a two-way assessment – the counsellor of the client, and vice versa, the client of the counsellor – and that the outcome of this assessment will be for both to make an informed decision whether to go ahead or not, or whether it would be more appropriate for the client to see another mental-health specialist, as noted above. The counsellor will want to make it clear, therefore, that there is no commitment at this stage.

Before making his decision, the client will want to know who the counsellor is, what kind of therapy she practices, that she has expertise and is accredited or in training, that he will be 'safe' with the counsel-lor, that her sole purpose will be to help him as best she can, that she will keep information confidential, and of course that she is caring and friendly. These will be some of the first things the counsellor will need to communicate, not only to help the client make a decision, but to establish and make explicit the CBC method of working (including setting and boundary conditions) for therapy if it does go ahead.

Clarifying the Relationship
Clarifying the nature of the therapeutic relationship is important as the client may well have mistaken assumptions about how therapy will be conducted, for example that it will be like the doctor–patient relationship

where the counsellor is the 'doctor' with all the expertise who will ask closed, symptom-based questions, make a diagnosis and 'prescribe' some treatment, and the client only has to conform to her instructions to be 'cured'. Or if the counsellor is a touch too friendly and informal, the client may think her role is like a befriender simply to chat to and even to go out with socially. Or in a residential setting, the client may label the counsellor as the equivalent of a warden whose job is to ensure he conforms to the rules and regulations of the residence.

Whichever set of assumptions he has, it is likely that the client may not realise that the counsellor wants to know *his* views, that her job is mainly to help him as best she can to resolve the problem as seen by him, and to help him reach for his goals. He may not realise that he, as well as she, will have to work hard and face emotionally challenging assignments if change is to occur, and that in the end he will need to become his own counsellor, in order to maintain his gains after discharge. Since these client assumptions may never be explicitly expressed, the counsellor checks them out by asking what he expects of counselling. She also introduces him to the CBC method of working, as this method itself makes explicit the goals and tasks and should help correct his misapprehensions.

The CBC Method of Working

When the counsellor introduces the CBC method of working to the client at this early stage, the focus and emphasis will be on just that – the method by which CBC is done rather than what the therapy itself consists of.

As we commented earlier, clients often have a populist idea of therapy which they get from the media, and are quite unprepared for the fact that they will need to undertake difficult, sometimes distressing, work. Failure to prepare the client for this work early on may lead to the client dropping out later. So the counsellor will want to address this first, and will not introduce him just yet to CBC theory, since this will better come after the next task – clarifying his problems. At that stage she will have a list of problems and goals, and then will be in a position to describe the main principle of CBC (that it is our cognitive appraisals that largely disturb us), and show him how this principle can be applied to his problems. He will then be able to make a fully informed decision and a commitment.

The CBC method of working, then, is outlined in principle, though not yet in detail (which comes in Task 8). This outline includes discussion of the length and frequency of sessions; a time-frame for therapy as a whole; agenda setting for each session; between sessions work by the client; a focus on identifying and defining problems, goals and tasks in a specific and concrete form.

The method of working also includes clarifying the role expectations of client and counsellor, in which the client is the 'expert' on his problems and is seeking guidance on how to overcome them, the counsellor is the expert on clarifying the nature of problems and on methods to overcome them, and they work together collaboratively as a team, jointly working towards overcoming the problems. Introducing the client to this structured method of working will ensure the client is fully consulted and engaged in a focused way of working, rather than the less helpful ways implicit in his assumptions described earlier.

Action Summary

1 Brief yourself on the client (before actually meeting him) from his problem and biographical data sheet and any referral letter, if available.
2 Be thoughtful about dress and manner, to avoid triggering any client attitudes which may interfere with rapport-building.
3 Greet the client warmly and firmly, and by name. Make a judgement as to whether it will be appropriate to be on first-name terms with your client. This choice depends both on the client's and your preferences about the relative formality/informality of the relationship within the constraints of the boundary conditions.
4 Introduce yourself briefly, giving your name and professional status.
5 Say who referred him and the reason for the referral and ask the client if the referral and reason accurately reflect his wishes and needs.
6 Ask if he has any thoughts or feelings about being referred. If the client seems tense, explore the reason for this and clarify any misunderstanding. It may also sometimes help to start on a lighter note by engaging in small talk (for example, his journey to the clinic) and to take down or check formal details like name, address, telephone number, marital status and occupational status.
7 Ask the client what he expects from counselling. Then tell him that your specialty is CBC, and that this has a particular 'method of working' and a particular theory. Explain that you will describe the method of working now, and the theory later on, after he has talked about his problems and goals. Then give a brief account of the CBC method of working, that the aim is to help clients solve problems and become better able achieve their goals, that it involves quite a lot of practically and emotionally hard work for you both, you in listening and guiding, and him in working at gaining new insights and putting these into practice. Tell him that each session will have an agenda, and that you

will be helping him to describe specific problems, identifying goals for each problem, working on solving the problems with various types of work, both in session and 'home' work between sessions. Tell him you will help him to learn self-help techniques, so he can maintain his gains after discharge (specific guidance on this issue is given in Chapter 11). Ask him how he feels about this pragmatic way of working, and whether he could see himself engaging in such a way.

Case Example

Counsellor:	Hello, Mr Dell. *[Offers chair.]* Make yourself comfortable. I am Joan White, I am a cognitive behavioural counsellor, and as you know we are meeting today at the suggestion of your GP, Dr Smith. Before we start I'd like to ask you how you feel about coming here to see me. Feel free to say what you think.
Client:	Well, I have read a bit about cognitive behaviour therapy and I'm keen to try it.
Counsellor:	That's good, that you are keen to try it. Any other thoughts or concerns?
Client:	I'm quite embarrassed about it . . . and I'm wondering what is going to happen, whether it will work.
Counsellor:	That's understandable that you feel embarrassed, so let me say, without at all making light of your problem, it is not unusual, and we see quite a few people with similar problems.
Client:	That's a relief. I thought it was just me.
Counsellor:	No, not at all. Now as you know your GP gave you the diagnoses of depression and social phobia, do you agree with those?
Client:	Well, yes, I suppose so, I just get so anxious that I feel I can't go on and then I get depressed.
Counsellor:	OK, we will certainly talk about that in detail, but first let me ask you what you expect from cognitive behavioural counselling?
Client:	Well, it's a talking therapy, isn't it? I'd like to talk about it but I don't see how talking is going to help. I'd like to know more about it.
Counsellor:	I agree talking is important but not enough on its own. So let me tell you a bit about it. The aim of CBC is to

help you overcome your problem by thinking, feeling and behaving differently and it's a well-researched approach with good evidence for its efficacy. It does involve quite a lot of hard work for both of us. Each session will have an agenda in which we will identify the problems and possible solutions, and agree various types of work, both in session and 'home' work between sessions. I will help you to learn self-help techniques as we go along, so you can maintain your gains after discharge. How do you feel about this way of working?

Client: It's not going to be easy, but I'll try anything, I'm desperate.

Task 3. Establishing a Therapeutic Bond

Task 3 is to establish a therapeutic bond with the client. Unlike the other tasks which are discrete events to be completed in sequence, the therapeutic bond is continuous, and underlies all the other tasks. We place it here as the counselling skills involved are essential to completing the next task (Task 4), which is to get a clear and accurate account of the problem. These two tasks are not independent – one facilitates the other, and in fact the therapeutic bond facilitates all subsequent tasks in CBC, and we describe aspects of it where appropriate in subsequent tasks.

Briefing

How does the counsellor help the client to talk freely and openly about problems about which he may feel distressed and ashamed? She needs to have as a minimum three qualities or attributes which make up the therapeutic bond – to be able to understand accurately, to have positive regard for the client and to be genuinely herself. And she needs to communicate each of these – through specific verbal and non–verbal counselling skills. We will deal with each of these qualities in turn.

Accurate Empathy

The client will talk more openly if he is given space and time to express himself and to feel that he is truly understood. So the first task for the counsellor is to reach for an accurate understanding of the problem from the client's perspective, and to communicate this understanding to him.

This is what Carl Rogers described as *accurate empathy*, and Ellis described as *philosophic empathy*, and which is one of the key components of person-centred counselling (Rogers, 1951, 1961), and which research has shown to be one of the core conditions of effective psychotherapy.

The counsellor puts aside her own opinions in order to be as open as possible to gaining the deep, unbiased understanding of the client's view that defines accurate empathy. She not only listens actively and closely observes the client's body language, but she also encourages him to express himself freely by her use of verbal and non-verbal counselling skills. And to ensure she truly understands accurately, she will regularly ask him for this feedback.

Although the counsellor puts aside her own opinion and judgements about the content of the client's disclosures, she nonetheless uses the *ABC* structure, outlined in Chapter 1, as an organising framework in her head, to help her to clarify the key aspects of the problem and their relationship. She will have already started this process when she received the referral. But now, face-to-face with the client, she will be listening for *A*, the problem situation and the activating events within it; for *B*, his beliefs and other cognitions about the *A*; and *C,* his consequent feelings and his actions. As we shall show, she will use these headings to make sure she is not missing key information, and if necessary to guide her use of listening skills in order to elicit information that the client is omitting.

Unconditional Positive Regard

The counsellor's first task, then, is to help the client feel his views are understood by her accurate empathy. In the process of achieving this, she will also be part way to her second counselling task, which is to have, but also to communicate, Roger's second core condition, namely *unconditional positive regard*, or as Ellis described it, *unconditional acceptance*. Her aim is to be completely non-judgemental, and unconditionally accepting of him as a person, regardless of what he says or does or has done, and to communicate this acceptance to him. With unconditional positive regard the client will more likely feel his views are not only understood but he, as a person, is valued and respected despite whatever failings he may be reporting.

Genuineness

In order to have and to communicate unconditional acceptance, the counsellor also is genuinely and authentically herself in the relationship – *genuineness* is the third of Rogers's core conditions. Genuineness will underpin the sincerity of her empathy and acceptance of him as a person.

The counsellor will use these and other qualities and skills to build the therapeutic bond with the client. This bond is vital if the client is to lower his guard, overcome any shame that may be preventing him from disclosing his problems, be more willing to accept her guidance, and later to carry out the difficult work involved in therapeutic change, or alternatively to express his doubts and reservations about her and her therapeutic approach.

The qualities we have described here are expressed and communicated by means of a number of counselling skills which are now outlined below in the Action Summary.

Action Summary

The strategy of the counsellor is sometimes referred to as the funnel approach, first broad and open, and then narrowing down to specific detail. So you will want to begin by giving your client maximum freedom to choose what problems he wants to present and how he wants to present them, to be sure to get the full client perspective, but then within that perspective, bringing the focus to the adversity (A), the consequent emotional and behavioural reaction (C), and later the beliefs (B). Here we describe some of the basic counselling skills you can use to achieve these objectives.

1. *An open invitation*. Give the client an explicit open invitation to talk – an open question that is non-directive, imposes no constraints on the content other than it is the problem he needs to focus on – and give a reasonable time allocation.
2. *Listener body language*. Adopt good *listener body language*, including eye contact (70 per cent or more of the time), proximity in the 'personal' zone (2.5 to 4 feet), friendly and expressive facial expression, open posture (arms and legs uncrossed), and postural orientation and (initially) forward lean to the client (indicating an open attitude from the counsellor to encourage openness from the client).
3. *Verbal following*. Use *verbal following* – brief listener responses that follow closely what a client is saying, giving the client the opportunity to explore and elaborate his own line of thought. These include head nods and other emblematic gestures, 'mmhmms', 'yes', 'no', 'OK', 'I see what you mean' and end-of-sentence repetitions. Also use silences judiciously in conjunction with

observations and questions that encourage the client to elaborate, such as 'Can you say a bit more about that?' or 'I noticed you were silent – were you thinking or feeling something at that point?'

4 *Questions, paraphrases, reflections and summaries*. There are a number of established verbal-counselling skills that can be used to facilitate the client to disclose sensitive but core issues.

   a First there are *open and closed questions*, used at this stage purely to encourage client disclosure but later as we shall show, in the form of Socratic questions, to guide the client to their own solutions. Open questions impose the least constraint on the content and give the client the most freedom to select material, while closed questions impose the most constraint, inviting the client to answer yes or no or to give concrete information. There is a place for both, open questions for opening up an issue, closed to fill in with specific, missing information. Open questions can also be used to obtain essential specific information, so an open question like 'What problem would you like to talk about?' can be used to open up an issue, but a question, also open but specific in focus can be used to follow up, such as 'Can you give me a specific example of that?' All questioning needs to be used judiciously, as too much can be experienced as interrogative and is one way of causing rupture in the therapeutic alliance (though these too, would be explored using the same counselling skills).

   b Second is *paraphrasing of content*. Here you briefly summarise the facts of the situation as described, in your words but as accurately as you can. The paraphrase should be used quite frequently, and is designed to a) show the client you have understood and, at the same time, b) check that you really have and c) unobtrusively guide the client to the relevant issues and keep on track. The paraphrase is particularly useful for getting facts and inferences at point A and B in the *ABC* framework.

   c Third is *reflection of feeling*, used in conjunction with paraphrasing, to reflect the feeling and impulse being expressed, either explicitly or implicitly. Again this is done fairly frequently and is also designed to show understanding and to check understanding is accurate. Reflection of feeling and associated impulse or action tendency is done tentatively and can be couched as a question. It is useful for getting information at point *C* in the *ABC* framework.

   d Fourth is *summarising*, which combines paraphrasing of content and reflection of feeling, and is used to bring together material over a longer period of time. The purpose of summarising is to give a structure to what the client has said by ordering the main points in his story. By summarising you can achieve two things. First you help your client

get greater clarity about his *own* thoughts and feelings (often bringing a sense of order out of chaos) by reflecting back to the client a
summary of the key issues. Second, you can structure the material
within the *ABC* framework, and by summarising in this way, you begin
the process of guiding your client to a tentative *cognitive* explanation of his problem. This cognitive explanation is known as a cross-
sectional formulation or case conceptualisation in CBT, and you are
already preparing for a later task here to guide your client to this cognitive explanation.

Case Example

We combine the case example for Task 3 and Task 4 and this appears in
the next chapter (Chapter 4), where we show how our counsellor Joan
White uses the counselling skills described here to elicit and clarify the
problem from the client's perspective.

4

Preparation Stage II – Will this Help? Clarifying Problems, Goals, the Cognitive Approach, Commitment

In Chapter 3, Preparation Stage I, we described the counsellor's tasks from first receipt of the referral and the initial screening before meeting the client, handling the first meeting, introducing the CBC method of working, and guidance on the essential counselling skills for establishing and maintaining a therapeutic bond.

In the current chapter (Chapter 4) the counsellor helps the client to express and clarify (and herself to understand) the problems from his own perspective, to choose the problems to be worked on, to help the client clarify what he wants to do about each problem, to introduce him to the cognitive perspective, to guide him to a new understanding of his problem within the cognitive perspective. At this point she invites him – and herself – to make an informed decision, and if this is favourable, to make a commitment to the CBC method of working. The counsellor will encourage the client to follow the steps in the client guides throughout the process.

In summary, this chapter includes the following tasks:

1 Clarifying the First Problem from the Client's Perspective.
2 Clarifying the Client's Goals for the First Problem.
3 Clarifying any further Problems and Goals and Drawing Up a Problem List.

4 Introducing the Cognitive Perspective as One Approach.
5 Reaching an Informed Joint Decision and Commitment to the Method of
   Working.

Task 4. Clarifying the First Problem from the Client's Perspective

Briefing

The counsellor uses her counselling skills (Task 3) in the current Task 4, namely to help the client to describe his problem from his own point of view, and then to clarify the key aspects of the problem that need to be tackled in CBC. This task is also spelled out for the client in the Preparation Guide and Worksheet (see Appendix 1).

The counsellor knows from the ABC framework that one key aspect in the client's account will be the adverse event itself (A), and another will be his emotional and behavioural reaction to it (C). At this early stage she only wants the client to note these two aspects of the problem (A and C), adhering closely to how the client expresses it, and not yet the mediating beliefs (B), which she will explore later (Task 7).

The counsellor will not want to introduce the client to the ABC terminology yet either, as her first priority is to encourage him to express himself in his own words and for her also to use ordinary language in her summaries. So in the briefing that follows below, we assume the counsellor will 'think ABC', that is use the framework in her head only, to guide her enquiry and organise the information. Later on (in Task 10), she will introduce the client to the ABC terminology, and show him how the information he provides about his problem can be classified in terms of these categories.

Invite Client to Describe Problem

So in detail, the counsellor invites the client to describe the problem he wants to work on. As we have just noted, she assumes the client will be experiencing the problem as a disturbed emotion (C) and an adverse event (A). He may have fleeting negative automatic thoughts (NATs) and/or images, which he would construe at this stage as a factual part of the adverse event. She listens for both, namely she 'listens' for the emotion (though it may be expressed as much in body language as verbally), which she will identify in her mind as the C (the emotional/behavioural problem), and for the adverse event (A) which triggered the C, which the client may express as one or more NATs. She formulates his answer in her own mind in terms of the C and A ('he says he gets anxious (C) when activating event (A) happens'), and then summarises for the client as 'so you get very anxious whenever you meet strangers', and points out these two aspects of the problem.

When the Client Thinks A Causes C

Clients will usually describe a problem in terms of an adverse event and an emotional disturbance (A and C), because most clients think negative events directly cause their distress – to put this in terms of the ABC framework, they are 'A–C thinkers', often completely unaware of the mediating beliefs (B). This means they think A (adverse event) 'causes' C (emotional consequence), so for example they assume their unhappiness at C is caused by a current event A like a critical comment or rejection, or a historical event like abuse in childhood. This way of thinking is common in everyday expressions like 'Mary made me angry', referring to a current event or 'it was the way he was brought up', referring to an early event. They are rarely aware that their C is largely the consequence of their beliefs B of events A rather than the events themselves. We show below how the counsellor will deal with the 'A–C thinking' issue as part of the process of socialising the client into the cognitive perspective.

Is the Problem as Presented an Emotional (C) or Practical (A) Problem?

Sometimes the client may not give the counsellor information about both A and C, but only one or the other. The client may only give her the C (e.g. how depressed and withdrawn he is) as this *is* the problem from his point of view. We call this the 'emotional (C) problem'. Or he may just give her the A (the adverse events, e.g. Mary rejected him) as he may construe his problem in terms of these negative events. We call this the 'practical (A) problem' (Dryden, 2006). In these cases the counsellor will accept the problem as *presented* in this way as the problem to work on, but she still wants the A and C, and will therefore ask for the A when only C is given, and C when A is given.

When the Client Thinks His Beliefs (B) Are Adverse Facts (A)

Since most clients are A–C thinkers, the counsellor knows her client is often unlikely to *knowingly* give her his beliefs – the Bs. Actually he may give her his beliefs, but doesn't think of them as beliefs, but thinks they are simply facts, and therefore part of the A, the adversity. For example, he may say 'Mary rejected me', but thinks this is a fact, an adversity, an A. The counsellor knows this is an inference, which is one type of belief, B. Alternatively the client may say he 'felt rejected' where he thinks of the inferred rejection as a feeling at C. In both cases she notes the distinction in her head, does not explain it to the client yet, but will do so later (Tasks 7 and 9). So she simply summarises the A and C as the client presents it, with his implicit inference at A or C.

After summarising the A and C (but in ordinary language), the counsellor then asks whether it is the emotional problem (C) or the practical problem – the adversity (A) that the client wants to work on. The answer is accepted in this way as the problem as presented.

Client Completes Preparation Steps 1 to 3

The client has now hopefully clearly identified his problem (or the first if several) for CBC. As this is the client's first task, this is a good point for the counsellor to introduce the client to the Client's Guides and Worksheets (Appendix 1), a series of practical steps that will help him carry out his tasks for therapy. The counsellor explains that it is important for him to keep a record of the steps he takes in therapy, that she will provide him with suggested steps throughout the process. The steps in the Preparation Guide are designed to help him make an informed decision, and if he agrees, to prepare for CBC.

The counsellor gives the client a copy of the Preparation Guide and Worksheet, and asks him to complete the first three steps.

The first asks him to write an account of the problem in general terms. This will be the problem as presented, that is either an emotional problem or a practical problem.

The second step asks him to describe how he usually feels and behaves when faced with this type of problem.

The third step asks him to describe the kind of event in general terms that typically happens or he imagines might happen when he has this problem.

Action Summary

1   Your aim is to clarify the problem as experienced and described by the client, in terms of the two aspects, the adverse event and his disturbed reaction, (A and C), using the counselling skills. Once you have enough information

about the client's A and C, you summarise the problem in these terms, being careful not to say A *causes* C but rather A is the event that activates or *triggers* C. This wording is important as it clarifies both components of the problem – the A, the adverse event, which is the practical problem, and C, the emotional/behavioural consequence, which is the emotional problem – but avoids reinforcing the A–C thinking trap that the client may be in. The client is unlikely to express a belief *as* a belief (B) so identified Bs will still be missing at this stage, but this is fine, and will be identified later.

2 If you do not have enough information about both C and A, for example if the client gives you information about C but not A, you use the counselling skills to elicit information about A, or conversely if the client only gives information about A but not C, you ask for information about C.

3 You clarify whether the client is presenting his problem as an emotional/behavioural (C) problem, e.g. 'my problem is I am anxious and avoidant (because people will probably be critical)' or as a practical (A) problem, e.g. 'my problem is that people will probably be critical (and I am anxious and avoidant because of that)'. Why this difference in presentation is important will be addressed in Task 5, goal setting.

4 You summarise the problem as now presented, using ordinary language rather than the ABC terminology at this stage. You identify the two aspects of the problem in your summary.

5 You introduce the client to the Client Guides and Worksheets and the rationale for their use. You give the client a copy of the Preparation Guide. You suggest the client writes a description of the problem as presented in general terms on the Preparation Worksheet – Step 1. You also suggest he writes down two of the key aspects, the adversity and his reaction to it – Steps 2 and 3.

Case Example

Counsellor: OK Brian let's now turn to the problem or problems. I have got the GP's account but I would like to hear it directly from you in your own words. So can you describe the first problem that you would like us to work on? (*Joan starts with the counselling skill Open Invitation to Talk, but phrases it in a way that shows that it is going to be a collaborative working effort and not a diagnosis with a prescription.*)

Client: Well the main problem is that I have great difficulty fulfilling part of my coursework, which is to give presentations to the whole class, which is assessed by the tutors. I just can't seem to do it. It doesn't sound much but it got so bad that I dropped out of uni for a year and nearly didn't go back.

Counsellor: Mmhmm, I see, so you dropped out for a whole year and nearly didn't go back. (*Joan uses the skill Verbal Following – minimal encouragers like head nods, 'mmhmm's' and end-of-sentence repetitions. Verbal Following is a non-directive skill in that it encourages the client to talk but doesn't try to lead him. She also adopts the counselling attentive posture throughout.*)

Client: I have come back to repeat my second year but I just don't think I am going to be able to do it.

Counsellor: What makes it so difficult that you don't think you are going to be able to do it? (*Joan used the skill Open Question but more directively to begin to focus Brian towards talking about the nub of the problem.*)

Client: All I know is I get in a complete state every time.

Counsellor: So you get really panicky and probably tend to freeze up (*Joan reflects the feeling and associated behaviour, which is C in the ABC framework.*)

Client: Yes, and this happens every time I try to give a presentation in front of my peer group and the tutors who are assessing me. This happened before when I was at teacher-training college.

Counsellor: Yes I see, it keeps on happening whenever you have to give one of these presentations. (*Joan paraphrases the content, which is the A in the ABC framework.*)

Client: That's right, and of course then they are all looking at me and judging me every time. I feel a complete nervous wreck and they can obviously see that, and will be thinking I'm completely incompetent – or worse. I can never face that again, and that's why I dropped out for a year, and that's why I get so down.

Counsellor: So every time you try to give your presentation, you panic and freeze, think they can see that and imagine they're all thinking you're incompetent or worse. Is that right? I can see that you then get very depressed about it all. (*Joan offers a tentative summary of the main problem as it generally occurs, including the adverse event (A), Brian's thoughts about that (B) and his consequent feeling (C), and the effect the problem has on his life subsequently.*)

Client: That's right. Except I don't think I'm imagining it – it's pretty obvious that's how they must be thinking. How do I get over that?

Counsellor: OK, I understand what you're saying. (*However Joan makes a mental note that Brian thinks it's a fact (A) that people think he's incompetent, not his inference (B), an example of A–C thinking.*) So Brian, would I be right in saying that the problem you want us to work on is your panic and freezing up, because that is what is affecting your presentation, and through that, people's opinions of you?

Client: Yes, except I sometimes think I really am incompetent. (*Brian tries to hide tears. Joan makes a mental note that Brian has a self-downing belief 'I am incompetent', and others can 'see' that.*)

Counsellor: That's what you believe. (*Brian nods.*) All right, that is clearly very distressing for you. (*Brian nods.*) If it's OK with you Brian we will be sure to include that distressing belief as a central part of the problem we will deal with. So let's make a start by writing down this general problem, and then looking in a bit more detail at the key aspects. (*Joan gives Brian a copy of the preparation guide and suggests he completes the first three steps, namely a description of the problem and two of the key aspects – his emotional and behavioural reaction and a description of the situation that typically triggers that reaction.*)

Task 5. Clarifying the Client's Goals for the Problem

Briefing

So far the counsellor has asked: What is the problem? Now her question is: What is the goal? As soon as the problem is reasonably clear (Task 4), the counsellor helps the client to shift his thinking from problems to goals, from a problem-focused to a solution-focused (or problem-solving) orientation (the present Task 5). This problem to goal shift in focus is important because clients often become so 'stuck' in their problem-focused thinking that they lose sight of their goals, and instead tend to ruminate around the problem with analytic, abstract questions like 'Why am I like this?' or 'Why do they pick on me?' Such questions rarely yield answers, so the client is stuck in a loop in which he is constantly reminding himself that his problem appears to be unsolvable.

From Emotional/Behavioural Problem to Emotional/Behavioural Goal

When the client has presented an emotional/behavioural (C) problem, such as anxiety and avoidance, the counsellor asks, 'How would you prefer to feel and behave in reaction to this event?' At this stage she accepts any answer that suggests less disturbance, such as 'not so anxious', 'calmer', and any behaviour that is more functional, so long as it is realistic. If the client suggests an unrealistic emotional goal like 'completely relaxed' she suggests, 'What about concerned in place of anxious?'

From Practical Problem to Practical Goal to Emotional/Behavioural Goal

When the client has presented a practical (A) problem, such as, for example, facing a job interview, the counsellor asks, 'What do you want to achieve with regard to this practical problem?' However, practical (A) goals, are not directly the goals for CBC, but are goals for the client to aim for (and which the counsellor may later be able to help with) once he has overcome his disturbance and dysfunctional action tendencies with the help of CBC. The counsellor therefore explains (or preferably Socratically helps the client to realise) that he will be better able to achieve his A goal (i.e. find a solution to his A problem) once he has achieved his C goal (i.e. overcome his emotional C problems). So in brief, to achieve the A goal, first achieve the C goal, which brings the counsellor back to the question, 'How would you prefer to feel and behave in reaction to this event?'

Client Completes Preparation Step 4

Once the client has described how he would like to feel and behave when faced with his problem, the counsellor asks him to write this down on the Preparation Worksheet (Step 4). He should then have completed the first four steps.

Action Summary

1 If the client has presented an emotional/behavioural (C) problem, ask 'How would you prefer to feel and/or behave in reaction to this event?' At this stage accept any answer that indicates less disturbed and more functional.
2 If the client has presented a practical (A) problem, ask 'What would be your goal as regards this problem?' Help the client see that he will be better able to achieve this practical goal if he achieves his emotional/behavioural goal first.
3 Ask the client to complete Step 4 on the Preparation Worksheet.

Case Example

Brian has Presented an Emotional/Behavioural Problem:

Counsellor: So the problem is your panic and freezing up. How would you prefer to feel and act in this type of situation – what would be a good goal?
Client: Well I'd like to stay completely calm and relaxed obviously.
Counsellor: OK, that would be good. Would you consider 'concerned' rather than 'completely calm and relaxed'?
Client: Yes, OK, that sounds more realistic.
Counsellor: Well, let's note that as your emotional/behavioural goal on the worksheet.

If Brian had Presented a Practical Problem, the Dialogue Might be:

Counsellor: So the problem is you think your presentation is poor and people are critical. What would be your goal as regards this problem?
Client: Always to give a really cool presentation (gives an A goal).
Counsellor: OK, what are the chances of doing that given you are panicking, shaking, can't think (C problem).
Client: Practically no chance.
Counsellor: So what do we need to do to help you to achieve your goal of giving a cool presentation?
Client: I suppose it's to get over my panicky state (suggests C goal) but I'll never do that either.
Counsellor: Well, let's go a step at a time. What's the goal for us to work on in CBC?

Client:	Get over the panic, obviously.
Counsellor:	And feel and do what? What would be an alternative emotional and behavioural goal?

Counsellor and client then negotiate 'concern' as the emotional goal and approaching rather than avoiding the situation as the behavioural goal, and record this on the worksheet.

Task 6. Clarifying Further Problems and Goals and Drawing up an Initial Problem List

Briefing

Now that the counsellor has the first presented problem and associated goal, she can invite the client to disclose any other problems and associated goals. This invitation could be postponed until after she has introduced the cognitive perspective in Task 7 and the informed decision has been made in Task 8. If the counsellor suspects CBC may not be appropriate or the client seems ambivalent or not at a stage of readiness, she may not pursue Task 6 at the point.

The client may have several other problems. These other problems may be entirely separate or dynamically related to the first, such as anxiety with or followed by depression, anger followed by guilt and so on. Like the first problem, these too may be emotional/behavioural problems (C problems) or practical or health-related problems (A problems), and are clarified and goals established for them in the same way as the first problem, as described in Tasks 4 and 5.

Once clarified, the client is encouraged to write these problems and goals down on separate preparation worksheets, and also write them down in a Problem List. He is then asked to rank order them in terms of their priority for him, putting first that which he wants to address first, followed by the second and so on. The list is not written in stone, and priorities may change, and other problems may occur during the course of sessions. Some problems may be sufficiently similar that they can be dealt with together. As many of the problems as possible will be dealt with in the available time frame, if this is limited.

Action Summary

1 Make a decision whether to explore and list further problems now or leave until after client and counsellor have reached an agreement about the relevance of CBC in this case, the focus of Task 8.
2 If the decision is to go ahead, then ask if there are further problems, and repeat Tasks 4 and 5 for at least some of these. Explore any connections or themes between problems.
3 Ask the client to prioritise the problems, and whether they should continue to give first priority to the first presented problem.
4 Ask the client to write the final list down in a Problems List, in order of priority. Then return to the problem with top priority.

Case Example

In Brian's case the counsellor is satisfied that CBC is relevant. She therefore offers Brian the choice of exploring further problems now or waiting until he has made an informed decision later. Brian decides to explore further problems now.

Counsellor: What other problems would you like us to explore?
Client: Well, I do get very depressed as Dr Smith says.

Counsellor and Client discuss the depression problem, during which it is clear that it is almost entirely a consequence of the first problem, which led to his dropping out of university for a year and seems to threaten his main life and career goals. A decision is made to focus solely on the first problem for the time being, and to return to the depression problem only if it does not ameliorate after resolving (or failing to resolve) the first problem.

Task 7. Introducing the Cognitive Perspective as One Approach

Briefing

Now that the counsellor and client have established the problems and goals, the next tasks are to look at whether CBC is the best, or one of the best, ways of overcoming the problems and achieving the goals, and if so, whether to go ahead with CBC. Before the client can make a judgement about this, he has to have a good understanding of what the cognitive approach is. So the counsellor's current task – Task 7 – is to introduce the cognitive perspective, make sure the client understands it, and to check out whether the client is persuaded that CBC is a good way to tackle his problems.

So far in this practitioner guide we have focused on the A and the C in the application of the ABC framework. We now explicitly turn to the B, the beliefs, in other words the cognitive component in the model, and Task 7 is about introducing this to the client in the most facilitative way.

How to Introduce the Cognitive Component

Having clarified the problems and goals in terms of adverse events and consequent disturbances (As and Cs), the counsellor has prepared the ground for introducing the rationale for the cognitive approach. This is because the A and C are the anchor points which we need to have in place before introducing the cognitive B between the A and C.

This is when the counsellor can guide the client to realise he is an 'A–C thinker' as noted earlier. The task therefore, is to introduce the client to the mediating role of the B, that emotional disturbance is largely the consequence (C) of the beliefs (B), given the adversity (A). This is the aim of Task 7, namely introducing the cognitive perspective as the approach being offered. But this task of 'socialising' the client into the cognitive ABC has to be handled with care, because it transfers emotional responsibility to the individual.

A–B–C Thinking and Emotional Responsibility

Socialising the client into the cognitive ABC framework means persuading them to give up the AC way of thinking and adopting the ABC way, that is, their distress is caused not so much by (or even in severe cases not only by) adversities but by the beliefs they have about them. However, this task needs to be undertaken with considerable care. Putting the B into the AC is good news for the client but could be seen as bad by the client. It is good news in that, though difficult, the client can change his beliefs (B), and therefore he can significantly change his distress and dysfunctional behaviour (C), and thereby improve his effectiveness in dealing with negative events (A). This is in contrast to the AC way of thinking, in which he appears to be the helpless victim of events outside of his control.

However, the ABC way also means that the client needs to accept that his unhealthy negative emotions and dysfunctional behaviours are a consequence largely of his own beliefs, and to that extent he is responsible for them. The adverse events obviously contribute significantly, but as Ellis (1994) puts it, his irrational beliefs contribute the larger part of the variance. But if the counsellor tells him this, he may think she is blaming him for his own unhappiness! This in turn may lead him to unnecessarily feel guilt, shame or anger *in addition* to his original distress, with potentially negative consequences for the therapeutic bond, and possible premature termination of counselling. This is what the counsellor needs to be aware of in planning her approach to socialising the client into the cognitive perspective.

Our approach to Task 7, then, is designed with these concerns in mind. First, the counsellor asks the client for his own 'theory' about his problems and assumes this will be an AC account. Second, she gives an example of an ABC account which is not related to his problem. Third she gives an ABC account which he can clearly relate to his problem. Throughout this process she adopts a mainly Socratic style of drawing out the implications of AC v. ABC, rather than a didactic teaching style. If he can gain the insight for himself, he will be less likely to misinterpret it as a criticism.

Introducing the B

First, then, the counsellor asks for the client's own theory about his problem. Most clients have ruminated about their problems, seeking a solution, and usually not finding one because they are trapped into the AC thinking pattern. The counsellor draws the client's attention to his AC way of thinking, and Socratically draws out the disadvantages of this, namely that if his distress (C) is directly caused by adverse events (A), and if the adverse event doesn't change, his distress will not change. So the only possible goal in this way of thinking is to change the situation. Even at his most optimum level of functioning, he may not be able to change the A, but while he is in a disturbed frame of mind, he will be considerably less able (and probably has not been able) to change A, or could make the situation worse, or could create an adversity that wouldn't otherwise exist. In addition some adverse A's can't be changed, such as the death of a loved one.

So in the next step the counsellor asks the client to suggest another way (other than the A–C way) of construing the problem which might be more productive. The counsellor introduces (or preferably Socratically draws from the client) the idea of the B between the A and the C, namely that events at *A* are always viewed in a certain way, and that this view itself, if distorted in a very negative, may contribute greatly but unnecessarily to the person's distress.

Using an Illustrative Example

The counsellor illustrates with a simple, non-threatening example that is unrelated to the client's own concerns but will give him the intellectual insight into the principle. A good example is one which requires the client to supply the B, such as the one given in the Case Example below. This asks the client what a person would have to be believing to react in three different ways, such as anxiety, anger or neutrally, to the same activating event – a noise at the window late at night. To give this more experiential realism, the client can be asked to vividly imagine the event and each of the three reactions, and then suggest three different beliefs that would lead to the three different reactions.

Using the Client's Problem and Goal

If the client clearly understands this example, and seems favourably disposed to the idea that C is to a great extent the consequence of B, then the counsellor asks the client to think about his own problem and goal he has identified on the Preparation Worksheet in a similar way. For example, he has identified two different emotions, namely his emotional problem and emotional goal. What belief might he have that is leading to his emotional problem, such as anxiety? What alternative belief could he have that would lead to his emotional goal, such as feeling calm or concern? If the client cannot think of an alternative, the counsellor tentatively suggests some and he chooses one. She also encourages him to notice the difference between the two, including the presence and absence of biases such as all-or-nothing thinking, selective attention, relying on intuition such as emotional reasoning, and self-reproach (Burns, 1999). We offer more guidance on such inferential biases in Task 10 and distinguish these from evaluations, as we also discussed in Chapter 1.

Client Completes Preparation Steps 5 and 6

If the client agrees, the counsellor invites him to write down his anxious-making belief under 'Biased (or possibly biased) belief', and the alternative under 'Alternative belief' – Steps 5 and 6 on the Preparation Worksheet.

Seeking an Informed Decision

If the client can complete this example based on their own problem, then the counsellor explores whether the client thinks this approach, namely the cognitive approach, might be helpful in tackling his problems. Examination of the now filled in Preparation Worksheet explicitly shows the relationship between the events, beliefs and consequences and is a useful aid for this discussion. Our experience is that often the client might agree that this approach is worth exploring, but is sceptical that it will work, especially if they are depressed, as the depressive style of thinking is intrinsically pessimistic.

We suggest the counsellor tells the client that she accepts his scepticism, that it is indeed part of their depressive outlook (and clients usually accept this) and that the counsellor is only asking the client if they think the approach makes sense and is worth exploring in CBC.

If the client understands the role of B and agrees the approach makes sense and is worth exploring, Task 7 has been completed, and the counsellor goes on to Task 8, either immediately in the same session, or at the first of the next session. If the client is still uncertain and wants to think about it, then the counsellor invites the client to come to the next session ready to make a decision – Task 8. In both cases the counsellor gives the client a handout summarising the cognitive approach to read, or CD or DVD recorded demonstration of CBC. The counsellor can at this stage introduce the client to the specific ABC framework, though our preference is to keep this for Task 10, and to stick to ordinary language descriptions at this stage.

A Self-monitoring Homework Experiment

One further approach the counsellor uses to help persuade the client that it is the beliefs that mainly cause the emotions (the B–C connection) is by inviting him to carry out a homework task in the spirit of an experiment, before the next decision-making session. The client is asked to monitor his emotions during the week, and when he experiences emotional distress about one of the problems he has presented, he also notes the thoughts or images that are going through his mind simultaneously with the emotions. So, for example, if he finds himself worrying or ruminating, he tries to identify the distressed feeling, and then the negative thought that will automatically accompany the feeling. He makes a note both of the feeling and the negative automatic thought (NAT). In this way the client should discover for himself that disturbed emotions invariably follow NATs or other types of negative beliefs.

Adverse Event	Beliefs/NATs	Disturbed Emotion
3	2	1
	Alternative Belief	**Emotional Goal**
	5	4

FIGURE 4.1   *Daily Thought Record (DTR)*

The client can use a Daily Thought Record (DTR, Figure 4.1 and Appendix 1), based on the Preparation Worksheet they will now be familiar with. This version of the DTR can be used in a graded way, depending on the level of complexity the client is comfortable with. So, for example, at a minimum the client could fill in boxes 1 and 2 (the disturbed emotion and the belief or NAT respectively, or they could add a brief description of the adverse event, box 3, or they could also construct an alternative emotional goal (4) and an alternative more helpful belief (5), in the way described in the Thought Monitoring Steps provided in the Preparation Guide (Appendix 1).

Action Summary

1 Elicit the client's own 'theory' of what is causing his C problem (emotional disturbance and behavioural dysfunction).
2 Draw the client's attention to this as an AC theory, if it is, in which the C problem is apparently caused by/is the consequence of the adversity A. If the client offers an ABC theory, agree with this, and show how it is different from an AC theory.

3 Guide the client, preferably Socratically by questions, but if necessarily didactically with a short explanation, to the disadvantages of the AC theory.

4 Ask the client for an alternative explanation, and guide him to the role of the B between the A and the C. Illustrate with an example, such as the 'noise at the window' scenario which shows three alternative Cs to the same A. Ask the client what he would have to be inferring in order to experience each emotion, and make tentative suggestions if he has difficulty doing so. Ask the client to imagine each scenario, to give added realism.

5 If the client understands the example, use the same format for the client's own problem, and invite him to identify two beliefs about the same adversity, a biased one that leads to his problem emotion and an alternative that should lead to a healthy negative emotion he would prefer to have (his emotional goal). Get the client to imagine each scenario to better experience the B–C (belief-consequent emotion) connection. Get him to write the two beliefs in the relevant belief boxes on Preparation Worksheet, Step 4.

6 Ask the client to evaluate whether this cognitive approach might be worth exploring with regard to his own problems, even though he may be sceptical about the outcome. If the client agrees the approach is relevant, give the client an explanatory handout (explanations of cognitive behaviour therapy are widely available, for example downloadable for free from www.babcp.com), and go to Task 8. If they disagree and do not want to continue, suggest alternative routes to getting help and/or refer back to the referrer. If they are uncertain and want more time to think about it, give them an explanatory handout and preferably a CD or DVD recorded demonstration, and invite them to a further session ready to make a decision.

7 If the client is willing, invite them to carry out the Self-monitoring Homework Assignment as described in the Briefing.

Case Example

Counsellor:	(*with the preparation worksheet in front of them*) You have written how you felt panicky and you froze – that is the emotional and behavioural problem you want to get rid of, and replace it with your emotional/behavioural goal of feeling concerned. (*Brian agrees.*)
Counsellor:	What do you think is causing your panic? If we can identify and change the cause (or reason), we should be able to change your panicky feeling to the feeling you want?
Client:	I see what you mean. That makes sense, in theory anyway.

Counsellor: OK, so what do you think, in theory, is the cause of your panic?

Client: Well, obviously it's the people – my assessors, my peers – thinking I'm rubbish isn't it?

Counsellor: (*noting the A–C thinking*) So if it's a *fact* they think you're rubbish that will directly and automatically cause you to panic and freeze up? That leaves you totally vulnerable, almost like a helpless victim of whatever they think?

Client: Well, it feels like that, and I do feel helpless.

Counsellor: Can you think of another way of looking at this, in which you wouldn't be so helpless?

Client: No, other than somehow stopping them thinking that way.

Counsellor: That would be nice, but might not work! So how about this: We all view our adversities in a certain way, and our views differ, more or less optimistic or pessimistic. You view these trying situations in a certain way. Suppose your view is excessively pessimistic, wouldn't that make you feel worse?

Client: I suppose, but I think it's realistic.

Counsellor: OK, you think it's realistic, and you could be right, but you could also be wrong couldn't you? (*Brian nods.*) (*At this point Joan presents the 'noise at the window' scenario and asks him to carry out the exercise as described in the Action Summary above. Joan helps Brian to see that each emotion follows from a particular inference – e.g. anger if he thinks it's his partner back late again and forgot to take a key, anxiety if he thinks it's a burglar, neutral if he thinks it's the wind blowing.*)

Counsellor: If you look at your own emotional problem and emotional goal on the worksheet, what different beliefs might you have about the situation to have these two different emotional reactions?

Client: Well I know what I'm thinking to feel panicky – they think I'm incompetent! But to feel concern I'd have to think the opposite, that they think I'm fine, but that's ridiculous, I'm not.

Counsellor: Can I suggest that to feel concern you might think, not 'they think I'm fine', but 'some might think I'm incompetent but some might not, and instead be quite understanding?

Client:	I suppose so.
Counsellor:	So let me ask you: is it a belief or a fact 'they think I'm incompetent?' Is it a belief or a fact 'some might understand?'
Client:	Beliefs, not facts.
Counsellor:	If you believe 'they might think I'm incompetent' that makes you have what feeling?
Client:	Panic.
Counsellor:	And if you believe 'some might think I'm incompetent but some might not, and be quite understanding' that would lead to what alternative feeling?
Client:	OK, maybe more concerned than panic. But I don't believe the second one.
Counsellor:	But it's a *belief* nonetheless, not a fact, and therefore could be true or false? (*Brian agrees.*)

(*Joan asks Brian to write the two beliefs down on the worksheet following Step 5. She then points out – or asks Brian to point out – that it is clear, from the filled-in worksheet, that it is the beliefs that lead to the emotional consequences, given the adverse situation.*)

Counsellor:	This is the aim of CBC, to help people change their beliefs when those beliefs magnify the adversity and so cause them to be unnecessarily distressed and dysfunctional. (*Joan and Brian then discuss further the pros and cons of the CBC approach.*)
Counsellor:	Brian, what do you now think about the relevance of CBC to your own problem?
Client:	It makes sense, and I'd like to really try, though I am a bit sceptical to be honest.
Counsellor:	That is all I ask, that it makes sense to you and you are prepared to really try. Don't worry about being sceptical, that's to be expected at this stage. (*Joan gives Brian a handout on CBT to familiarise himself further with the approach.*)

The Counsellor then introduces the Self-monitoring Homework Assignment and the DTR (Appendix 1 and Figure 4.1). Brian expresses willingness to carry this out as part of the preparation before making an informed decision, so Joan takes him through the task as described in the Briefing (also described in the Thought Monitoring Steps 6 to 9), using the DTR to record their observations.

Task 8. Reaching an Informed Joint Decision and Commitment to the Method of Working

By the end of Task 7, the client should have had sufficient information and experience about what the cognitive approach means to judge whether it has credibility for him as an approach which, in principle, should be able to help him.

Equally, the counsellor is sufficiently 'informed' about the client and the client's problem to judge whether the cognitive approach is appropriate to help him to achieve a positive outcome.

The time has come for both counsellor and client to make an explicit decision together, whether or not to go ahead with CBC, and to make a commitment to the work that this entails, as described in the CBC method of working. If either or both decide against going ahead, the counsellor needs to suggest alternative avenues of help, or refer back to the referrer with a request that they explore alternative channels, as discussed in Task 1.

Commitment to the CBC Method of Working

If both client and counsellor make a joint decision to pursue CBC, the counsellor negotiates the commitments entailed in the CBC method of working, which means that this method will be adhered to by them both from this point on. She gives the client a handout of the following points, and they go through all the points together. The points include the following:

- *Session length.* Sessions are traditionally about 50 minutes long, though this can be varied by agreement, depending on the type of problem and the stage reached. So, for example, if the client is undertaking a re-experiencing account of a traumatic event, one and a half to two hours maybe required, whereas towards the end of counselling and the client has learned how to become their own counsellor, half an hour may be sufficient. However, it is important they both agree to start punctually and to end at the agreed time.
- *Session frequency.* The frequency of sessions will usually be weekly, though this can also be varied by agreement, with two or three times a week at the beginning of counselling, particularly in cases of more severe distress and disturbed behaviour. Frequency will be tapered towards the end, reducing to once fortnightly, once a month with a three- and six-month booster session when required.

- *Time-frame*. An approximate time-frame is agreed in conjunction with goal setting and bearing in mind the severity and complexity of the problem, at the end of which they agree to review progress towards the goal, and a decision whether to terminate and discharge or to continue for a further period, at the end of which counselling will be terminated unless there are exceptional grounds for considering a third extension. The counsellor seeks the client's agreement that the client will, over the course of counselling, learn how to become his own counsellor, that the counsellor will coach him how to do so, and that he will take increasing responsibility for the session agendas. We suggest the counsellor familiarises herself with the Ending Stage (Chapter 11), particularly Task 18, for guidance.
- *Agenda*. A mutually agreed agenda is set at the beginning of each session, to ensure the relevant issues are prioritised and focused upon, and collaboration is maintained. Items that will usually be included are:

  o Brief review of the last period since the last session.
  o Review of the last session, including new insights or problems.
  o Assessment of current mood, either a brief questionnaire such as the Beck Depression Inventory – II (Beck et al., 1996), or the Beck Anxiety Inventory (Beck et al., 1988) or a more informal SUDS rating where 0 = no disturbance and 10 = maximum disturbance.
  o Review of homework set from previous session. This is discussed as a separate point below.
  o The main topics for the session. This will take up a major part of the time. Some topics will be brought by the client, such as new problems or issues to do with an ongoing problem. Other topics will be introduced by the counsellor, such as the task and steps reached in this guide. So in the present session the counsellor will be negotiating this task, namely Task 8 and the mutual commitments, and anticipating and setting up the work of the next, Task 9.
  o Setting of new homework. This is discussed as a separate point below.

- The agenda 'gives permission' to the counsellor to keep the client on track and if necessary bring him back to the topic, while always being sensitive to and responding to the client's needs. It is useful to summarise each point and encourage the client to make notes.
- *Between-session homework*. The type of homework will be dictated by the tasks appropriate to, and agreed at the stage of counselling reached, so in this Preparation Stage the focus for homework will be mainly on facilitating problem clarification and goal setting, gaining the cognitive-emotive insight and the associated Self-monitoring Assignment, if undertaken. In general, new homework could be a continuation of the previous homework, such as continued but expanded thought monitoring, plus new homework linked to the next task. A common guiding framework for

homework and goal setting generally is summed up in the acronym SMART, which stands for

- ○ Specific
- ○ Measurable
- ○ Achievable
- ○ Realistic
- ○ Time-frame (a date for completion)

- Setting homework can be time consuming and time needs to be set aside at the end of the therapy session, and time also set aside at the beginning of the next session to discuss the previous session's homework. A basic session and homework report form is provided in Chapter 9.

Action Summary

1 Ask the client whether he understands the main principle of CBC (and satisfy yourself that he genuinely does, such as by asking him to tell you what the main principle is), check he thinks it could be helpful and he wants to try it. Share with him your view that you also think it is relevant (if you do). You can now optionally ask him to write a statement giving his informed consent to receiving CBC and signing and dating it.
2 Write out a list from the method of working points listed above, go through them with your client item by item, and ask for his (and give your) agreement to work this way. You can both sign and date this if you wish.

Case Example

After considering the method of working list, Brian shows he understands CBC and what it would entail, says he thinks CBC is relevant and could be helpful, wants to try, and is happy to sign and date an informed consent statement. Joan and Brian also jointly agree to follow the method of working.

5

Beginning Stage I – What's the Problem Specifically? Cognitive Assessment of a Specific Example

Once the informed decision and the commitment to go ahead has been made, the CBC process moves from the Preparation Stage, which was covered in Chapters 3 and 4, to the Beginning Stage in this and the next chapter. This chapter (Chapter 5, Beginning Stage I) focuses on cognitive assessment in two Counsellor Tasks and five Client Assessment Steps, while the next chapter (Chapter 6, Beginning Stage II) focuses on cognitive conceptualisation and constructing alternative functional goals and beliefs in a further two Counsellor Tasks and four Client Goal Planning Steps.

Task 9. Elicit a Specific Example of the Problem

Briefing

The counsellor asks for a *specific* example of the problem the client prioritised in his Problem List, and described in *general* terms on the Preparation Worksheet. She needs this specific example in order to carry out a more in-depth ABC assessment and conceptualisation of his problem and goal setting within the cognitive framework. Ideally the example should be typical of the problem, should be vivid (can be visualised or imagined) and recent or currently re-experienced (a current problem). The client is encouraged to visualise *where* he was, *when* it happened, *who* else was present, *what* actually happened and any other concrete detail. Equally if the client is anticipating an adverse event, this should also be described in specific detail as he imagines it. If the client had carried out the Self-monitoring Homework Experiment and as a result recorded any specific problems which may have arisen during the week, then one of these could be used to provide an example.

In carrying out this task, the counsellor is helping the client move from the general, more abstract level of a *type* of problem so far identified in Task 4, to a concrete example of such a problem, which has occurred or which is anticipated. The counsellor then uses the same procedure she used in Task 4 to encourage the client to describe this specific example in his own words and in his own way. For the moment she goes with whatever he gives her, so long as it is specific and contains an adversity and a problematic emotional/behavioural consequence.

The counsellor gives the client a copy of the Assessment and Goal Planning Guide and Worksheet (Appendix 2) covering Steps 1 to 6, and invites him to follow this guide just as he did the Preparation Guide, starting with Step 1 by writing down the specific example of the problem.

Action Summary

1   Ask the client for a specific example of the general problem he wrote down on the Preparation Worksheet. Explain why you need a specific example. Get him to imagine in concrete detail, answering the four questions – where, when, with whom and what happened.
2   Ask the client to write this specific example on the Assessment and Goal Planning Worksheet.

Case Example

Counsellor: We now need a specific example of the problem you have described in general terms on the Preparation Worksheet. This will enable us to do a thorough assessment of a specific situation, your actual thoughts and images about that situation and more precisely how you felt and what you did or had an urge to do.

Client:	That shouldn't be difficult. They are so vivid in my mind.
Counsellor:	OK, then, choose one that is typical of the problem and you can remember and visualise well. Maybe one came up when you were doing the self-monitoring homework task that you could use. Say where and when it happened, who was there and what happened.
Client:	OK. In my first year of uni, I had to do a presentation after Christmas. It was a group presentation and it was assessed, so there was not only my peer group but the tutors all there. I was terrified, I just wanted to run. I made a complete mess of it, it was awful. (*Joan invites Brian to write this description down on the Assessment and Goal Planning Worksheet, Step 1.*)

Task 10. Cognitive Assessment of the Specific Example

Briefing

A fundamental task for the counsellor is to help the client become aware of the normally elusive and out-of-awareness beliefs that largely cause his disturbance. She has prepared the ground in the preparation stage, but now builds on this with a much more in–depth cognitive assessment of his problem, which is intended to be a discovery process for the client.

In the current Task 10 the counsellor engages the client in jointly carrying out an ABC assessment of the specific example of the problem which the client has written down on the Assessment and Goal Planning Worksheet (Step 1). The counsellor will help the client to identify the activating event (A) and the specific disturbed emotional consequence (C), and then the mediating beliefs (B), using the steps in the Assessment Guide.

This is also the point when the ABC framework and terminology can be explicitly introduced. The natural place for this will be the start of a new session, usually between the second and fourth. Since the counsellor has prepared the ground with the client already, this more formalised assessment and conceptualisation should be partly familiar to the client, except this time with specific examples of problems. The counsellor will invite the client to write down the steps as they go along in the worksheet with the help of the guide (Appendix 2) and optionally also on a whiteboard.

The counsellor proposes that she and the client carry out a detailed assessment and conceptualisation of the specific problem he has written down in Step 1. She introduces and explains the ABC model, revisits the principle of the B–C connection, shows how the general problem he described on the Preparation Worksheet can be framed in terms of the ABC model, and that this framework will now be used to analyse the specific example of the problem now in front of them.

The counsellor uses the ABC categories to identify the components of the specific problem, namely A (the adverse event that triggered his disturbance), his C (consequent disturbance) and the B (his mediating beliefs that made the event an adversity and led to his disturbance). She prefers to begin the process by first eliciting the problem C, then the adverse event A, then the beliefs B.

Step 2: Elicit the Disturbed Feeling and Dysfunctional Behaviour – the Consequent Problem C

The counsellor asks the client to hold in mind the specific example he has written down for Step 1, and to focus on and describe the disturbed *emotion* he experiences, and any unhelpful action or action tendency that is associated with it. This will be the consequent emotional and behavioural problem (C).

The Disturbed Emotional Consequence

Since the client believes he is facing an adverse event (A), the emotion he describes will inevitably be *negative*, which is appropriate. (The client may later discover, after the Middle Stage intervention, that there is no adversity after all, for example when a health-anxious client discovers in fact he has no physical health problem. At that point he should no longer have a negative emotion, but up to that point, a healthy negative emotion is appropriate.)

However, the counsellor is seeking to draw out a problematic, unhealthy emotion, so she asks what *disturbed* emotion was he experiencing (or be likely to experience). The emphasis here is on an emotion which is dysfunctional and unhealthy, to distinguish it clearly from a functional and healthy negative emotion (see Chapter 1). Dryden (2009) makes a distinction between a number of 'unhealthy' and 'healthy' negative emotions, such as between depression and sadness, anxiety and concern, emphasising that the healthy alternative can be deeply felt, but not disturbing. Others also make distinctions, for example between dysfunctional worry that would characterise Generalised Anxiety Disorder and from functional worry (Wells, 2009).

The Problematic Behavioural Consequence

Having identified a disturbed emotion, she then asks for a description of any problematic *behavioural* consequences he might have, given the adverse situation. This might be an actual action he carried out, or an action tendency that he wanted to carry out but repressed. These actions and action tendencies are integrally related to the emotion, and certain actions are characteristic of certain emotions, such as avoidance and escape that go with anxiety.

These evolved actions would be functional if, for example, the anxiety was a reaction to real danger. It would then be a highly adaptive *safety seeking behaviour*, but the counselling process is designed to help the client discover that he is not facing a real danger, and that the safety seeking behaviour is in fact maladaptive (Salkovskis, 1991) in that it prevents effective problem solving. In Chapter 6 we describe how the counsellor shows the client that this pattern of behaviour will often prevent him from discovering his 'danger' belief is invalid. For example, a client is helped to realise that by compulsively hand washing she prevents herself from discovering that there is effectively no risk of contamination.

Sometimes, however, the counsellor helps the client discover that his safety seeking behaviour can actually *create* an adverse situation when previously there was none, in a self-fulfilling cycle. For example, by defensively staying silent the socially anxious client unwittingly appears cold and disinterested, and *then* gets rejection. At this and other points, she shows the client in a simple diagram that the ABC sequence is cyclical; namely, not only does A lead to B lead to C, but C can lead to and modify A, and the cycle repeats again. This cycle is described in Chapter 1 and techniques for overcoming it are described in Chapter 6.

The counsellor ensures the client identifies and understands in principle, the role of the behavioural consequence (C) in preventing disconfirmation of his beliefs and potentially 'contaminating' the situation (A) in a self-fulfilling cycle.

Client Completes Assessment Step 2

Having identified the disturbed emotion and the dysfunctional behaviour for the specific example, the counsellor asks the client to write them down on the Assessment and Goal Planning Worksheet (Assessment Step 2, Appendix 2) under C: Consequent Problem Emotion/Behaviour.

Step 3: Ask for a Factual Description of the Specific Adverse Event – the A

The counsellor asks the client to continue to hold the emotion (C) in mind, and to provide as best he can from memory, a literal, factual description of the specific adverse event (A) in which he experienced this emotion (C). If he gives insufficient information for an 'external' event, she prompts him to report when and where the event happened, with whom, and what was happening exactly. When the event is 'internal', such as a physical sensation, an intrusive thought or a hallucination, he describes the event in detail, but still needs to pin it down to time and place. In both cases the client is encouraged to bring to mind an image of the event with all the sensory modalities, either from a memory or as they imagine it would be, and to describe this image.

The adverse event (A) being focused on in this assessment could be the start of an ABC episode or it could be in the middle of a cycle of ABC episodes – A–B–C–A–B–C. In the example above, by defensively staying silent at C, the socially anxious client unwittingly appears cold and disinterested, and *then* gets rejection at A. In this case the situation A comes in the middle of two episodes, and is 'contaminated' by the client's behaviour at C. He then draws further biased inferences and extreme evaluations at B, leading to further dysfunction at C.

Before recording the event A, the counsellor ensures the client agrees that his description is as factual as possible, and not an interpretation or inference. The client is asked: 'Is this your factual description of the event or your interpretation of it?' When the client complies with a factual description, the counsellor also points out that even this factual description of A may contain errors, as memories are themselves prone to bias, and it is advisable to precede the memory description with the words 'as best as I can remember …' In addition she ensures his description of A reflects its position in a cycle of episodes and the description includes an account of the effect of his own behaviour on the situation.

Client Completes Assessment Step 3

If the client confirms his description of the adverse event is, as best as he can remember, a literal, factual description and not an interpretation or inference, she asks the client to write the description down on the worksheet under A: Adverse Event as actually remembered or imagined (Assessment Step 3, Appendix 2).

Step 4: Elicit the Biased Inferential Belief (B¹)

The counsellor's next task is to elicit the biased or probably biased inference that is leading to his emotion (C), namely to identify what he was inferring about the adverse event he has just described that was so disturbing (such as anxiety-provoking, depressing, etc.). This inference is the first of two types of belief (B¹) she will seek that will 'explain' his disturbance. The second is his evaluation (B²) of the event, which is the focus of Step 5.

Explaining and Recognising Inferences

Inferences are thoughts (B¹) the client has about the meaning of the adverse event (A). The counsellor explains that an inference is a belief that goes beyond the evidence, such as a prediction, and therefore might be true *or* false. Technically speaking an inference is the act or process of deriving a conclusion based on what one already knows or on what one assumes. The statement(s) given as evidence for or that supposedly lead to the conclusion are known as premise(s). The rationale for identifying them is that very biased negative inferences contribute to (though do not directly cause) disturbance, but can be challenged and changed in CBC, as part of the process of overcoming disturbance.

The client may have difficulty in recognising inferences since he may usually see them not as thoughts (B) at all but as factual aspects of the adverse event (A), 'and you just have to accept facts'. The counsellor therefore helps him recognise his inferences by the form they take.

An inference may take the form, implicitly or explicitly, of an 'if … then …' statement. *If* (factual description of the A) *then* (inference B of what this means). So a client may assert that if the client's friend crossed the road (A) then it means (B) she was avoiding him. There may then be a second inference, given the first. So if she was avoiding him (first inference B) then it meant she was rejecting him (second B). Alternatively, the friend crossed the road *because* she wanted to avoid him, and so on. These conclusions do not, of course, follow from the premises.

Identifying and Eliciting Biased Inferences

After this explanation, the counsellor seeks to elicit the client's actually or probably biased inferences, and to help the client discover how they may be contributing to (though not themselves evoking) his disturbance and often self-defeating behaviour.

Techniques for Eliciting Inferences

A technique for obtaining the *relevant* inferences, namely the ones that are contributing to the disturbance and behaviour, is called inference chaining in REBT, or downward laddering or the downward arrow technique in CT. One form of questioning in inference chaining uses the 'if … then … ' format. So:

- 'If that happens (description of adverse event A), what meaning does that have for you that you find disturbing (description of emotion C)?'

The question can be repeated to get deeper inferences and, as discussed next, one or more evaluations. Inference chaining often produces several inferences, one following from the other in an 'if … then' sequence. So in the example above:

- 'My friend crossing the road (A) means she was avoiding me.'
- 'My friend avoiding me (first inference B) means she doesn't like me any more (second B).'

Counsellor and client select one to be the focus of the ABC assessment, preferably but not necessarily the one at the bottom of the chain, and which leads to the evaluations, which we address next.

Eliciting Biased Inferences

Since the client is facing an actual or perceived adverse event (A), the inference as well as the emotion will be negative, and just as with the negative emotion, it is desirable and healthy that it should be so, even if the event turns out not to be adverse. However, the counsellor is anticipating a probably *biased* negative inference, one that is likely to be contributing to an unhealthy, disturbed emotion and a tendency to behave in a self-protective but self-defeating way. The emphasis here, then, is on a biased and inaccurate negative inference, to distinguish it clearly from an unbiased and more accurate one.

The task now is to identify the type of bias that probably characterises the client's inference (B^1). Common forms of bias were originally identified by Aaron Beck in the early 1960s, and comprehensive lists are available in any good CBT practitioner book, such as Judith Beck's Cognitive Therapy (1995, p. 119), Robert Leahy's Cognitive Therapy Techniques (2003, pp. 32–33) or the classic client self-help book by David Burns called *Feeling Good: The New Mood Therapy* (1999, pp. 42–49).

The counsellor can use such lists to help persuade the client that his inference may be biased, though he is likely only to accept this as a possibility since at this stage he remains convinced they are true. Once he accepts the possibility, she and the client identify the kind of bias that might characterise his inference. Once this identification has been done, the counsellor explores with the client whether he would now be open to the idea that it is not just possible but probable that his inference is biased, contributing as it does to his unhealthy negative emotion.

We suggest many of the biases can be grouped into the following three:

* All-or-nothing thinking, also known as polarised, dichotomous, 'absolutistic' or categorical thinking, and also underlies over-generalising, and the tendency to magnify (e.g. failures) and minimise (e.g. achievements). This is where the client infers an outcome in only one of two categories, such as 'always' 'every' 'never' 'totally' 'extremely' instead of on a continuum or dimension such as 'some', 'partly' or 'relatively'. For example, 'if I don't get this job, I will *never* get another one'.
* Negatively biased arbitrary inference, including jumping to conclusions, mind reading and fortune telling. This is where the client views an ambiguous or neutral event and systematically but arbitrarily draws a negative conclusion. For example, 'my raised pulse means I have heart disease' or 'crossing the road means he doesn't like me'. This can be combined with all-or-nothing thinking to produce '.... I have a fatal heart disease' or '... he doesn't like me at all and never will', etc. A variation of this negatively biased arbitrary inference is negatively biased selective attention, also known as mental filter, where only the negative possibilities are focused on and all others are overlooked or discounted.
* Internal or external negative attributional bias. This is where the client systematically attributes the cause of an adverse event either to himself (internal attribution), as in personalisation, or to the other person or situation (external attribution). When combined with all-or-nothing thinking, this is shown in the tendency to always attribute to oneself or always attribute to the other.

Checking the Distinction between an Event (A) and an Inference (B¹)

At this point it is important for the counsellor to check that the client understands and agrees there is a distinction between his factual description of the adverse event (Step 3) and his inferences about the event, for this is the distinction between the event A and the inference (B^1), which contributes significantly to the disturbance. This is part of the insight process of bringing the B into the ABC.

One way the counsellor draws out the distinction is with a similar question she asked in Step 3: 'Is this a factual description of the event or your (strongly held) inference/interpretation or opinion?' This question is important, as the client may otherwise be unlikely to reflect on the difference, and will continue to mistake his inferences for facts, particularly if the inference is encoded in an image of the event. The counsellor can ask the client to explain the difference, or if he seems unclear, to explain the difference herself, namely that the description is what he thought actually happened, whereas his inference is a judgement he believes is true but could be false. If he still seems unclear, the counsellor repeats the 'tap at the window' exercise in Task 7. Further guidance is also given in Task 1 of the Middle Stage.

Client Completes Assessment Step 4

Once the client recognises his inferences are possibly or probably biased and accepts the distinction between the factual event (A, Step 3) and his inferences (B^1) about the event, she asks him to write the biased inference down on the Assessment and Goal Planning Worksheet under B^1: Biased Inference about A (Assessment Step 4, Appendix 2). He may prefer to qualify the bias as probable or at least possible. She also asks him to rate his conviction level in the inference on a 0–10 scale where 0 means no conviction and 10 means absolutely certain. In making this rating he is also acknowledging that this is an inference (B^1) and not a factual event (A), while insisting that he may still think it is true.

Step 5: Seek an Extreme Evaluative Belief (B^2)

The counsellor and client have now reached the last, but arguably the most important, step in the ABC assessment of the specific example of the problem (Assessment Step 1). They now have the disturbed C, the description of the event A, and the negative inference B^1. Staying with the same specific example of the problem, the counsellor is now looking for the second type of belief, the evaluations (B^2). She asks the client to identify what it was about the activating event *as inferred* that was so disturbing, that is, not just distressing but truly disturbing. In other words, if we assumed the inference was true (as the client thinks) what would be so disturbing about that? For example, if the client's friend really was rejecting him (inference) what would be so disturbing about that?

The counsellor explains that whereas an inference is a belief that something is true or false, an evaluation is an assertion that something is good or bad and, in the case of negative emotional problems, always bad. However, the kind of evaluations the counsellor is looking for are extreme evaluations, that the adverse event as inferred was not only bad but was *catastrophically* bad or *awful*, was absolutely *intolerable*, and meant that the client himself, the other people or life in general was totally *bad* or *worthless*. We see here the all-or-nothing bias discussed earlier, but this time applied to evaluations.

These are the dysfunctional evaluations or 'hot beliefs' which follow from an extreme and inflexible rule of living that certain negative events (As) absolutely must not happen (or conversely that certain positive events absolutely must happen). This rule is described as an irrational Demanding Philosophy by Ellis (1963) and is one of a number of beliefs that Beck (1976) calls Dysfunctional Assumptions. When the client has this extreme rule of living, and the adverse event goes against or might go against the rule, then he will also very probably draw the extreme negative evaluations, because they follow from the rule.

The counsellor helps the client recognise when he has the extreme rule of living and the extreme evaluations that follow when the rule is broken. The rule and these derivatives are as follows:

- *Extreme Rule of Living*. The event as inferred *absolutely should never* have happened, or *must never* happen, but if it did, or does, some or all of the following beliefs would also be the case.
- *Catastrophising belief*. The event as inferred was *absolutely awful* or *catastrophic*, or would be if it happened.
- *Intolerance belief*. The event as inferred was *absolutely intolerable* and the client *cannot* cope at all, or it would be intolerable if it happened and the client would not be able to cope.
- *Self or Other Depreciation/Core Belief*. The event as inferred showed or proved that the client was *totally bad, worthless, useless or flawed*, or would be if it happened. Or the event showed that another person was *totally bad or worthless*, or would be if it happened.

These evaluations are implicit (that is hidden) in the inferences, and are made explicit (that is revealed) by the counsellor's assessment, as these statements show. For example, when the client believes his friend might reject him (the event as inferred), he might believe the following:

- He absolutely must not be rejected like this (implicit demand or dysfunctional assumption or rule of living), but if he is, that would prove or show that he was worthless (implicit core belief).
- That would be catastrophic (implicit catastrophising belief),
- And absolutely unbearable (implicit intolerance belief).

The counsellor will be listening for these evaluations, which will often be accompanied by a visible change in affect, which brings us to another key point about evaluations.

Not only do clients think that their adversities are facts ('the pulse means I probably have a heart problem'; 'the critical comment means they think I am stupid'), but they then tend to think that this 'fact' directly causes their distress. In truth the 'facts' are nearly always inferences as we have just seen, but even the 'inferences' are not just inferences but contain within them evaluations, and it is the evaluations and not the inferences that lead to emotional consequences. So implicit in the inference 'I probably have a heart problem' is the implicit evaluation 'and that would be catastrophic'.

Because it is evaluations that lead to emotional distress, there will often be a visible change in affect as shown in body language, when the client gets close to his dysfunctional evaluations. The counsellor can pick up on this, draw attention to it and ask the client what was in their mind when they showed the affect change.

For example, one technique the counsellor uses to get evaluations is a continuation of inference chaining until the client shows a change in affect and maybe on the point of expressing one or more of the above statements. Alternatively the counsellor can ask directly whether it would be bad or awful, barely tolerable or intolerable if the event happened. When self-esteem or the esteem of another is clearly involved, the counsellor can ask what it means about him or another person, or more directly whether they are making a judgement about the person's behaviour or about the person themselves.

One important technique the counsellor uses in inference-to-evaluation chaining is to assume the client's biased inferences are true. The client still thinks, of course, that the inferences are true, as none have yet been challenged, but it is essential for the counsellor to have the client at this stage continue to imagine the inferences are true, in order to get to the evaluations.

As with inferences, the counsellor draws out the distinction between evaluations, which are a B, and factual descriptions, which are an A. She can repeat a similar question as before: 'Is this a factual description of the event or your (strongly held) evaluation?' Again this helps the client reflect on the difference, and register the difference firmly in his mind. Alternatively, the counsellor might need to explain the difference, for example that the description is what he thought actually happened, whereas his evaluation is a value judgement that could be right or wrong, or a gross exaggeration, for example, something judged absolutely awful that is more realistically judged as relatively bad or even not bad at all. The counsellor also ensures the client understands the difference between an evaluation and an inference, that the latter is a true–false judgement, the former a good–bad judgement.

The Client Completes Assessment Step 5

Once he accepts the distinction between his evaluations, factual descriptions and inferences, she suggests he writes his evaluations down on the worksheet (Assessment Step 5, Appendix 2). In the B^2 box we provide space for the four Extreme Evaluations, namely Demanding (to include 'musts' and 'absolute shoulds'), Awfulising, LDT (Low Disturbance Tolerance) and Self/Other/Life Downing. She also asks him to rate his conviction level in the evaluations on a 0–10 scale where 0 means no conviction and 10 means absolutely certain. As with inferences, this rating also underlines the distinction that these are beliefs not facts, while acknowledging that he may still think they are true.

Coaching the Client to Capture His Bs

Having now completed the ABC Assessment of the specific example, the client has hopefully learned that it is his dysfunctional beliefs B (inferences and evaluations) that mediate between the adverse event A and his consequent distress C. The counsellor's next task is to coach the client to apply this insight, to learn the skill of capturing the elusive negative automatic thoughts (NATs) and beliefs in his everyday thinking so that he can start to identify and in due course challenge and change them. We introduced the first steps of this approach in the Self-monitoring Homework Experiment in Chapter 3, and build on this now that the client has a better understanding of the As, Bs and Cs and the connections between them.

So the counsellor first reviews how the client managed in carrying out the self-monitoring steps during the week. Together they review each of the steps and look at his thought record (DTR, Figure 4.1 and Appendix 1), and identify any difficulties, for example in noticing disturbed feelings, noticing any dysfunctional thoughts occurring at the same time, recording these, and any further steps the client managed to do in identifying the event, the emotional goal and an alternative belief.

Next the counsellor introduces a new form and guide, the ABC Diary (Appendix 2), based on the DTR, but which allows for some of the new ABC conceptualisation now introduced. The client is asked to carry out the emotion and thought monitoring as before with the new form, except this time in terms of the ABC categories, and to try to identify at least two beliefs – one or more inferences and preferably two or more evaluations. At this stage he only fills in the top half of the ABC diary, namely the ABC Assessment, since the bottom half of the diary, namely ABC goals, will be the focus of the next chapter (Chapter 6). The actual steps for filling in the ABC Diary are provided in the Assessment and Goal Planning Guide, Appendix 2.

Action Summary

1 The counsellor asks the client to hold in mind the specific example he has written down for Step 1, and to focus on and describe the disturbed *emotion* he experiences, and any unhelpful action or action tendency that is associated with it. This will be the consequent emotional and behavioural problem (C). The counsellor ensures this is an unhealthy not a healthy negative emotion.

2 The counsellor asks for a description of any problematic *behavioural* consequences he might have, given the adverse situation. This might be an actual action he carried out, or an action tendency that he wanted to carry out but repressed. She ensures that this is a dysfunctional action and action tendency, related to the unhealthy negative emotion, such as avoidance or escape, withdrawal, aggression, etc. She then asks the client to write both the identified emotion and behaviour on the Assessment and Goal Planning Worksheet (Assessment Step 2, Appendix 2) under C: Consequent Problem Emotion/Behaviour.

3 The counsellor asks the client to continue to hold the emotion (C) in mind, and to provide a literal, factual description of the specific adverse event (A) in which he experienced this emotion (C), or a description of a predicted event he is anxious about. The counsellor ensures this description is factual and does not contain his beliefs about the event (inferences or evaluations). She asks

the client to write the description down on the Worksheet under A: Adverse Event as actually remembered or imagined (Assessment Step 3, Appendix 2).

4   The counsellor elicits the probably biased inferences (B^1) that are contributing to his unhealthy emotion (C), namely the inferences about the adverse event (A) he has just described that was so disturbing, and to rate his level of conviction in the inferences. She helps him identify the *type* of bias in the inferences, and to be sure he is clear about the difference between an inference and a fact, and the difference between a biased and unbiased inference. She asks him to write the biased inference down on the Worksheet under B^1: Biased Inference about A (Assessment Step 4, Appendix 2).

5   The counsellor lastly elicits the extreme evaluations (B^2) that are leading to his unhealthy emotion (C), namely evaluations of the adverse event (A) given the inference (B^1), and rate his level of conviction in the evaluations. She helps him identify the type of irrationality in his evaluations, and to be sure he is clear about the difference between facts, inferences and evaluations, and between rational and irrational evaluations. She suggests he writes his evaluations down on the Worksheet (Assessment Step 5, Appendix 2).

6   The counsellor helps the client to see how he can use his understanding of the As, Bs and Cs to further monitor his thoughts on a day-to-day basis. Counsellor and client review his homework using the DTR, deals with any difficulties with this, and building on this, she introduces the ABC Diary and the steps (Appendix 2) and asks the client to carry out a similar task, again on a daily basis between the present session and the next.

Case Example

Counsellor: (*after Brian has described a specific example of the problem, Assessment Step 1*) You have described a specific problem, and we are going to analyse it as before, but this time in terms of our ABC framework. (*Joan explains the model – see Briefing – and Brian explains it back, showing he understands quite well.*).

Counsellor: (*seeking the problem emotion C*) Let's identify your consequent emotion, C. If you would bring to mind that situation, and tell me what disturbed emotion you were experiencing?

Client: Oh, I felt awful, just awful.

Counsellor: What emotion words would you use to capture that – anxious, panicky, or feeling down? (*Joan asks Brian to pinpoint a specific unhealthy negative emotion.*)

Client: At that point it was panic, terror, full on, 10 out of 10.

Counsellor: And the symptoms?

Client: My heart was beating so fast I am sure it was visible to people around me, my face was going bright red, my eyes went all blurry, my mouth was going dry so I had trouble getting my words out and my hands shook so much I had trouble holding the paper.

Counsellor: So it was that bad that it was visible?

Client: Oh everyone could see what a state I was in.

Counsellor: (*seeking the problem behaviour C*) How did you cope with that? What did you actually do, or want to do?

Client: I wanted to run away, but I couldn't do that. There wasn't much I could do. I avoided making eye contact with anyone. I tried to grip the paper really hard to hide the shaking. I had written out word for word what I wanted to say as my mind goes completely blank once I start. And I spoke quickly and quietly and for as short a time as I could get away with – about two minutes when we were supposed to do five.

Counsellor: So you did those things to try to hide your anxiety. We call that safety-seeking behaviour, understandably trying to protect yourself. It's a natural response to threat – we all do our best to avoid or escape from threat when we see it coming. What would happen if you didn't do that?

Client: It would be a disaster, just awful, a lot worse.

Counsellor: Did it work?

Client: Not much. For example the worst part was when I suddenly lost my place ... I stood there for what felt like an eternity, and rummaged through my paper, until I finally found my words. I am not sure whether any of it helped.

Counsellor: It is unlikely it helped, for example gripping the paper hard is likely to make you shake more, not less. Your 'safety' strategy of writing it all out probably made the situation worse for you, but let's come back to that point. For now could you fill in box C on the Worksheet. You are writing under C for consequent emotion and behaviour. (*Brian writes.*)

Counsellor: (*seeking a description of the adverse event A*) Now could you describe the adverse situation that triggered these emotions and safety-seeking actions. Try to stick to the facts – what a camera would record. Try to visualise it in your mind.

Client: Well, the room was very small and hot and crowded. There weren't many windows. It felt difficult to breathe. I'm sure when I was talking the assessors were frowning, muttering and very close, too close. I think students were smirking. Everyone else looked and sounded so confident.

Counsellor: (*seeking the biased inferences, B^1*) OK, if you could write that down on the Worksheet under A for adverse situation. Now imagine again you are in the situation and your panicky feeling is at a peak. What are you imagining and predicting about that situation that's making you panic?

Client: They're all staring at me.

Counsellor: And what do you think they see?

Client: They can see my pulse is racing and that my face is going bright red, stumbling over my words, hands shaking, and I know it's going to get worse unless I can camouflage it somehow.

Counsellor: You say it like it's a fact. You say 'they can see that … etc.', you 'know' it's going to get worse. But actually may I suggest it's an inference or assumption or prediction you're making – you think they can see that … etc., you predict that it's going to get worse.

Client: What do you mean by inference or assumption or prediction?

Counsellor: (*Joan explains they are all inferences and what an inference is – see Briefing – emphasising that an inference might be true or false, depending on the evidence.*) So would you agree that these are inferences, not facts? They're what you think people are seeing and thinking or you predict what they will think.

Client: I suppose so, though they feel like facts to me.

Counsellor: They feel like facts because you are convinced they are true, but it is possible, though very unlikely in your mind, that they are false.

Client: I see what you mean, when you put it that way.

Counsellor: So would you write this in the B^1 inference box on the Worksheet, but I suggest write it as an inference, 'I think they are or predict they will …' or 'I'm convinced they are, or will ...', not as a fact 'they are, they will ...' (*Brian writes, 'I'm convinced they are all staring at me shaking, going red in the face, heart racing.'*) How convinced are you?

Client: Completely convinced, 10/10.

Counsellor: OK, now to get your next inference, let's assume you're right that that is what they see; what panic-making thoughts do you have about that?

Client: That they will think I'm a complete idiot. (*Brian bites his lip.*)

Counsellor: That's another inference do you agree? (*Brian writes in B^1 inference box 'I'm convinced they think I'm a complete idiot'.*) And how much do you believe that they think that?

Client: Same, 10/10.

Counsellor: Because you believe these inferences (B^1) are true, they are contributing a great deal to your anxiety – remember it's your beliefs, in this case inferences, at B about the event A that largely makes you experience the consequent disturbance at C. (*Brian nods.*) And because you believe them, you try to avoid the predicted threat, that they will all think you're an idiot, etc. But it is just possible that these inferences are giving you a picture that is biased and there is actually no, or very little, threat, but you never discover this because you're avoiding it, and so go on believing it, go on getting anxious, and the problem remains. So can we look at this crucial idea, at the possibility that your inferences are seriously biased?

Client: OK, possible but I don't think they are.

Counsellor: Here is a list of common biases people have (*gives list from Burns, 1999*), especially when they get emotional. One of them is the all-or-nothing bias, which causes a tendency to magnify, so do you think that is a possibility, you could be magnifying the visibility of your symptoms, like you say 'face burns bright red'?

Client: Possibly but unlikely.

Counsellor: OK, so let's write 'magnification' under the heading? 'Biases'. (*Brian writes.*) Another bias is the 'negative mental filter', where there is selective attention only to the negative and all other attributes are overlooked or discounted. There are only negatives in your description. (*Joan explores some others, including mind reading, and attribution to self rather than the situation, and Brian makes a note of them.)*

Counsellor: In summary we have several inferences which you have written down with their possible biases. Just to recap, are these inferences or facts?

Client: They are inferences.

Counsellor: What is the difference?

Client: *(describes the difference between inferences and facts and Joan is satisfied she understands clearly)* I suppose they are inferences but I do think they are true, though I wish they weren't.

Counsellor: Could you rate your conviction level in them on the worksheet – 0 = you are not convinced, 10 = you are totally convinced? *(Brian rates them all 10 out of 10.)*

Counsellor: *(seeking the extreme evaluations B^2)* Biased inferences are very important in keeping you anxious and avoidant. But your evaluations are even more important. Can we assess your evaluations now, and can I explain what I mean by evaluations? *(Brian agrees to both requests, and Joan explains the difference between inferences and evaluations – see Briefing – emphasising that the former are assertions that are true or false depending on the evidence, the latter are good or bad value judgements.)*

Counsellor: OK, let's go back a step. You're convinced your inferences are true, so let's just assume that for a minute, so that we can find out what your unhelpful evaluations are. You say people could see how you looked and because of that they thought you were a complete idiot. *(Brian agrees.)* What panic-making thoughts do you have about them thinking you are an idiot?

Client: *(long pause)* It's just terrible. I can't bear it. It actually then feels like its true, and I will be thrown out of university, a failure. *(Brian becomes tearful.)*

Counsellor: They are your evaluations, do you agree? You can see the emotional impact these evaluations have on you. *(Brian agrees.)*

Counsellor: Just as the inferences are possibly biased, your evaluations are possibly absolute and extreme and therefore unrealistic.

Client: Again possibly but not likely.

Counsellor:	Here are four evaluations that we believe are extreme and which lead to emotional disturbance. (*Joan goes through the four extreme evaluations described in the Briefing. She points out their 'absoluteness': certain events absolutely must or must not happen; it is absolutely catastrophic and awful if they do or don't happen; it is absolutely impossible to bear if they do or don't happen; and I, you or life is absolutely bad or worthless if it does or does not happen.*)
Counsellor:	Brian, do you recognise any of these evaluations?
Client:	(*smiles*) Yes, I do. I was saying it would be terrible and I can't bear it. They're extreme. And I'm an idiot, that's pretty extreme too.
Counsellor:	So for now let's just record on the Worksheet these evaluations that you have and your conviction level in them, 0–10. (*Brian notes his three extreme beliefs on the Worksheet.*)
Counsellor:	(*summarises with the help of the ABC assessment*) With all these catastrophic predictions here at B, it's no wonder you are panicking and behaving self-protectively at C, to save yourself from the threat A that you see as potentially catastrophic. But suppose you were wrong in your beliefs B, you would be saving yourself (safety behaviour C) from a danger that wasn't there, or only mildly there (A), but you never find this out, and go on remaining unnecessarily anxious at C. Worse than that, you could create a real adverse situation A when there previously wasn't one. These are vicious-circle traps that CBC will help you identify and escape from.
Client:	OK, I can see what you're saying. But how do I start to get hold of these beliefs?

Joan uses Brian's question as her cue to review Brian's homework using the DTR, and to help him build on this by using an adapted form, the ABC Diary (Appendix 2), to continue to learn how to monitor and capture his thoughts during the next weeks. The method is described in the Briefing for this task, and in the ABC Diary steps (Appendix 2).

6

Beginning Stage II – What are We Aiming For? New Thinking, Feeling and Action Goals

Task 11. Conceptualising the Problem: B–C Connection and Vicious Circles

Briefing

Does the client still think his distress is directly caused by adverse events out of his control – what we have called A–C thinking (Task 7)? Or has he now gained the cognitive insight that his distress is mainly caused by his beliefs (B)? This is probably one of the most important and yet most resistant to change issues in the CBC process, and is one that we therefore return to again later.

Having explicitly drawn out the role of the inferences and evaluations in Task 10, the counsellor now asks the client this question: 'What mainly causes your emotional/behavioural problem (C) – is it A, the adverse event you described, or your beliefs (B), your inferences and evaluations?' If the client answers B, his beliefs, she asks him why; to make sure he really understands and is not simply giving her the answer he thinks she wants to hear. She is looking for an answer of the form, 'My feelings and my behaviour are mainly the consequence of my negative beliefs about these events'. She summarises the point as 'the B–C connection'.

However, if despite the coaching so far and the thought-monitoring homework the client is still saying it is the activating event (A) that causes his problem (C) she returns to Task 7 and again guides the client from A–C thinking to A–B–C thinking, but this time draws his attention to the inferences and evaluations which he wrote down on the Assessment Worksheet, Steps 4 and 5, and which shows graphically the mediating role of the beliefs.

Sometimes the client will still insist that he 'knows' that his inferences and evaluations are correct. The counsellor then checks out whether by 'knowing' he means he thinks it is a fact or it is his conviction that 'statement x' is the case. He may say he understands intellectually but feels emotionally that he 'knows' his inferences and evaluations are correct. The counsellor can explain, with examples, that his inferences and evaluations are experienced as part of, and colour his images of, negative events, and images are experienced at an emotional level like facts, just like actual perceptions. Usually by this stage clients will agree it is a strong conviction, although they may yet harbour doubts, as we shall see.

The counsellor wants to make sure the client understands that the way to solve his problem (C) is by changing his beliefs (B) since his problem is largely the consequence of his beliefs rather than the activating event (A) alone. This then leads to her next question, which is that if he wants to *change* the way he feels and behaves, what does he have to change, A or B? If he agrees he needs to change the B, and even if he is pessimistic about being able to do this, this is recorded, written down, to register the importance of this insight.

Vicious Circles

The B–C (B leads to C) connection not only explains emotional and behavioural problems in a linear sense, but in a circular sense, as described in Chapter 1. A problematic B–C connection can be at the heart of several vicious circles, or a composite 'vicious flower' where a number of circles can be represented in the petals of a flower diagram, as described by Butler et al. (2008) for anxiety problems, and Moorey (2010) for depression. We will just describe two of the most important.

First, the client predicts (B) that there is going to be a catastrophic adverse event (A) when in fact there is no such risk, or the risk is mild or moderate. Because of the B–C connection in his case, he anxiously avoids (C) the presumed event (A), thus never learning that it will never happen in the form his belief (B) predicts. The counsellor's task is to help the client discover not only the B–C connection, but how his avoidance of A prevents disconfirmation of his belief, preserving the B–C connection and maintaining the problem.

Second, the client not only believes (B) there is a catastrophic event (A) when there isn't one, but in attempting to avoid the assumed adversity in A he actually creates a real adversity when previously there wasn't one. The counsellor's task is to help the client discover that his avoidance or safety-seeking behaviour C actually 'contaminates' in an adverse way the previously relatively neutral situation A.

The counsellor reminds the client that he will be better able to replace the vicious circle with a virtuous circle once he has changed his beliefs and replaced an unrealistically negative with a realistic B–C connection.

Failure to make the above points clear will leave the client without a rationale for working on changing the B and therefore undermine any commitment to carry out the difficult tasks that this will require. However, our experience is that even now the client will have doubts about the cognitive theory of disturbance, and we return to this issue from yet another angle at the beginning of the Middle Stage.

Action Summary

1 The counsellor checks whether the client has a genuine understanding of the mediating role of beliefs (B) between adverse events (A) and emotional and behavioural consequences (C).

2 If the client is still unclear about the mediating role of beliefs, she returns to Task 7 and again guides the client from A–C thinking to A–B–C thinking, this time drawing his attention to the inferences and evaluations which he wrote down on the Assessment and Goal Planning Worksheet, Steps 4 and 5, and which shows graphically the mediating role of the beliefs. She also draws attention to what he has learned by thought monitoring and filling in the ABC Diary between sessions.

3 To help the client to be clear about the difference between a fact and a belief, the counsellor ensures the client knows the difference between 'knowing' a fact and 'knowing' something with high conviction.

4 The counsellor checks whether the client agrees that to change his unhealthy (C) he should change the mediating (B) and that is the main aim of CBC.

5 The counsellor helps the client understand the two types of vicious circle which he is vulnerable to, that arise due to the influence of dysfunctional beliefs (B) on (C) and subsequent effects on (A), often maintaining a problem or making it worse.

Case Example

Counsellor:	Lets just take stock, and look at the Worksheet now that we have completed the ABC assessment of the problem, and whether this helps us understand and explain your problem. What do you now think causes you to be so disturbed in these presentations? Is it A, the adverse situation, the way people regard you, or is it B, your catastrophic beliefs about that situation?
Client:	I think its both. If I didn't care I wouldn't be bothered, so it's partly my beliefs.
Counsellor:	And if it's partly your beliefs that cause your disturbance, and your beliefs were wrong, what would be the way to overcome your problem?
Client:	Well to change the beliefs.
Counsellor:	That's true, but there is a risk that you will unwittingly prevent yourself from ever changing them.
Client:	How could that happen?
Counsellor:	It can happen like this: Your catastrophic prediction (B) leads you to behave in a safety-seeking way to try to avoid a catastrophic outcome that actually isn't realistic – getting very poor marks, being judged a failure, thrown out of university and so on. But you never find this out. In technical language, your safety-seeking behaviour prevents you from disconfirming your prediction, and since that's what's causing your anxiety, that could maintain your problem indefinitely.
Client:	Like a vicious cycle.
Counsellor:	Exactly, but there is a *real* danger for you. Your own safety-seeking behaviour C could actually make you appear worse not better, and provoke a real negative reaction from others, that is create a real adverse situation A when there previously wasn't one. This is another vicious cycle.
Client:	How can I avoid these problems?
Counsellor:	By learning how to change your beliefs to more benign ones, and that's what we come to in the next sessions. If you could do that, how would you feel and behave?
Client:	Better, not panicking, just concerned. (*Points to the difference between the problem C and the goal C on the Worksheet.*)

Counsellor:	And if you were concerned and functioning better as in the goal C, how could that affect the way you dealt with the adverse event?
Client:	I'd be able to deal with it better. This makes sense in theory, but … .
Counsellor:	We will come to the practice very soon!

Task 12. Eliciting the Specific Emotional/ Behavioural Goal and Functional Beliefs

Briefing

The client may now agree that the most effective way to change his problematic feelings and behaviour and improve his capacity to solve or overcome his adverse problems (A) is to change his beliefs (including mainly his inferences and evaluations), though he may still be sceptical that he can do so. Before trying to change the Bs, however, which is the focus of the next stage, the Middle Stage of CBC, he needs to do two things. First, he needs to make explicit the specific emotional/behavioural goal that he wants to change *to* – how does he want to feel and behave instead of disturbed and acting in a self-defeating way? Second, he needs to find and make explicit alternative, functional and realistic beliefs which will more likely lead to his emotional/behavioural goal. He made a start on both tasks for the problem in general terms in the preparation stage. He now needs to establish the concrete detail for the specific problem.

Assessment Step 6. Ask for a Specific Emotional/ Behavioural Goal – C

The counsellor asks for a specific emotional/behavioural goal for the Specific Example of the Problem. One suggestion that clients sometimes suggest is to feel neutral or calm, which was touched upon in the Preparation Guide, but may not have been resolved at that stage. Feeling neutral or calm might be appropriate, for example, where the adverse event is in reality non-existent, as in panic disorder or health anxiety where there has been a medical health check and there is no basis for the anxiety or depression. Another suggestion often proposed in CBT is to experience less of the disturbance, such as 'mildly anxious' or 'mildly depressed' to replace 'severely anxious' or 'severely depressed'. This could be appropriate, it is argued, where there is genuine adversity and not the magnified adversity that he has imagined because of his dysfunctional belief system.

However, we prefer an alternative approach in most circumstances, as we outlined in Chapter 1. The counsellor makes a clear distinction between an unhealthy negative emotion like anxiety with associated avoidance, and a qualitatively different negative emotion which we call 'healthy', such as 'healthy concern'. Implicit in healthy concern is a tendency to approach and deal with the adverse event as best they can, in contrast to 'unhealthy' anxiety where there is a tendency to avoid or escape from the adversity. When the counsellor judges there is a likelihood of genuine adversity, she therefore recommends a healthy negative emotion qualitatively distinct from a disturbed negative emotion such as anxiety or depression.

If the client still opts for a practical goal of changing the adverse event (A) without changing the emotional/behavioural consequence (C) first, she reminds him of the rationale for going for an emotional behavioural goal that was explained in Task 5. She may explain again, or get the client to explain, that his present emotional/behavioural problem is not only disturbing him, but also interferes with his ability to deal with the adverse situation and probably makes it worse. In particular, his self-protective, safety-seeking behaviour can influence the adverse event in a negative way, for example by saying nothing in a social situation to avoid sounding 'stupid', the client may unwittingly create a negative impression. The counsellor then explores what alternative emotion and behaviour might be more helpful, and whether this alternative might then be a goal to aim for. When clients struggle to construct alternatives, the counsellor can tentatively make suggestions. A number of suggestions are provided in Dryden (2009).

Client Completes Assessment Step 6
The client writes his specific emotional/behavioural goal on the Assessment and Goal Planning Worksheet (Appendix 2) under 'Options for Change, C: Emotional/Behavioural Goal'.

Guide the Client to Alternative Functional Beliefs and Images
The counsellor asks the client what now needs to happen in order for him to reach his emotional/behavioural goal that he has chosen, completed in Step 6. The answer she is looking for, and if necessary guides him to, is that he needs to replace his disturbance-making beliefs and

images, completed in Steps 4 and 5, with alternative, functional beliefs and images. She therefore suggests they jointly generate alternative functional beliefs and images which would lead to his emotional/ behavioural goal if he changed to them.

There are three options that the counsellor can draw upon, namely to help the client change his biased inferences (B^1), his extreme and rigid evaluations (B^2), and the actual imagery that the adverse event (A) is based on in the client's mind. The desirable alternatives to these dysfunctional beliefs are more accurate and less biased inferences, functional and rational evaluations, and more realistic and positive imagery. These three options are *options*, and the counsellor will make a judgement, based on the type of problem and the client's needs, whether to utilise one, two or all three of them. How she makes this judgement will be a focus of the Middle Stage. She will also help the client to weaken his conviction in the dysfunctional beliefs and strengthen his conviction in the alternative, functional beliefs during the Middle Stage, but at this stage only asks the client to nominate the alternatives.

Discovering functional alternative beliefs is not easy for the client, so the counsellor helps the client prepare to do this by asking him to put himself into the healthy emotional state that is his goal, such as feeling concerned but not anxious. This can be facilitated by imagining a time when he has actually felt this way. If this proves difficult, he can prepare with calming systematic muscular relaxation, or mindful breathing or similar preparation exercises as described, for example, by Gilbert (2009) and then to try to 'feel' himself into and experience the healthy emotion. He then may be more able to bring to mind helpful alternative thoughts and images, with the counsellor's help. The counsellor also accepts that the client may not have much conviction in the validity of these alternatives, but explains that this is to be expected at this assessment stage and that his doubts will be the focus of the next stage.

Assessment Step 7. Ask for an Alternative Unbiased Inference to B¹

The counsellor suggests that, whilst in the healthy emotional state of mind, *and* while holding the adverse event (A) in mind, the client generates one or more alternative inferences about the adverse event that can compete in a positive way with the biased inferences (B^1). The client then writes these down on the Assessment and Goal Planning Worksheet in the box headed B^1 Alternative unbiased inferences (Assessment Step 7, Appendix 2).

Inevitably some clients have difficulty identifying more realistic, unbiased inferences because of the mental filtering effect of their bias, so they may need the counsellor's guidance. One method is to encourage the client to try to step outside their own perspective with its 'built-in' bias and imagine the perspective of another person, maybe what a friend or what an average person or role model might infer. The counsellor herself can sometimes be the 'other person'.

Usually the client will have greatly and unrealistically magnified the negative event in some way, or even created a negative event where none actually exist. This is largely due to one or more of the biases we outlined in Task 10, and one method the counsellor uses in this case is to draw the client's attention to the bias they should have identified in Assessment Step 4, and to have them choose an inference without the bias, that is for example the *opposite* of, or goes against the bias. For example:

- With the all-or-nothing biased inference, someone with a blushing phobia might have 'everyone will notice', whereas an unbiased inference might be 'some or none might notice', with the emphasis on 'everyone' versus 'some or none', and 'will' versus 'might'.
- Similarly an anxious client with the mind-reading bias whose friend crossed the road might have 'crossing the road means she doesn't like me', whereas an alternative, non-biased inference might be 'maybe she didn't see me, or there may be other reasons', or if she crossed the road to avoid him, it was not because she didn't like him but because 'she wasn't wearing any make-up!'. The bias here is a negative arbitrary inference with a mental filter '... she doesn't like me' compared with the openness in the unbiased alternative to a wide range of possible reasons.

Sometimes there is genuine adversity, where the bias lies not so much in magnifying the adversity but in misattributing it to a cause which cannot be changed easily, if at all. The counsellor's task here is to help the client think of an alternative inference which attributes the cause to something which he can change for the better. For example, suppose the client's inference that the friend crossed the road to avoid him is true. Maybe the friend is avoiding the client because the client himself was previously unfriendly. This commonly happens when the client's own safety behaviour 'contaminates' the social context and creates a more adverse situation in a vicious cycle that maintains the problem. As we showed in Task 10, the counsellor helps the client discover that by defensively staying silent the socially anxious client unwittingly appears cold and disinterested, and *then* gets rejected as a consequence. This changes the attribution from something seen as unchangeable e.g. 'I am unlikeable/unlovable' to something changeable, namely his social behaviour.

One advantage of guiding the client to identify an unbiased alternative as part of the Beginning Stage assessment rather than the Middle Stage intervention is that it facilitates cognitive change without the counsellor appearing to be explicitly trying to get the change, which can sometimes evoke resistance. The client may have the experience, 'Oh, yes, I didn't think of that'. Making the alternative explicit is not always advised, however, and in panic disorder in particular it is better tactically not to do so, so as to maximise the impact of a provocation test of the biased catastrophic inference like deliberate hyperventilation (see Middle Stage, Task 3), as a result of which the alternative emerges anyway.

Assessment Step 8. Ask for Alternative, Realistic Evaluations

The counsellor suggests that, whilst in the healthy emotional state of mind, and while holding the adverse event (A) *and* negative inferences (B^1) in mind, the client generates at least two and preferably all four alternative, realistic evaluations that compete in a positive way with the four extreme evaluations identified in Assessment Step 5. The client then writes these alternatives down on the same Assessment and Goal Planning Worksheet, in the box headed B^2 Realistic Evaluations, under the four alternative headings provided (Assessment Step 8, Appendix 2). Space is provided under these headings for the client to briefly describe each of the realistic evaluations (Preferring, Non-awfulising, High Discomfort Tolerance (HDT) and Self/Other/Life Acceptance).

The counsellor offers quite specific guidance on these four realistic and helpful alternatives, namely Preferring is the alternative to the Demanding rule of living, and Non-awfulising, HDT and Self, Other and Life Acceptance, are the alternatives to the three extreme evaluations that follow from Demanding, and that were described in Task 10, assessment Step 5. This guidance can take the following form:

- Preferring. The alternative to the demanding rule of living is a strong *preferring* but non-demanding rule of living (Dryden and Neenan, 2004). So the alternative to the client's demanding rule that negative events like the one he faces absolutely must not happen, is that he *strongly wishes* negative events do not happen but does not demand what he strongly wishes. For example the client might say about his friend rejecting him: I really hate being rejected but do not demand I never am.

- Non-awfulising. Just as extreme beliefs follow from the demanding rule, so relative and non-extreme beliefs follow from the preferring rule. So *negative events are bad* but never absolutely awful: It was bad she rejected me but hardly catastrophic.
- High Discomfort Tolerance (HDT). Similarly, *negative events are hard to tolerate* but never absolutely intolerable: It was really hard to bear/cope with but I can bear/cope with it.
- Self, Other, Life Acceptance. Finally, *negative events may show our fallibilities* but never that we are totally bad or worthless: *I unconditionally accept myself as a fallible person* despite the rejection (and other failings and adversities). Similarly I unconditionally accept the other as a person despite their rotten behaviour.

Assessment Step 9. Ask the Client to Imagine an Alternative to the Adverse Event (A)

Whilst in the healthy emotional state of mind, the counsellor asks the client to try to imagine a more positive alternative to the actual adverse event (A) as remembered, that would be likely if he behaved in the situation in accordance with his behavioural goals. In other words, he tries to change the remembered image of the adverse event by imagining a more positive outcome, such that the now 'rescripted' image provides him with an alternative to the original description of it (Step 3 of the assessment guide). This description could be either a positive, neutral or milder aversive version or outcome of the event A. Having settled on a rescripted image, the client describes this on the Assessment and Goal Planning Worksheet, in the box headed A: Adverse Event Rescripted (Assessment Step 9, Appendix 2).

Counsellor and Client Review Assessment Steps 6, 7, 8 or 9

With the Worksheet in front of them, the counsellor and client review the completed assessment and goal planning stage, comparing the ABC Goals – healthy emotional behavioural goals (Step 6) alternative inferences (Step 7), the alternative evaluations (Step 8) and the alternative image (Step 9) – with the problem emotion/behaviour, and probably biased inferences, extreme evaluations and memory of the event (Steps 2, 3, 4 and 5). The counsellor uses this opportunity to non-directively give the client space to reflect on the implications of the assessment and goal planning discoveries, and to explore for himself the choices he wants to make, in preparation for the Middle Stage. of therapeutic change.

Whether one or two or all three of the alternatives will be used in the process of therapeutic change will be finally decided in the Middle

Stage. However, we recommend that all three are elicited and recorded and reflected upon at this assessment stage, to give maximum choice of treatment strategies.

Coaching the Client to Capture Alternative Bs

If the client has carried out the ABC Diary keeping before this task, the counsellor reviews and deals with any difficulties. She then suggests he repeats the task for the following week but this time she asks him to fill in both the top half of the ABC Diary, namely the ABC Assessment as before, but also now the bottom half of the Diary, namely ABC goals, which have been the focus of this chapter. The steps for filling in the ABC Diary are provided in the Assessment and Goal Planning Guide, Appendix 3.

Preparing for Cognitive Behavioural Change

The counsellor and client have completed the assessment, conceptualisation and goal setting – the Beginning Stage of CBC. The counsellor will want to be sure that the client has gained two important insights that will prepare him for the next, Middle Stage of CBC, namely cognitive behavioural change. First, the counsellor again checks that the client understands and agrees that his dysfunctional cognitions are the main reason for his emotionally disturbed and self-defeating behavioural reaction to adverse events. Second, that the alternative cognitions he has identified should lead to healthy negative emotional and functional behavioural consequences. For example, she asks the client what would lead to the healthy emotional and behavioural consequences. The answer she is looking for is that it is mainly the alternative cognitions and not the adverse event itself. She will re-address this issue from a different angle at the beginning of the Middle Stage.

She also checks that he wishes to continue to the next stage and is willing to commit himself to the work involved in cognitive behavioural change.

Action Summary

1 The counsellor asks the client to specify a healthy emotion and functional behaviour he would prefer instead of the unhealthy emotion dysfunctional behaviour which currently is his problem (C). This is the specific emotional/behavioural goal for the specific example of his prioritised problem. The

counsellor guides the client to choose a health *negative* emotion in most circumstances, rather than a completely neutral or even positive emotion.

2   The counsellor elicits one or more unbiased inferences as alternatives to his biased inferences (B^1). She suggests that, whilst in the healthy emotional state of mind, and while holding the adverse event (A) in mind, the client constructs one or more alternative inferences about (A) which can compete with and which do not have the specific bias he identified in his inferences (B^1).

3   The counsellor elicits at least two non-extreme, rational alternatives to his extreme evaluations (B^2). She suggests that, whilst in the healthy emotional state of mind, and while holding the adverse event (A) *and* negative inferences (B^1) in mind, the client generates alternative evaluations that compete with and which to not have the specific distortion of his extreme evaluations (B^2). The counsellor offers quite specific guidance on these realistic and helpful alternatives (see Briefing and Case Example).

4   The counsellor suggests that whilst in the healthy emotional state of mind, he tries to imagine a more positive possible alternative to the remembered adverse event (A) that would be likely if he behaved in the situation in accordance with his behavioural goals, and viewed it in terms of his alternative beliefs.

5   The client writes down the alternative inferences (Step 7), the alternative evaluations (Step 8) and the alternative image (Step 9), on the Assessment and Goal Planning Worksheet (Appendix 2).

6   If the client has completed the ABC Diary as homework, this is reviewed, and the client asked to repeat the homework, but this time adding the ABC goals to the diary.

Case Example

Counsellor: (*seeking the client's emotional and behavioural goal*) We will come to the practice very soon! But first we need to agree your goals for the specific problem and your alternative beliefs for achieving them and write them down on the worksheet. So instead of panicking and behaving dysfunctionally, how would you like to feel and act in response to this specific presentation situation?

Client: I will go with healthy concern again. (*Writes on Worksheet, Assessment Step 6.*)

Counsellor: That's a good choice. Why do you choose it?

Client:	It means I am alert for things going wrong but still facing up to it.
Counsellor:	I agree. And what about the action.
Client:	Well, my goal is to give a really cool presentation, no shaking, nothing.
Counsellor:	That would be good but as you point out, healthy concern implies facing up even when things go wrong.
Client:	Yes, I see, so I'd like to be able to cope even if I'm shaking and going red. (*Writes on Worksheet, Assessment Step 6.*) Can't see it happening though!
Counsellor:	What do you need to change to make it happen?
Client:	My beliefs. (*Points to the Worksheet as this clearly shows the B–C connection.*)
Counsellor:	(*seeking alternative beliefs*) That's right, because by changing your possibly distorted beliefs for undistorted ones, you can change how you feel and act. You have three possible options for change – your inferences, evaluations and even the image you have from how you remember the event, since as we've agreed you could have anxiety-making distortions in any or all of them. So we need to look for alternatives that definitely have no distortions. So that's the next task. You will find it easier to think of these alternatives if you try to put yourself into that *concerned* frame of mind, so try to do that first. Maybe you can remember a time when you felt that way rather than panicky, or think of someone who is a bit of a role model for you, who approaches problems with this frame of mind.
Client:	(*after a pause*) OK, I think I've got it.
Counsellor:	Good. So holding that frame of mind, what shall we start with?
Client:	The inferences.
Counsellor:	OK, you have two 'possibly biased inferences' written down here. Try to think of two alternatives to these inferences. For example, instead of the all or nothing bias which leads you to magnify your symptoms, what could you have without the bias?
Client:	You mean instead of thinking 'all or nothing' I should think of them as somewhere in the middle, maybe not that bad or obvious? (*Joan agrees, Brian writes, 'If my*

symptoms aren't that bad or glaring, people may not notice so much', Assessment Step 7, but he rates this only 3/10 for conviction.)

Counsellor: And what about the magnifier and the mind-reading filter which gives you, 'They all think I'm an idiot'. If you get rid of those biases, what have you got?

Client: Well, I don't know what they're thinking; my symptoms may not be that obvious, so what about 'it will vary, some think that I'm an idiot, some don't, some don't even notice'.

Counsellor: And some may even be sympathetic to your anxiety and not be judging you, especially if they have had a similar experience. *(Brian settles on, 'People will vary, some negative, some neutral, some even positive.')*

Counsellor: So this could lead to a virtuous circle couldn't it – healthy concern helps you draw unbiased inferences like these, unbiased inferences helps you to have healthy concern *and* healthy behaviour. Do you think it could lead to this virtuous circle?

Client: It would make it easier for me to give my talk, look at the audience more and so on.

Counsellor: And might that have an effect on the audience reaction?

Client: They would respond better to me.

Counsellor: So to summarise, change B to change from the problem C to the goal C, and you are then more able to change A, the practical goal. But we have only so far identified one type of B, the inference (B^1). Let's look at alternatives to the other type of B, the evaluations (B^2), that you have written down here. What do you suggest?

Client: I said it would be terrible and I couldn't bear it. They are extreme, so realistically it would be very bad, and that's not extreme. And I could bear it, but that's not true!

Counsellor: What about 'it would be *very hard* to bear?'

Client: Yes that's true, and that's not extreme. I also said I really am an idiot. So I am not a complete idiot.

Counsellor: What about 'I'm a fallible human who behaved idiotically (or behaved anxiously)'?

Client: I could live with that.

Counsellor: You'll find these alternatives come a lot easier if you also give up your demand and just stick with your strong

	want – I don't want them to think I'm stupid BUT … if they do its bad, its hard, I'm fallible….
Client:	OK, so 'I really *really* don't want this but … .(*Writes down the alternative B²s on the Worksheet, Assessment Step 8.*)
Counsellor:	Excellent, that completes the assessments. One last question before we go on to the treatment – what mainly causes your problem, your anxiety, is it the adverse situations you are facing or your beliefs about them
Client:	Oh, don't worry, I've got the message – it's mainly my beliefs!

Joan reviews Brian's thought-monitoring homework using the ABC Diary, and suggests he repeats this during the forthcoming week but adds the ABC Goals to the task, following the steps. Joan winds up the session by non-directively inviting Brian to reflect on the assessment and goal planning stage, and what implications this has for overcoming his problem.

7

Middle Stage I – Getting Realistic: Challenging and Changing Inferences

The aim of the Middle Stage of CBC is to help the client change those of his beliefs and images which are largely responsible for his emotional disturbance and self-defeating pattern of behaviour. The Middle Stage marks a shift from assessing and conceptualising the problems and setting goals and alternative beliefs, to doing the actual work that will produce the belief changes necessary for a therapeutic outcome.

We propose three options for belief change in the Middle Stage. The first entails changing the inferences, the second entails changing the evaluations and the third entails changing the imagery. Counsellor and client may choose to work on any or all of these options, depending on factors we outline later, but for the purposes of our guide, we address all three. However, we precede the options for change tasks with a vital check – whether the client has yet 'seen the light' and truly understands the mediating role of beliefs in generating disturbed emotions and behaviour and driving vicious cycles – the B–C connection. If the counsellor is satisfied the client understand this, then she skips this task and goes straight on to Task 14.

Choosing a Belief Change Option

After checking the B–C connection insight (if necessary), the counsellor and her client will make a choice between the three options, whether it should be option 1 which focuses on the client's inferences which may be biased (B¹), option 2 concerning the client's evaluations which may be extreme (B²) or option 3 concerning the client's perception of the adverse event itself which may be misrepresented in his memory. How do the counsellor and client select amongst these options? We will give guidance in the briefings to the tasks that follow, but in summary, we suggest the following:

- Choose the inference-level option when the inference is fairly discrete and specific and clearly wrong and can be relatively convincingly shown to be baseless, such as in panic disorder and some non-complex phobias. This option may be sufficient and no further work may be necessary. More experienced practitioners apply this option to more complex cases, and combine it with other levels of intervention, including evaluations, schemas and imagery. In describing this option we draw mainly on established cognitive therapy and cognitive behaviour therapy principles and practice.
- Choose the evaluation level option when there is 'low self esteem' and a consequent social emotion which reflects this, such as shame and guilt, plus intolerance of distress, plus an inference that is not clearly wrong and may even be right. Examples might include depression and generalised anxiety disorder. In describing this option we draw mainly on rational emotive behaviour therapy.
- Choose the imagery level option when an image is vivid and traumatic but is highly likely to be a misrepresentation of an adverse event. The clearest case would be post traumatic stress disorder but trauma imagery also occurs in other problems including social anxiety, agoraphobia, eating disorders and depression (Stopa, 2009). In describing this option we draw on recent developments in research and practice in imagery rescripting.

Sometimes the counsellor may want to include two or all three of these approaches, depending on the client's preferences and the complexity of the problem. Counsellors vary in their orientation and preferences. For example, a Cognitive Therapy (CT) practitioner will traditionally prefer the inference-level options initially, and only if the client shows signs of not responding will they want to investigate deeper low self-esteem and core belief problems and turn to the evaluation level option. A Rational Emotive Behaviour Therapy (REBT) practitioner, on the other hand, will prefer to use an evaluation-level intervention followed by an inference-level intervention in most cases, on the basis that the evaluative-level change will make inference-level change much easier and relapse less likely. Our own recommendation is that if the counsellor and client agree to use the evaluation-level option, either alone or in conjunction with either or both of the other options, they should pursue this option first, for reasons explained in Task 3 below.

Chapter Structure for the Middle Stage

Following the format of the first stage, we also divide this stage into tasks for the counsellor and steps for the client. The tasks will comprise a Briefing, an Action Summary and a Case Example as in the first stage. This chapter (Chapter 6) contains Task 13. Checking the B–C Connection Insight and Task 14. The Inference Change Option. Chapter 7 contains Task 15. The Evaluation Change Option. Chapter 8 contains Task 16. The Imagery Change Option. Chapter 9 contains Task 17. Working Through.

Task 13. Checking the B–C Connection Insight

Briefing

Before attempting to facilitate belief change, the seasoned counsellor may want to check whether the client yet understands and is fully prepared to engage in the belief-change approach, whether he has 'seen the light' and realises that it is dysfunctional cognitions that often largely create emotional and behavioural disturbances – the B–C connection. She may omit this task if she is satisfied from her last check that he has B–C connection insight, but if in any doubt, she will check again at this point, for the reasons we shall now describe.

Experience repeatedly shows that the cognitive model seems quite counter-intuitive, particularly to those in most distress (Chadwick, 2006). The beliefs (B) that actually mediate between adverse events in the real world (A) and distress (C) are not the focus of awareness like the adverse events themselves but are like conceptual spectacles *through* which we see those events and by means of which those events are 'coloured'. The beliefs, like spectacles, are not themselves noticed. Largely because of this, the beliefs about adversities are often not recognised as beliefs but are seen as an aspect of the actual adversities themselves. So the 'catastrophic' nature of the adverse event is 'out there' and really happening. The beliefs are experienced as facts. This deeply entrenched intuition is held about all types of cognition – images, inferences and evaluations.

One of the main objectives of the Beginning Stage has been to address this problem. However, the A–C (A leads to C) intuition (discussed in Task 4 of the Beginning Stage) is often so entrenched that the counsellor needs to be ever vigilant that the client genuinely recognises and accepts the B–C (B leads to C, given A) connection, as otherwise pursuing the options for change may make no sense to the client, and may have little beneficial effect on him or may even worsen his problem.

Even when the client has identified his inferences and evaluations (assessment Steps 4 and 5), the client may still be harbouring doubts that these are really beliefs and not facts, but not sharing these doubts with the counsellor. He may think that, in theory, beliefs mediate between negative events (A) and emotional disturbance (C), but *in his specific case* these are actually facts, and that he knows this because they 'feel' like facts. This is especially compelling when associated with a powerful feeling like anxiety which is physically experienced. This is because clients often have a meta-cognitive belief (a belief about beliefs) such as 'if it *feels* true, it is'. This is one form of the emotional reasoning bias.

So the counsellor checks whether the client has a meta-cognitive belief *about* the specific inference: 'Because it feels so true, does that seem to make it true?' If the client agrees, that this is intuitively what he believes, the counsellor can introduce the first of many empirical challenges of beliefs. How she helps the client do this in general is dealt with in the next task on Challenging Inferences. A successful challenge of the meta-cognition 'If it feels true, it is true' will make it more likely that the client will accept that his inference really is a belief and not a fact, and the inference itself can then also be challenged as to its validity. Once the client accepts his beliefs are truly mediating beliefs, the counsellor reminds the client to qualify them with the prefix 'I am having the thought that . . .', so, for example, 'she has rejected me' becomes 'I am having the thought that she has rejected me'. Having qualified it as a thought, he then proceeds to challenge it, as described in the next two tasks.

Action Summary

1 The counsellor checks again whether the client understands and accepts the B–C connection.
2 Even when the client says he understands and accepts the B–C connection, she checks whether he still has an intuitive 'felt sense' that it is true, and if so helps him recognise that this is also a challengeable meta-belief about a belief.

Case Example

Client: I understand and accept the B–C connection, but I still
               have this almost physical sense when I am anxious that
               the threat is real and not just a belief.
Counsellor: You experience the physiological arousal in your body
               and it seems to say 'danger'?
Client: That's right.
Counsellor: Maybe you have a belief, or really a belief about a belief,
               that if the threat feels real physically, or more exactly
               physiologically, then it is real, but that is another belief,
               or meta-belief, which you can also challenge along with
               the other beliefs. So if you are agreeable I suggest this
               is what we do, since belief change is what we now plan
               to tackle.

Task 14. The Inference Change Option

Briefing

When to Choose the Inference Change Option

A key criterion for selecting the inference change option is when the
counsellor knows from the ABC assessment that there is good evidence
that the inferences the client is drawing about the type and degree of
adversity are either simply not true or extremely exaggerated and
improbable, and alternative, more benign and unbiased inferences are
either clearly true or highly probable. For example, the client with panic
disorder has a catastrophic inference that his raised pulse rate means he
has heart disease and is going to die of a heart attack, even though he
has been thoroughly checked out and found to be in perfect health. An
inference-level challenge, if successful, would prove the alternative inference that his raised pulse is harmless. Other problems of this type would
include some health anxieties, some phobias, some obsessive compulsive
disorders where a catastrophic outcome is predicted if checks are not
made, and some aspects of social phobia.

Explore Why it is Important to Change an Inference

With the completed Assessment and Goal Planning Worksheet in front
of them, the counsellor and client review the ABC assessment of the first

presented problem (or an alternative, urgently prioritised new problem that has been through the assessment process), and decide to focus on one of the biased inferences (B^1) as the target to change *from*, and the alternative inference to change *to*. The counsellor asks the client for his understanding of the AB^1C problem and goal conceptualisation. She listens for his understanding that:

- his emotional and behavioural problem (C) is partly a consequence of his very negative and probably biased inference (B^1)
- the alternative unbiased inference would contribute significantly to his emotional and behavioural goal
- he therefore needs to change from the negative to the alternative inference, but
- he has high conviction in his negative and low conviction in the alternative and
- needs to reverse this such that the former is low and the latter high.

The counsellor therefore seeks the client's agreement that the task before them is to find a way he could reverse his conviction levels in the two inferences, which he needs to do if he is to give up the negative inference and adopt the alternative as the means to achieve his goals. (The counsellor also shares her own conviction levels, which are genuinely the reverse of the client's, namely low in the negative and high in the alternative.)

She begins to address the task of helping him to change his conviction with the question, 'What makes your inference so convincing, and the alternative so unconvincing for you?' There are usually two answers, namely the client thinks:

- First, that his inference is true, as there is compelling evidence for it, as opposed to the alternative, and though it is distressing, it is realistic to accept it and unrealistic to change it.
- Second, his inference is more helpful or protective in some ways than the alternative and therefore it is pragmatic to hold on to it.

The counsellor suggests they address both points in this order, the evidence issue first, the pragmatic issue second. Turning to the evidence issue, the counsellor explains that there are two methods of testing the empirical truth of both inferences. The first is by weighing the evidence for and against both of them, the second is by testing the evidence, by putting those inferences that can be tested, such as predictions, to the test in behavioural experiments.

Weigh the Evidence

In this task the client is shown how to weigh the evidence for the selected biased inference (B^1) and alternative inference and to compare them, the aim being to weaken the former and strengthen the latter. For this task we provide an Inference Change Worksheet with guidance steps for the client in Appendix 3 and the Action Summary for the counsellor below. The Inference Change Worksheet replicates the Assessment and Goal Planning Worksheet, but introduces three new boxes – a box for evidence for the client's biased inference (B^1), a box for evidence for the alternative and a box for describing the results of a behavioural experiment to test them both. The client transfers the information asked for from the first worksheet to the second (Client Step 1).

Inference Change Steps 2 and 3

The counsellor asks the client to list all the evidence he can think of both for their inference and the alternative, and to write this down on the Inference Change Worksheet (Client Steps 2 and 3). It is easier for the client to find evidence for the inference he believes than for the alternative due to the ubiquitous confirmation bias, i.e. that people in general look for evidence that confirms their beliefs, and very rarely look for disconfirming evidence, so the client may need help with this aspect of the task. The methods used earlier to help identify alternative inferences in Assessment Step 7 can also be used now to find evidence for these alternatives. So one method is to look for evidence as if from the perspective of another person, maybe that of a friend or 'the man in the street', and here the counsellor herself can be a proxy for such a person and give her own version of evidence for the unbiased inference. The other method suggested earlier is to look for evidence that is the opposite of, or goes against the bias, which is not usually difficult as the biased inferences should be clearly improbable to the counsellor's eye.

Inference Change Step 4

Once the client has written down evidence for both inferences on the Inference Change Worksheet, the counsellor invites him to examine the quality of this evidence, as there are a number of traps that the client may fall into that give the impression of having valid evidence when there is none. This type of gentle interrogation can also help to elicit alternatives.

One trap the client may fall into is to resubmit the same evidence that formed the premise for his biased inference (B¹) as if the conclusion was self evidently true, e.g. :

- Biased inference (B¹): 'Feeling dizzy and light headed means I have heart disease.'
- Question: 'What is the evidence that feeling dizzy means you have heart disease?'
- Answer: 'The symptoms of feeling dizzy and light headed.'

Here the question is: 'But what is the evidence for that conclusion. Feeling dizzy, etc. could mean many things.' This can open the way for the alternative inference, which is that the symptom was due to over breathing, as shown in our example.

Similarly, the client may submit further biased inferences as 'factual' evidence for their main biased inference (B¹). So, for example:

- Biased inference: 'John crossed the road means he doesn't like me.'
- Evidence for inference: 'By crossing the road John was obviously avoiding me.'

Here the client is illegitimately but probably unconsciously using another inference 'John was obviously avoiding me' as if it was a fact to support his inference 'he doesn't like me'. The question is: 'But what is the evidence that John crossing the road means he is avoiding you? He could be crossing the road for many reasons.' Again this can open the way for an alternative inference.

In cases where the client's inference-as-evidence is true, e.g. John really was avoiding our client, the client is next invited to question his inferred conclusion, that it means John doesn't like him, since John could be avoiding the client for many reasons, so yet again opening the way to explore alternative inferences.

The counsellor reminds the client about the difference between facts and inferences, and that only facts can be used as evidence for inferences, not further inferences which themselves need verifying. She can also repeat the inference chaining technique, which lays out clearly how one inference leads to another, giving the appearance of compelling proof when there is little, if any.

The counsellor recommends that if she and client agree that the evidence being evaluated doesn't hold up, then he should cross it out (Client Step 4), as it can no longer support his inference.

Inference Change Step 5

After the client has reviewed the quality of the evidence, the counsellor asks him to weigh up the evidence for the two inferences, decide which has most support, and to rate his level of conviction in both (Client Step 5). The counsellor at this point is hopeful for a shift in the balance toward increased conviction in the unbiased inference.

Testing the Evidence

Despite carefully weighing and comparing the evidence for the biased versus the alternative inference, the client may remain unconvinced. He recognises in his head but not in his heart that the evidence for the alternative is greater. This is the familiar intellectual versus the emotional insight problem. In this case the counsellor introduces the client to the method for testing the evidence by behavioural experiment. In this approach the client agrees to put his inferences to a real-world hypothesis-testing experiment to see if it is true or false.

One type of experiment, and the one we most recommend, is the hypothesis A v. hypothesis B type, or in our case, the probably biased inference (B^1) v. the alternative inference. Another type just tests hypothesis A. The counsellor therefore suggests they design a behavioural test of one of these, the former being to confirm the alternative and disconfirm the biased inference, since this is the client's goal.

To be effective, a behavioural experiment needs to be able to show definitively whether an inference (hypothesis) is true or false, confirmed or disconfirmed. Most common-sense inferences are constantly being tested, revised or abandoned as evidence for and against them is discovered in informal 'experiments' in everyday life, but the biased inferences that create problems tend to persist, often for very long periods of time, despite often never having had evidence for them, due to the vicious cycle effect (see Assessment Task 11).

For example, the panic-disorder client who experiences frequent symptoms like dizziness continues to predict a heart attack is imminent despite never having had one. This is because they assume the inference is true and act accordingly in a safety-seeking way, like sitting or lying down or holding on to something, and then thinking 'that was a close shave', which seems like confirming evidence. They never find out that nothing happens, so never get their inference disconfirmed, so the person goes on believing it and taking avoidant action. The behavioural experiment, therefore, is designed both to confirm the alternative and disconfirm the biased inference. An illustration of the problem and a typical experiment is shown in Case Example 1 (John) in the Options for Change Guide (Appendix 3)

Inference Change Step 6
In designing the hypothesis A v. hypothesis B type of behavioural experiment, counsellor and client need to do three things:

- First, they formulate the main inference and alternative as contrasting hypotheses (technically speaking, a hypothesis and a null hypothesis) which can be *dis*confirmed and confirmed respectively by a specific intervention. The main inference predicts an outcome following the intervention; the alternative predicts the opposite outcome.
- Second, they decide on a specific behavioural test. The main inference predicts that a bad outcome will not occur (i.e. be prevented) if 'safety behaviour' designed to stop the outcome is used, and will occur if it is not used. The alternative 'null' hypothesis predicts the opposite, that a bad or less favourable outcome will more likely occur if safety behaviour is used, and less likely occur if safety behaviour is not used.
- Third, they run the test twice, in which the client agrees to first use, and second give up using his safety-seeking behaviour. The first prevents exposure to a 'bad' outcome; the second exposes him to it.

The hypothesis A only experiment simply tests the main hypothesis. The client predicts a bad outcome if safety behaviour is not used or a 'provocation test' is used. If the bad outcome fails to occur when tested in either of these ways, this disconfirms the hypothesis.

A classic example of the hypothesis A v. hypothesis B experiment is used in social phobia (Clark and Wells, 1995) and is the test used for our running Case Example. The client first uses and second drops his usual safety behaviour while doing a presentation simulation to the counsellor and some colleagues. To his surprise the second presentation produces a significantly better response than the first.

Another classic experiment is typically carried out in panic disorder, where the client, instead of carefully avoiding doing anything that would provoke dizziness, provokes it deliberately by over breathing for five minutes – the so-called 'hyperventilation provocation test' (see Case Example 1, Appendix 3). This test confirms the alternative hypothesis ('the dizziness is caused by hyperventilation') but more powerfully disconfirms the biased inference ('symptoms like dizziness are caused by heart disease and deliberately provoking them will lead to heart failure').

A wide range of problems can be subjected to the experimental test approach, either in the consulting room (as can be done with the hyperventilation provocation test) or as in *in vivo* homework, with the client trying this alone, or with the counsellor or a relative or friend as a co-counsellor. An excellent practical guide to designing and implementing behavioural experiments for a wide range of problems is provided in the *Oxford Guide to Behavioural Experiments in Cognitive Therapy* (Bennett-Levy et al., 2004).

The results of behavioural experiments are compelling for clients for two reasons. One is that, if successful, they actually disconfirm the biased inference and provide evidence to confirm the alternative. The second is that they 'promote greater cognitive, affective and behavioural change than purely verbal cognitive techniques lacking an experiential component … so that patients do not get into the position of saying "I can see the alternative, but I still don't feel any different"' (Bennett–Levy et al., 2004, p. 15).

Client Completes Inference Change Steps 6 and 7

With the help of the counsellor the client designs and carries out an experimental test to disconfirm his inference and confirm the alternative. He writes down the experiment and the result on the worksheet (Client Step 6). The client then rates his level of conviction in each inference and re-rates the intensity of his feelings (Client Step 7).

Action Summary

1 The counsellor ensures the client understands that to reach his healthy emotional and behavioural goal he needs to change his beliefs, and that they will in this session address first the inferences, and help him learn how to change for the healthy alternatives.
2 The client copies across from the Assessment and Goal Planning Worksheet to the Inference Change Worksheet all the information asked for in the boxes (following Inference Change Option Step 1, Appendix 3). This will include the A (Adverse event), B[1] (Possibly Biased Inference) and Alternative Inference, the C Problem and C Goal.
3 The counsellor asks the client to list all the evidence he can think of that would support his (probably) biased inference (B[1]) and the unbiased alternative and write them on the Inference Change Worksheet (Steps 2 and 3).

4   The client examines the two lists and, with the counsellor's help, questions the quality of the evidence. Is it reliable evidence? Would it stand up in a court of law? If the evidence doesn't stand up to scrutiny, she suggests he crosses it out – a symbolic deletion (Step 4). The client weighs up the two lists of evidence carefully and considers which of the two inferences has the strongest support. He then re-rates his level of conviction in each inference and the intensity of his feelings (Step 5).

5   If the client's conviction hasn't changed substantially, the counsellor introduces the idea of carrying out a real-life behavioural experiment. Together they design, and he is invited to carry out an experiment, either with the counsellor as part of the session, or with the counsellor or a relative or friend acting as a co-therapist between sessions as homework. The purpose of the experiment is to *dis*confirm his inference (B^1) and confirm the alternative. The experiment may need to be carried out several times. The client writes down the experiment and result on the worksheet (Step 6).

6   After the experiment he re-rates his level of conviction in each inference and re-rates the intensity of his feelings (Step 7).

7   Counsellor and client agree that for homework he continues thought monitoring using the ABC Diary, but adds today's inference task, as described above and in the ABC Diary steps.

Case Example

Counsellor Joan starts by checking the client understands clearly from the Assessment Worksheet that:

*   his biased beliefs lead to his emotional problem (B^1 to C problem)
*   the alternative beliefs lead to the emotional goal (B^1 alternative to C goal)
*   he needs to change from B^1 to B^1 alternative, but
*   his conviction levels are B^1 high, B^1 alternative low, and
*   he needs to be B^1 low, B^1 alternative high

Counsellor:	So you agree this is the task to help you reverse your conviction levels. So what makes your inferences so convincing and the alternatives not?
Client:	Well, mainly because they seem so true, so valid and they somehow protect me, get me prepared for a potential disaster. Better safe than sorry.
Counsellor:	OK, that's two points. One is that there seems such good evidence for their truth; the second is that they help you in some way. (*Client agrees.*) Let's start with

the evidence issue. There are two ways of looking at this. One is to note all the evidence we can think of for your inferences compared to the evidence for the alternatives and weigh it all up and see which comes out best. The second is to put your inferences and the alternatives to the test, like we can test predictions in behavioural experiments. What do you think of this approach?

Client: Well, yes, I have got to try.

Counsellor: If you are agreeable then, here is an Inference Change Guide and Worksheet with steps like before. (*Both go over the Guide and Worksheet and the client completes Step 1.*)

Counsellor: OK, Step 2 in the Guide is to brainstorm all the evidence we can think of for your inferences B^1. Let's start with your first inference, 'they're all staring at me' or at your anxiety symptoms to be exact – shaking, going red, pulse racing. What's the evidence?

Client: It's so obvious. I can feel it so strongly I just know they're a dead giveaway and everybody will be just staring – people do.

Counsellor: And what's the evidence for your second inference – because of the first being true, they all think you are an idiot?

Client: Again it's obvious; we know that's how people think when they see someone screw up that much.

Counsellor: Anything else?

Client: I can feel their eyes boring into me. (*Brian tries to think of any other evidence.*)

Counsellor: Now, Step 3 in the Guide is to look for evidence for the B^1 alternatives, First, 'if my symptoms aren't that bad, people may not notice so much'.

Client: My symptoms may not be as bad and visible as they feel.

Counsellor: That's right, how you experience them from the inside (your face feels it's burning) is not the same as they look from the outside, and such symptoms always *feel* worse than they *look*. Also you are not looking at people so you have no evidence that people even notice, you just imagine they do?

Client:	I can see I might be building a picture in my mind but I have no evidence it is true. (*Joan and Brian continue to explore evidence for other alternatives.*)
Counsellor:	Let's go on to Step 4: does the evidence hold up, is it valid? So evidence for your first belief, you feel it 'strongly', it's a 'dead giveaway'.
Client:	It's the same point – how it feels to me on the inside isn't the same as how it looks on the outside, and I don't know how it looks.
Counsellor:	I agree. So what is the jury's verdict on that evidence?
Client:	Throw it out! (*Brian crosses it out. Joan and Brian examine the quality of the evidence for all the B^1 inferences and alternatives.*)
Counsellor:	We're on to Step 5 now. So weigh up the two lots of evidence carefully and consider which of the two sets of inferences has the strongest support. Then re-rate your level of conviction in each inference and re-rate the intensity of your feelings in the C boxes. Has there been a real change? (*Joan and Brian systematically go through the process, and Brian shows a moderate shift in his conviction ratings.*)
Counsellor:	Now that you have weighed the evidence, are you convinced your B^1 inferences are not true and the alternatives are true?
Client:	Sorry to disappoint you, and myself, but I'm not really. I can see very clearly in my head that you are right but at a gut level I just have this strong sense that my beliefs are right, I can't easily explain it.
Counsellor:	Don't worry at all. It's important at this stage that you have what we call intellectual insight but it's to be expected you won't have emotional 'insight'. What we need to do now is to put both sets of inferences to a real-world test, and if that works, you may find it more convincing at a gut level.
Client:	OK, that's encouraging, and makes sense.
Counsellor:	So what we need to do is design an experiment where we pit yours and the alternative inferences against each other and see which one 'wins'. The aim, frankly, is to confirm the alternative and disconfirm your biased inferences, since this is your goal if you remember?

(*Brian agrees. Joan and Brian discuss and then design an experiment.*)

Counsellor: So we have agreed on the following experiment. Your main inference is that a terrible outcome (you screw up and look like an idiot) will be *less* likely if you use 'safety behaviour' and more likely if you don't. The alternative predicts the opposite, that a bad outcome will more likely occur if safety behaviour is used (because it makes the situation worse), and less likely if safety behaviour is not used. Is this a fair summary? (*Brian agrees.*). OK, so you will give a presentation to us, like you would at uni, but twice, the first time using and second time not using your safety-seeking behaviour. Giving up safety-behaviours means you look at and engage members of the audience, you don't read from a script but ad lib and that you let any shaking and blushing show. We will video both of them.

Client: This sounds terrifying.

Counsellor: Well, also remember in the second take to try to adopt and feel the 'concern' not 'panic and terror' mindset. And if it isn't too much to think about, keep in mind at least one of the alternative inferences, such as 'if people notice they are probably sympathetic and interested'. Now before we start, let's just be clear what your exact predictions are, such as just how red in the face you will look. (*Brian writes down the experiment on the worksheet, then carries out both tests in front of the counsellor and some colleagues, then watches the video playback. This is Client Step 6.*)

Counsellor: How did it go?

Client: I feel quite shaken up, but at the same time feel it worked to some extent. I thought I did OK despite feeling anxious, and the video shows I was better than I thought, and the symptoms weren't that obvious either, so it did go against my negative predictions.

Counsellor: Excellent, I thought you did very well! Has there been a change in your conviction?

Client: Definitely more so, and more at an instinctive, gut level (Step 7). But I still feel quite anxious, that it could still go disastrously wrong.

Counsellor: Well, we have another intervention – to challenge your
               evaluations. We will come to this in our next session.
               But before that, do you think what we have done in this
               session today can be added to your homework? When
               you carry out your thought monitoring next week, and
               notice a negative biased inference comes to mind,
               and you choose an alternative unbiased inference,
               why don't you weigh the evidence for each as you have
               today, and also look for an opportunity to put them to
               the test.
Client: What could I do?
Counsellor: Well, why not try some positive assertion or express an
               opinion – something you would normally avoid – and
               drop any safety behaviour. Make predictions from your
               two beliefs and see which one turns out right, much like
               we did today.
Client: OK, I will see what I can do.
Counsellor: *If you are agreeable, let's be a bit more specific than that.*
               Let's write this down on your Session and Homework
               Report Form.

8

Middle Stage II – Changing Hot Thoughts

Task 15. The Evaluation Change Option

Briefing

The main criterion for choosing the Evaluation Change Option is when the counsellor has discovered or suspects from the assessment stage that the client has, or is vulnerable to developing, an extremely negative view of himself (core belief), a significant other or life circumstances, is grossly magnifying the badness of adverse events, or has an extremely low threshold for tolerating adverse events, whether external or internal. These extreme evaluative beliefs lead to disturbed emotional consequences and are common in anxiety, depression and anger-related problems. They are the products of what Albert Ellis, the inventor of REBT, described as an irrational demanding philosophy and Aaron T. Beck, the inventor of CT, identified as aspects of dysfunctional assumptions and schemas. Like all evaluations they are distinct from inferences in that they are concerned with good–bad appraisals and not simply true–false judgements. They are 'hot thoughts' in that they directly lead to emotional consequences, as opposed to inferences which indirectly lead to emotional consequence *through* the evaluations. The counsellor will have helped the client to identify his extreme evaluations and healthy alternatives in the assessment stage, and will now be helped to change from the former to latter.

Start with the Evaluation Option
We recommend that, if the evaluation option is chosen, it is undertaken *first* if possible, before the other change options, and while the client's biased inferences are still in place and unmodified.

First, the aim of this option is to enable the client to respond with a healthy negative emotion to the worst-case scenario, which is a persuasive argument for the sceptical client, and helps inoculate the client against relapsing if and when future adverse events recur.

Second, if the inference option comes first and the biased inferences have been successfully changed and are less negative, it is then rather more difficult to evoke and change the underlying extreme evaluations, unless and until the client becomes disturbed again, and then the problem may become more resistant to change.

Third, inference change becomes easier once the extreme evaluations have changed first, and behavioural experiments and the dropping of safety behaviours becomes less difficult for the client to undertake.

Although it is preferable to undertake evaluation change first, we still recommend using this option if inference level change has not been successful or only partially successful. For example the evaluation change option can be offered when the client appears to have made some progress in inference change, but though he now accepts the adverse outcome is unlikely or even very unlikely, it would still be so awful that he could not bear it and he therefore must be certain it will not happen at all. This is a classic evaluation level problem. Our ongoing Case Example illustrates this situation.

Explore Why it is Important to Change the Extreme Evaluations
The process for conducting this task starts in a similar way to the inference change option (Task 14) but then differs markedly. So, with the Assessment and Goal Planning Worksheet in front of them, the counsellor and client review the ABC assessment of the selected problem, and agree to work first on the extreme evaluations listed (B^2) as the target to change *from*, and the realistic alternative evaluations, also listed, to change *to*. The counsellor asks the client for his understanding of the AB^2C problem and goal conceptualisation. She listens for his understanding that:

- his unhealthy emotional and behavioural disturbance (C) is largely a consequence of his extreme and rigid evaluations (B^2), given his inferences (B^1)[1]
- the alternative realistic and flexible evaluations would more likely lead to his healthy emotional and behavioural goal, and may help change his inferences also, so
- he needs to change from the extreme and rigid evaluations to the alternative realistic and flexible evaluations, but
- he has high conviction in his extreme evaluations and low conviction in the alternatives.

The task therefore is to find a way the client could reverse his conviction levels in the two sets of evaluations, which he needs to do if he is to give up the former and adopt the latter. She therefore asks, 'What makes your extreme evaluations so convincing, and the alternatives so unconvincing for you?' She Socratically draws out three answers, namely that he believes the following:

- First, that his extreme evaluations are true, as he thinks they are realistic and has compelling evidence for them, as opposed to the alternatives, and though it is disturbing, it is realistic to accept them and unrealistic to change them.
- Second, his evaluations are more helpful than the alternatives and therefore it is pragmatic to hold on to them even though they make him more disturbed.
- Third, his evaluations are more logical and therefore it makes sense to hold on to them.

The counsellor suggests they challenge all three claims, the aim being to reverse his conviction levels such that the extreme, irrational evaluations become weakened so they can be given up and the alternative rational evaluations strengthened so they can be adopted. There are several methods developed mainly in REBT for achieving these evaluation changes, of which we select three for this guide. Comprehensive accounts of these and other methods can be found in a number of REBT-focused texts such as Dryden and Neenan (2004). The first evaluation change method is a cognitive technique of disputing the validity of both sets of evaluations, namely disputing the evidence for them, the helpfulness and usefulness of them and their logical coherence. The second is an experiential imagery technique in which the client learns how to change to a healthy

---

[1] When the client has already received the inference change option and made progress in inference change but is still anxious about the possibility of a catastrophic outcome, he is now asked to describe a 'worst case scenario' and provide the biased inferences from that example.

negative emotion by changing his evaluations. The third is a behavioural technique designed to help the client discover experientially as well as intellectually the validity of the alternative and the lack of validity of the extreme evaluation. This is somewhat different from the behavioural experiment described in Task 14, as we shall show.

Evaluation Change by Disputing

In this task the client is shown how to dispute the evidence for the truth, utility and logicality of both the extreme and the alternative flexible evaluations and to compare them, the agreed aim being to weaken the former and strengthen the latter.

The Disputing Steps 1 to 5

For this task we provide an Evaluation Change Worksheet with guidance steps for the client to follow in Appendix 3, and the usual Action Summary and Case Example for the counsellor below. The Evaluation Change Worksheet also replicates the Assessment and Goal Planning Worksheet, but introduces spaces for the client to indicate whether he thinks each evaluation is true, useful or logical, after disputing them. The client transfers information from the former to the latter Worksheet (Client Step 1).

The counsellor knows, and she helps the client to discover, that unlike inferences which can be false or biased but can also be true on occasions, the client's extreme evaluations are irrational, meaning that they can *never* be true, are never possible in the real world and are therefore unrealistic, unhelpful and illogical, whereas the alternative evaluations are rational, meaning they are realistic, helpful and logical. In a sentence, the irrational beliefs are never valid; the rational beliefs are virtually always valid (Ellis, 1994). One powerful way this difference is revealed for the client is through the process of disputing. The counsellor coaches the client how to dispute so that he will discover that his extreme evaluations are irrational and unrealistic and his alternative evaluations are rational and realistic.

Dispute the Evaluations in Pairs

She suggests he disputes the evaluations in pairs:

*   The demanding versus the preferring beliefs (Evaluation Change Through Disputing Step 2),

- o e.g. 'it absolutely must not happen' versus 'I strongly wish it wouldn't happen but it could'.
- The awfulising versus non-awfulising beliefs (Step 3),
  - o e.g. 'it would be absolutely awful if it happened' versus 'it would be relatively (slightly, moderately, very) bad but never absolutely awful'.
- The low tolerance versus the high tolerance beliefs (Step 4),
  - o e.g. 'it would be absolutely unbearable if it happened' versus 'it would be relatively (slightly, moderately, very) difficult to bear but I could bear it'.
- The self/other/life depreciation versus the self/other/life acceptance beliefs (Step 5),
  - o e.g. 'I/you/life would be absolutely no good at all if this happened' versus 'I/you/life wouldn't have done any good specifically but that doesn't mean I/you/life is no good at all, just relatively imperfect and fallible and I unconditionally accept that reality'.

The Dispute Questions

She coaches the client in the three types of dispute questions, the empirical, the pragmatic and the logical, for the four pairs of evaluations. As he works through the disputes he marks off his conclusions on the Evaluations Change Worksheet. Instructions for the client are provided (Client Steps 2 to 5).

- Empirical dispute questions ask whether the evaluations are consistent with reality:
  - o What is the evidence for this belief?
  - o Can you prove this?
  - o Is this belief realistic?
  - o Which of these two beliefs is realistic?

  For example, 'Which is more realistic, that the bad event mustn't happen or you strongly wish it wouldn't but accept it could?' A similar format can be used for awfulising v. non-awfulising, low tolerance v. high tolerance and depreciation v. acceptance beliefs.

- Pragmatic dispute questions ask whether the evaluations help the person achieve their emotional, behavioural and practical goals:
  - o How does this belief help you?
  - o Which of these two beliefs is more/less helpful? For example, 'Which is more helpful to you, to absolutely demand the bad event doesn't happen, or to strongly wish it wouldn't but acknowledge it could?' As before, a similar format can be used for the other three extreme beliefs.

- Logical dispute questions can ask which of two conclusions is more logical (or makes more sense):

  - a) 'I would hate this to happen, therefore it absolutely mustn't' or b) 'I would hate this to happen but this does not mean it mustn't'.
  - a) 'It would be very bad if this bad thing happened, and therefore it would be awful' or b) 'it would be very bad if this happened but it would not be awful'.
  - a) 'It would be very hard to bear and therefore it would be unbearable' or b) 'it would be very hard to bear but it would not be unbearable'.
  - a) 'It would be bad if I did this, therefore I would be a totally bad person' or b) 'it would be bad if I did this but that wouldn't make me a bad person, I would remain a fallible human despite this bad behaviour, and I unconditionally accept myself as such'.

Rating the Effect of Disputing, Step 6

Finally the client weighs up the effect of all his disputes on the validity of his extreme evaluations compared with the alternative evaluations, and rates his overall conviction in each set of evaluations and compares these with his original ratings (Step 6).

If the disputing is carried out correctly, there is only one possible outcome, namely that the extreme evaluations are shown to be 'irrational', that is unrealistic, unhelpful and illogical, and the alternative evaluations are shown to be 'rational', that is realistic, helpful and logical. Unlike the inferences, which the client can rightly claim could still be true, no matter how unlikely, the irrational evaluations can never be true. If the client has not reached this conclusion, the counsellor can go the extra mile, drawing on a rich variety of sources (e.g. Ellis, 1994) of which the following is just a very brief summary.

First, nothing can be truly demanded, where 'demand' means that a person absolutely must conform or obey. It may be highly preferable or morally very desirable that a person conforms but often fail to do so. To demand is therefore always unrealistic, cannot be derived logically, and cannot be pragmatic because it can never be attained, thus resulting in unnecessary anxiety, depression and other disturbances.

Second, nothing can be absolutely awful where 'awful' means the worst possible or even worse than the worst possible. Events can be very bad but no matter how bad, it is always possible for something to be worse. To 'awfulise' is therefore also always unrealistic, cannot be derived logically and cannot be helpful because no matter how bad an event, 'awfulising' magnifies it and worsens the level of distress.

Third, nothing is absolutely intolerable because no matter how bad the event that happens, the sufferer actually bears it or it wouldn't exist. Events can only be very hard to tolerate. To believe something is unbearable is therefore also unrealistic, cannot be derived logically and is hardly helpful because it makes the bad event more distressing.

Fourth, nobody can be totally bad or worthless in their essence because no matter how badly or unworthily they behave they can always change their behaviour, which would be impossible if they were totally bad in their essence. It is always unrealistic to believe a global negative (or even positive) rating, not logical to do so and not helpful as it leads to anxiety, depression and other disturbances.

This should provide the client with the necessary intellectual insight, but may not provide him with gut-level conviction which is also necessary for emotional and behavioural change. To produce intellectual *and* emotional insight, the counsellor can recommend the next two techniques that employ imagery and behavioural assignments.

Evaluation Change Through Imagery

Successful disputation will often soften the 'catastrophic' appraisal of the worst case scenario, by bringing it into the domain of the relative and out of the domain of the extreme and the absolute. However, it is still an intellectual insight, and though this 'knowing in your head' that the irrational beliefs are not valid and the rational beliefs are valid is essential for emotional/behavioural change, it is still sometimes not sufficient. The client may still be feeling disturbed. The second, pragmatic dispute may not have been satisfied, for the client needs to actually experience a change in emotion with a change in beliefs. How can this be achieved?

If the irrational evaluations produce an unhealthy emotion and the rational ones a healthy emotion, then the client (or anyone) should be able to *experience* the change in emotion if he can replace the former beliefs with the latter. An exercise known as rational emotive imagery (REI) is designed to achieve this. This exercise should only be attempted after successfully completing the disputing task, after which the client should be able to disengage from his automatic evaluations more easily, and engage the alternatives.

Rational Emotive Imagery, Steps 7, 8 and 9

The counsellor asks the client to bring to mind as vividly as possible the adverse event (Step 7). He needs to re-experience the emotional episode as a whole – what actually happened (A), the automatically triggered irrational evaluations (B²) and the unhealthy negative emotional and behavioural consequences (C). This can be done by transporting himself, in imagination, back to the event or imagine it as if it was happening now. Usually the best way the client can do this is by getting in touch with the disturbed emotion and the rest of the emotional episode is likely to follow.

Once he is fully cognitively and physiologically in touch with the disturbed emotion, the image of the event that triggered it and the irrational beliefs that led to it, he indicates this with a raised finger. The counsellor then asks him to change the emotion from the unhealthy disturbance to a healthy negative emotion, for example from anxiety to healthy concern (Step 8). At the first attempt he may try to achieve this by changing the A rather than the evaluative beliefs, in which case the counsellor coaches him how to achieve the emotion change by changing the beliefs and keeping the negative event the same.

To work effectively REI needs considerable practice. The client needs to be able to 're-live' (or 'live' if it's a prediction) in imagery the bad event in all sensory modalities if possible, and to really experience the disturbed emotion as near as possible to the real thing. Once he is able to do this, the irrational beliefs will automatically come into his mind. Then the client also needs to be able to disengage from the irrational beliefs and re-engage the rational alternatives, and this also requires practice. The problem is that the irrational beliefs (and the biased inferences that are closely linked) are triggered automatically, and can only be disengaged by deliberate, mindful awareness, first of the irrational beliefs, then deliberately bringing the rational beliefs to mind. The counsellor therefore carefully coaches the client in reliving the bad event in imagination, and practising the switch from automatic, mindless thinking into mindful awareness of the irrational beliefs, disengaging from them and engaging the rational alternatives.

The counsellor then asks the client to practise the imagery exercise as homework during the week, at least two or three times a day, and to keep a record of how far they were able to relive the bad event A, experience the unhealthy emotion C, and in mindful awareness identify and disengage from the irrational beliefs (B²) and remember and engage the alternatives (Step 9). She then reviews this homework at the next session and helps the client make the exercise more realistic and emotionally evocative, and improve their mindfulness skills. If mindfulness meditation training (e.g. Williams et al., 2007) or detached mindfulness training (e.g. Wells, 2009) can be provided, this would enhance the effectiveness of this task.

Evaluation Change Through Behavioural Exposure, Steps 10 to 14

Assuming good progress with disputing and REI, now hopefully knowing in his head the rational beliefs are valid and the irrational are invalid, and having experienced emotional change through belief change, the client will still not have gained very much unless he can bring these cognitive and emotional/behavioural changes to bear on his everyday life and its adversities. Moreover, he has further work to do, on increasing his conviction in and engagement with the rational, self-accepting beliefs, of making them the automatic, 'default' set of beliefs to replace the irrational set, and constructing new emotions and behavioural skills in everyday life as a result. Guidance for the client are provided in the section Evaluation Change Through Behavioural Exposure Steps 10 to 14, Appendix 3.

Disconfirming an Irrational Evaluation

One aim of the behavioural approach is to further establish the client's conviction in the rational evaluations. Like inference change, evaluation change is much more compelling when experienced in a real-life behavioural experiment, as we noted earlier. What behavioural tasks can the client undertake *in vivo* that could give him the experience of disconfirmation of an irrational evaluation and confirmation of the rational alternative, and thus deepen his conviction? One approach is to set up behavioural experiments similar to those discussed earlier in the inference-level task section, though with a different emphasis. For example, a behavioural experiment can be designed to disconfirm the irrational self-downing belief 'I am totally useless/and or bad' (and confirm the alternative 'I am a fallible human who does useful and useless, good and bad things'). To do this, the counsellor first clarifies that by 'totally' he means a global evaluation of the whole 'self in its essence', and then collaboratively sets up an experiment to disconfirm this. This could be any action that the 'average' person would deem useful or good, as it only takes a single action that would be impossible for a wholly useless or bad person to show the belief to be false. The counsellor has to ensure no subtle safety behaviours may get in the way of carrying out the belief disconfirming task, and no hidden biased beliefs that are disqualifying his achievements.

Shame-attacking Homework Exercise

Another aim of the behavioural approach is to help the client use in real-life adversities his newly acquired, rational self-, other- and life-accepting beliefs, and to give up his habitual irrational self-, other- and life-condemning beliefs. The goal is not only to experience a healthy negative emotion like disappointment and concern instead of shame and anxiety, but to show more self-respecting and positively-assertive verbal and non-verbal behaviour instead of self-subordinating and negative body language that communicates for example 'I am ashamed'.

What behavioural tasks can the client undertake to do this, to practise evaluating with his rational beliefs instead of his irrational ones? One approach is the 'shame-attacking' exercise widely used in REBT. For example, the client practices engaging the unconditional self-acceptance (USA) belief (e.g. 'I unconditionally accept myself despite doing fallible things like this') and the high discomfort tolerance (HDT) belief (e.g. 'I can do this even though it's very uncomfortable'), whilst doing something 'shameful'. This act can be something overtly 'silly' like calling out station names or making a speech in a busy town centre, or an assertive act like disagreeing with someone who is likely to be critical in response, or turning down a *reasonable* request.

The shame-attacking approach can be particularly helpful with clients who are ashamed of some aspect of their involuntary behaviour or appearance, such as blushing, shedding tears, or showing visible signs of anxiety like shaking as in our ongoing Case Example. Here the client does more than just drop the use of safety-seeking behaviour like trying to hide the shameful feature, and instead displays it or even deliberately draws attention to it ('oh look I am blushing') while practising self-acceptance and HDT. The aim is not in this case to get disconfirming evidence of a biased inference but to be self-accepting and tolerant of discomfort even when the inference is true ('I accept myself even if or when I am red in the face and they criticise').

If successful the client will not only lose the feeling of shame and replace it with a healthy negative emotion like disappointment or concern, but also the negative body language, and is encouraged to behave in an 'anti-shaming' way with positive, self-respecting assertion. This starts a virtuous cycle, by constructing a new pattern of behaviour, of creating evidence confirming the rational beliefs, of increasing the likelihood of changing the adverse event – the practical problem (A) – and thus creating a more positive evidence base for generating new, positive inferences. Part of this change will be the likelihood of influencing in a positive way the reactions of others, leading in turn to a reversal of the negative maintenance cycle to an enduring positive cycle.

Coaching the Client in Behavioural Tasks

One way the counsellor coaches the client in carrying out the behavioural tasks just described is by using the REI exercise as a guiding framework for constructing the behavioural exercise (Client Step 10). In addition the client uses the imagery exercise as a rehearsal for the behavioural exercises, such that after many practices in imagination, he knows clearly what to do when it comes to the 'real thing', not only behaviourally but cognitively and affectively. Counsellor and client can extend this rehearsal function further by carrying out role-play and role-reversal simulations of the behavioural exercise. Preparation and rehearsal will take time, so it is usually better to delay the start of the behavioural tasks until the client is reasonably familiar with REI, which he carries out as daily homework between sessions.

Client Step 11

In REI, the client first brings to mind the presented problem, the As, Bs and Cs of the emotional episode. In the behavioural exercise, the client sets up as homework an event that replicates or emulates the presented problem, or anticipates and plans for one that is upcoming. Some home-work tasks can be planned in advance, like going into a supermarket or on a bus, taking an item back to a shop, talking to a stranger in the street. Some are regularly occurring adverse events, like a bullying relation-ship at work or home, but some cannot be predicted when they occur. However, they all can be prepared for.

Client Step 12

Where the task can be set up in advance, the client rehearses shortly beforehand in imagery, using the REI method. Then the client steals himself to enter the situation (A) and to be mindfully aware of the auto-matic irrational beliefs (B^2) and consequent disturbed emotion and action tendency (C). If the client has difficulty entering the situation, he can engage the high discomfort tolerance belief at this point. If this is still too difficult, he can set an easier task, such as a smaller public space with less people if the problem is in this domain.

Client Step 13

The client then instructs himself to change from the unhealthy to the healthy negative emotion, such as anxiety to concern, precisely in the way he has learned in REI, that is by mindfully disengaging from the irrational beliefs and re-engaging the rational alternatives, or those which are most relevant to the situation. If the client has difficulty identifying, disengaging and re-engaging, his skill can be shaped up in role-play and role-rehearsals with the counsellor, where the counsellor first demonstrates the skill.

Client Step 14

If successful his action tendency may change naturally, but if it doesn't, and even if he cannot change the emotion, he nonetheless rehearses the rational beliefs and behaves in a way that is consistent with the rational belief. So, for example, even if still anxious, he mindfully engages the belief 'I unconditionally accept myself despite … feeling anxious, thinking I look stupid, etc.' and behaves accordingly, such as continuing shopping, looking at people, as opposed to making for the exit, gaze avoiding, trying to hide, look small, etc.

Just as it is important to practise the REI exercise, it is also important for the client to carry out the behavioural exercise frequently, daily if possible for the first two or three weeks between sessions. The first attempts will be mainly learning the method without much change at B and C, but there will be progressive improvement in the effectiveness of the exercise.

Action Summary

1. The counsellor checks again that the client understands that to reach his healthy emotional and behavioural goal he needs to change his beliefs, and that they will in this session address his extreme 'irrational' evaluations, and help him learn how to change them for the non-extreme and rational alternatives.
2. The client copies across from the Assessment Worksheet to the Evaluation Change Worksheet all the information asked for in the boxes. This will include the A (Adverse event), B1 (Possibly Biased Inference) and Alternative Unbiased Inference B2 (Extreme Evaluations) and Realistic Alternative Evaluations, the C Problem and C Goal.
3. The counsellor coaches the client in the method of disputing evaluations. They preferably dispute the evaluations in pairs – the irrational and the

rational together, starting with the demanding and preferring evaluations. She coaches the client in the three types of dispute questions, the empirical, pragmatic and the logical (see Briefing, and Client steps, Appendix 3).

4   The counsellor and client then together dispute the remaining three pairs of evaluations, namely the awfulising versus non-awfulising, discomfort intolerance versus discomfort tolerance and finally the 'self' or 'other' or 'life' depreciation versus 'self' or 'other' or 'life' acceptance evaluations. He places ticks and crosses against his choices on the worksheet.

5   The client weighs up the effect of all his disputes on the comparative validity of the two sets of beliefs. He rates his overall conviction in each set of evaluations and compares this with the rating he gave originally.

6   If the client remains relatively unconvinced because he does not feel any different, the counsellor introduces rational emotive imagery (REI) as a method to experience a change of feeling following a change of belief.

7   The counsellor coaches the client in the REI method, as described in the Briefing and in the Evaluation Change Steps 7 and 8, Appendix 3.

8   The client is invited to practise REI three times a day between sessions, and to bring any difficulties to the next session (Step 9).

9   The counsellor suggests how the client can use REI as a framework and method of rehearsal for introducing the cognitive, emotional and behavioural changes he has learned into real-life situations he had difficulty with.

10 The counsellor coaches the client in the four steps to carrying out behavioural exposure exercises, such as the shame-attacking exercise – see Briefing and Evaluation Change Steps 10 to 13. If the client achieves evaluation change through these exercises, he records this on the Assessment and Goal Planning Worksheet.

Case Example

Our client has made some progress but still predicts his presentations could go disastrously wrong – he is still vulnerable to 'awfulising' – so counsellor Joan introduces the evaluation-change option (Task 3). This starts with a similar format but different content to Task 2 – see Briefing for detailed guidance. They review the ABC assessment again and agree this time to work on changing the extreme evaluations (B^2). The counsellor asks the client for his understanding that:

- his unhealthy (C) is largely a consequence of his extreme evaluations (B^2), given his biased inferences (B^1) which still have validity for him,
- the alternative evaluations would lead to a healthy (C), so

- he needs to change his B^2 to the B^2 alternative but
- his conviction levels are B^2 high, B^2 alternative low, and
- he needs to be B^2 low, B^2 alternative high.

Counsellor:	So you agree the task is to help you reverse your conviction levels. So what makes your evaluations so convincing and the alternatives not? (*Joan Socratically draws out from Brian that, compared to the alternatives, he thinks his evaluations are true and realistic, are more helpful and more logical – see Briefing for more detailed guidance.*)
Counsellor:	So how about discovering how to challenge and reverse all three claims, so your extreme evaluations become weakened, so helping you give them up, and the alternatives strengthened so helping you adopt them.
Client:	Ok, I agree but can't see how you can do that.
Counsellor:	(*introducing the disputing strategy*) Well, there are several ways. The first I want to introduce you to is by disputing your evaluations and the alternatives, the aim being to discover that it's only the alternatives that are valid. (*Joan gives Brian the Evaluation Change Guidance Steps and Worksheet (Appendix 3), and Brian completes Step 1, which is to transfer information from the Assessment and Goal Planning Worksheet to the Evaluation Worksheet.*)
Counsellor:	You've got your evaluations and alternatives under these four headings: demanding v. preferring, awfulising v. non-awfulising, LDT or low discomfort tolerance v. HDT or high discomfort tolerance, and self/other/life downing v. self/other/life acceptance. Let's start with your demanding v. preferring beliefs. You have a good preferring evaluation – 'I really *really* don't want this but …' but you haven't got a demand down yet. What do you think you are demanding about this situation?
Client:	That's easy; I absolutely mustn't screw up and have them think I'm an idiot!
Counsellor:	That's it I'm sure. Now your first claim was that your extreme beliefs are more realistically true than the alternatives, so let me ask you, which of these two beliefs is

	more realistically true, demanding you absolutely never screw up and absolutely never have them think you're an idiot, or really *really* preferring you didn't and they didn't, but accepting it could happen?
Client:	When you put it like that, obviously really preferring is more realistic.
Counsellor:	That's right, unless you have a handy Genie who can make your demands come true, but in the meantime ... (*using the examples as a guide, Brian completes the first part of Step 2 and ticks the preference belief and puts a cross against the demanding belief on the Evaluation Worksheet.*)
Counsellor:	Now your second claim was that your extreme beliefs were more helpful. So which belief is more helpful, demanding you absolutely never screw up and never get thought to be an idiot, or really really preferring that, but realistically accepting it could happen?
Client:	I see what you're getting at here. Demanding something impossible is not going to help.
Counsellor:	And the demand is going to fuel your anxiety too. Now the third claim you made was that your beliefs were more logical, made more sense. So does it make more sense to demand these things never happen, or wish to hell they didn't but ...?!
Client:	Again, more sense to wish and not demand.
Counsellor:	Another way of putting it is to ask: How does it follow that just because I badly don't want something to happen, it therefore must not?
Client:	It doesn't follow at all.
Counsellor:	So what's happened to your conviction in the validity of your demanding over your preferring belief?
Client:	Its absolutely the other way round, I can see that.

Joan then disputes the other three sets of beliefs for their validity, namely which is more realistic, helpful and logical. These are Steps 3, 4 and 5 in the Guide. Joan also coaches Brian in how to use dispute questions himself when the extreme evaluations come to mind when he ruminates and worries about his presentation problems. Brian is encouraged to practise this as homework during the week, to try to remember to use his disturbed emotion as the cue to 'look for the should' and to keep a log of the emotion, the extreme belief B^2 and the alternative. This coaching helps prepare Brian for becoming his own counsellor (Ending Stage, Chapter 11).

Counsellor: OK, we have come to Step 6 in disputing. So have a go at weighing up the effect of all your disputes on the validity of your extreme evaluations compared with the alternative evaluations. Rate your overall conviction in each set on a 0–10 scale (where 0 = totally unconvinced and 10 = totally convinced), and compare this with the rating you gave originally. (*Brian carries out these tasks, and shows that his ratings have improved in the right direction.*)

Counsellor: It seems you have achieved substantial belief change, and the thought of these presentations is evoking less anxiety, but I sense that, though you are less anxious, you still haven't really made the transition to the qualitatively different emotion of healthy concern?

Client: No, that captures it, I still have this uncomfortable edge that makes me want to run rather than face up to it, and I feel I could lose my gains.

Counsellor: (*introducing evaluation change through imagery*) It may be because you haven't yet had the *experience* of a change of emotion with the change of belief. This next exercise is designed to give you that experience. We call it Rational Emotive Imagery or REI. (*Joan hands the client a copy of the Evaluation Change through Imagery Steps, 7 to 9.*)

Counsellor: So try as you did before by getting a felt sense of healthy concern, where you have a tendency to approach a problem with care rather than run away as in anxiety. Think of a role model, or recall a time when you felt this way.

Client: OK, I've got it.

Counsellor: OK, now put that on hold for the moment, and relive as best you can the last really difficult presentation when you lost your place and you froze to the spot. Try to relive the moment, what you saw, heard, felt, even smelt and tasted if those were present. Re-experience that intense anxiety and the physiological arousal, face going red, shaking and so on. Raise your finger when you've got it. (*Brian raises finger after a couple of minutes.*)

Counsellor:	OK, now change that anxiety for healthy concern, and raise your finger again when you've got that. (*Brian pauses, then raises finger.*)
Counsellor:	(*after a pause*) OK, how did you do that?
Client:	I imagined everyone was being nice to me.
Counsellor:	OK, that's understandable, and you have done well, but I'd like you to repeat the exercise now, and this time I want you to try to keep the situation like it was, and change your anxiety for healthy concern by changing from your extreme beliefs to the realistic alternatives. Remember what we did with the disputes. And take your time; try to disengage from your habitual beliefs and re-engage with the alternatives as best you can.
Client:	OK, I'll try.

Joan and Brian go through the process three times, and Brian experiences an increase in effectiveness, of reliving, of switching the emotion and disengaging and re-engaging the beliefs. Joan then asks Brian to carry out the homework tasks in Step 10 and report his efforts at the next counselling session.

At the next session Joan and Brian discuss as a main agenda item the REI homework that Brian should have carried out since the last session.

Counsellor:	How did you get on with the REI practice?
Client:	OK, in the end, but I nearly gave up at first. I couldn't make it realistic enough when I tried to do it deliberately, either the situation or the feeling of anxiety. But then when it spontaneously came to mind I got anxious automatically, and I found I could do it then.
Counsellor:	(*introducing evaluation change through behavioural exposure*) Well done, you found a good way to make it work. (*Brian agrees.*). Now we have to bring this skill from the imaginary world into the real world. (*Joan points out Steps 10 to 14 in the Evaluation Change Guide (Appendix 3).*) So I suggest setting up two or three presentation situations, beginning with me and a colleague here in the consulting room, then with your friends or family if you can, and finally the real thing which you have coming up in a couple of weeks I believe? (*Brian confirms and agrees to the plan.*)

Counsellor: So first I suggest just a brief presentation where you just follow what you rehearsed in REI. Take a couple of minutes to prepare, using REI. Can I also suggest you try to be sure to include disengaging from your total self-downing belief 'I'm stupid' and engaging your self-acceptance belief 'I completely accept my fallible self'?

(*Brian carries out the task with some pauses and nervousness.*)

Counsellor: How did you get on?

Client: I managed the right thinking and feeling, but not the performance bit, but then I was accepting my fallible self!

Counsellor: Great, it was the perfect task for you, and the result is just what we want.

(*Brian repeats the task again with fewer pauses and less nervousness.*)

Counsellor: Notice how your 'performance' improves significantly even after the second try, with more flow and less pausing, more eye contact and expressive body language. You are getting the thinking, feeling *and* behaviour together now are you not?

Client: Yes I am, and I am able to speak from knowledge, from my head, rather than depending on a piece of paper, and that's much better.

Counsellor: (*introducing a shame attacking exercise*) I agree. Let's do it one more time, and this is an advanced task, equivalent to the black belt in judo. We want you to deliberately screw up, and then draw attention to it, by saying for example, 'There I go again, red in the face' or 'Sorry I've forgotten the next point. Oh yes I remember'. And while you're doing that be sure to be unconditionally accepting of your fallible self and be seen to be doing so!

(*Brian carries out the shame-attacking exercise and is asked for feedback.*)

Client: That seemed far easier than I could have imagined!

Counsellor: Well done. Now do you think you can repeat this, first with your friends or family, and then in the next actual presentation at uni, following the steps in the Evaluation Change Guide?

Client:	I know what to do and am keen to do it.
Counsellor:	Also look for other opportunities, less formal, ordinary conversations. Look for opportunities to speak your opinion for example. You are normally rather reticent I believe.
Client:	Yes I am and that would be good, to make use of this more widely than just the presentations.
Counsellor:	It is important to consolidate this by doing it as frequently as you can. So we will review at our next session.

9

Middle Stage III – Imagery Rescripting

Task 16. The Imagery Change Option

Briefing

One of the main difficulties in making progress in CBC is that clients continue to report the head–gut problem; that they understand intellectually that there is, for example, no real danger, but they still feel intensely anxious. Both inference-level and evaluation-level (B) interventions can often successfully overcome this problem, but sometimes clients fail to carry out the homework required to change their beliefs (B) because the anxiety or other unhealthy negative emotion is still so intense that they continue to avoid, escape or withdraw (C).

Recent research has shown that this can happen because the actual memory of the adverse event (A) contains traumatic material that remains unmodified by the interventions so far described. This was originally believed to characterise only PTSD sufferers but has recently been shown to be present in many other anxiety disorders, depression and psychosis (Butler et al., 2008; Grey, 2009; Stopa, 2009).

The trauma material or 'hotspots' in trauma memories actually contain not only images of real events (A) but also inferences and evaluations (B) encapsulated within them, but which are not accessible to normal conscious processing or updating. All of these cognitions – images, inferences and evaluations – are subject to various distortions. They are usually encapsulated within sensory fragments of memories, not contextualised into the person's autobiographical memory and therefore tend not to be experienced as historical events but as if they were happening 'here and now', in the present, or at least have current implications.

In some disorders they intrude involuntarily into consciousness as flashbacks or nightmares in imagery form, and because they are never updated and remain 'frozen in time', are re-experienced as if they were happening again in the present, and have the compelling perceptual quality of real events. Because they contain both adverse imagery (A) and beliefs (B), they continue to evoke emotional and behavioural disturbance (C).

As Butler et al. (2008) point out, images can be very convincing, and are often perceived as accurate reflections of past, present or future reality, and even as real premonitions of disaster. A person can experience upsetting images without being aware that there is input from memory, so that they are misled into thinking they signal current or future threat. Images and memories often appear to stop at the very worst point, not connecting to the fact that an event actually ended in a very different way.

An intervention designed to modify and update distressing memories is known as imagery rescripting. One approach to transforming the meaning of a memory is outlined by Butler et al. (2008) as follows:

- Identifying a significant memory. A distressing memory is identified by using the 'emotional bridge' technique (for a description see Butler et al., 2008, pp. 42–44), which helps the client identify an earlier memory that is colouring the person's present image, but which they were unaware of.
- Reliving the memory. The memory is relived in the first person, present tense, in considerable detail about the thoughts and feelings.
- Identifying the meanings given to the event, and taking belief ratings. The counsellor asks what the memory means about the self, others and the world, takes belief ratings, asks about emotions aroused and asks for affect ratings.
- Checking that these meanings still persist today.
- Evaluating evidence for and against the appraisals made at the time of the event. Guided discovery is used to search for additional information and alternative perspectives.
- Reliving the memory and prompting for updating by asking questions. The client relives the memory including beliefs made at the time, and the counsellor enquires what the client knows now that might lead to another conclusion.
- Transforming the memory by inserting imaginal material more in accord with realistic appraisals. If the beliefs and affect have not dropped significantly,

the client can experiment with an imaginary transformation. Several attempts may be made to arrive at a more realistic perspective.
- Checking the belief and affect ratings. The counsellor checks the ratings to ensure that a new perspective has been reached.

Imagery rescripting is a rapidly growing area of research and development to which the reader–practitioner is referred. A thorough treatment of this large area of work is beyond the scope of this guide (there have been at least six practitioner oriented books published in the last two years as well as numerous research papers), so we will confine ourselves to describing one type of imagery rescripting for 'trauma' memory in the present Task 4. Our account is based on Grey et al. (2002).

The purpose of imagery rescripting differs from the imagery methods so far described, such as REI, which assumes the memory of the adverse event A is reasonably accurate, and the client's task is to change his evaluation (B^2) of the event as given and interpreted at the inference level. The purpose of imagery rescripting is actually to change the content of the memory image itself which may fail to contain crucial information but actually contain factual inaccuracies as well as biased and dysfunctional beliefs.

Imagery Rescripting Procedure for a Distressing Memory of an Adverse Event (A)

The counsellor first explains the purpose of this procedure. If the client agrees, a whole session is put aside, allowing up to 90 minutes, in which he is asked to 'relive' the specific adverse event from beginning to end.

He is asked to describe the event from memory, in the first-person present tense as if it were happening now, giving as much detail as possible, including sensory, emotional and cognitive as well as factual information. It is advisable to begin and end the session by having the person return in imagination to a 'safe place' identified beforehand. Although unpleasant, the reliving is essential as much of the crucial content of trauma memories is not accessible to normal conscious processing.

The emotionally disturbing 'hotspots' in the event are identified and the client asked to identify the ABCs of the hotspot – what the person was feeling, what was happening and the beliefs about what was happening.

The counsellor looks out for indicators of dissociation from the hotspots, namely avoidance of, and protection from them, because of the highly distressing material. Such indicators include 'whizzing through' them or going into third-person or past-tense narrative. She then uses a 'rewind and hold' technique of asking the client to hold the distressing moment vividly in mind, and to go through it slowly, reporting what he sees, thinks and feels.

Once out of reliving, the now consciously accessible hotspots are available for cognitive intervention, and the client invited to assess and change the disturbing biased and extreme beliefs for unbiased and benign alternatives in the usual way, as well as correct any factual information that has been revealed and identify crucial information that was absent.

The counsellor explains that to take effect, the new information and alternative beliefs have to be re-introduced into the trauma memory, much like cutting and pasting new scenes into a film strip, and this will bring about change from a trauma memory to a more benign memory. This is the meaning of the term 'imagery rescripting'. This requires going back into reliving, stopping the narrative at the hotspots, and bringing the new information and alternative beliefs in at those points, with the help of the counsellor.

The explanation is followed by rehearsal of specific new information and beliefs and the moments at which they will be introduced. The new information and beliefs are written down on cue cards ready to be introduced. The reliving is then commenced, and when the hotspots are arrived at, the counsellor prompts the client to introduce the new material, or Socratically asks 'What do you know now, what do you believe now?', or provides the new information or belief directly.

The modified reliving is tape or digitally recorded, and the client encouraged to play the tape a number of times as homework in order to consolidate the changes, each time rating the intensity of affect on the 0–10 subjective units of distress (SUDS) scale.

The rescripted memory is then described in words and written down, and the description compared to their goal of how they would like to remember the adverse event, which they previously wrote down on their Assessment and Goal Planning Worksheet.

Action Summary

1 The counsellor checks out whether the client's emotional distress is still unhealthily high and making it difficult to carry out the behavioural homework. She therefore suggests that disturbing images and thoughts may be 'locked

up' in his memory of the adverse event, and that they should investigate this and explore a method called imagery rescripting.

2 Counsellor and client discuss this possibility and if it seems likely from the assessments so far completed, they embark on one of the imagery rescripting techniques as described in Butler et al. (2008), Grey (2009) and Stopa (2009). One such procedure is described in the Briefing above, in the case example below and in the Client Steps for Imagery Rescripting, Appendix 3.

Case Example

Brian is still very anxious about doing the next presentation at university, and is not sure he can overcome his action tendency to avoid doing it.

Counsellor: Give me an example of when you last felt this anxiety so intensely.

Client: Well I was just sitting at home relaxing, and it just pops into my mind automatically and I go into a cold sweat.

Counsellor: What pops into your mind when you feel the anxiety most intensely, is it the adverse event itself (A), or your beliefs about the event (B)?

Client: It seems strange but I think it's the event itself, I can't seem to identify what exactly is so disturbing.

Counsellor: (introducing the idea of imagery rescripting) It could be that you have a memory of perhaps the worst presentation (or even from years before from your teacher-training college, or even before that, at school maybe) that keeps intruding into your mind almost like a trauma flashback.

Client: Yes that's actually quite possible. Every time it pops into my mind I tried to push it away.

Counsellor: It could be that you have toxic imagery and beliefs locked up in that memory that you haven't been able to re-process with the cognitive therapy methods we have been using up to now.

Client: So that's why I can't seem to identify what's so disturbing.

Counsellor: Very likely. I'd like you to try a method specially designed for this problem called imagery rescripting, where you first try to relive the event by revisiting it and talking through in the first-person present tense as if you were actually there. Then we identify the 'hotspots' where the most distressing events and beliefs are locked up, then come out of reliving and do our usual cognitive interventions, identify new information and beliefs, then back into reliving and introduce the new material into those hotspots, so rescripting the imagery – bit like cutting and pasting new scenes into a film. What do you think?

Client: I have an intuition this is the problem, and I'll give it a go.

(Joan gives Brian the Steps for Cognitive Change through Imagery Rescripting in Appendix 3, and takes him through the steps, following the guidance from the Briefing above. So she helps him go through the reliving procedure, identify the hotspots and the ABC components, asks him to 'rewind and hold' those that he has most difficulty with holding in mind. He rates his anxiety in the worst hotspots in terms of SUDS. He then concludes, and comes out of reliving, and he and the counsellor discuss the hotspots.)

Counsellor: If we look at the hotspot that is most disturbing, what is in there that is triggering such high levels of anxiety?

Client: Well, it's that point where I lost my place and stood there for what seemed like an eternity with everyone looking at me. What I could see, frozen in that image, was me! It was like I was looking at myself as if through the eyes of one of *them*, and I saw this complete wreck, red as a beetroot, sweating, shaking, mouth open, and I was thinking this is going on for ever, I'm never going to find my place and I'll be a complete disgrace! I literally was at that moment a complete and utter idiot, it was awful and totally unbearable, and that's why I've been blocking it out.

Counsellor: So although you in one sense knew it was there, this was the first time you have 'seen' this image in your conscious mind. Now from our discussions, what new information and beliefs do you have?

Client: It didn't go on for ever, it actually only lasted probably a few seconds and then I resumed my presentation, albeit not very well. Also I now know I am not a complete idiot but a fallible person who at the worst behaved 'idiotically' at that point, it wasn't good but wasn't awful and it's not unbearable. (*Client remembers and introduces rational evaluations.*)

Counsellor: Excellent, well done. Let's write this new information and beliefs on cue cards, and let's go back into the reliving and introduce it at this particular hotspot, and so rescript that toxic image.

Probably at the next counselling session, Joan takes Brian through the second reliving and helps him introduce the new information. This episode is recorded. After completing the reliving, Brian rates his conviction much lower in terms of SUDS.

Counsellor: You have done extremely well. Would you now play the tape over at least once a day during the next week as homework, and rate the intensity of your anxiety after each playback. (*Brian agrees. Once the changes have consolidated and stabilised, Brian records his achievement on the Assessment and Goal Planning Worksheet.*)

10

Middle Stage IV – Working Through

Task 17. Working Through

Briefing

Unlike the other tasks in this guide, which all introduce specific techniques and methods for cognitive assessment and change, this task refers to the routine work of consolidating the client's understanding, learning and gains. The counsellor will want to draw on other CBT practitioner guides for further techniques for assessment and intervention, but we will not be introducing further methods in this guide. The current task then is meant to serve as a reminder for the counsellor to follow the Method of Working introduced as Task 8 (Chapter 3), and so serves as a blueprint for structuring session routines. We position it here in the Middle Stage as this is where most of the sessions will be conducted, but it applies equally to all the other stages.

The Agenda

Agenda setting should have been introduced earlier and the client's agreement sought at that stage (see Chapter 3, Task 8). The session agenda is used as a way of systematically organising and actioning the routine tasks of working through. Initially the counsellor takes control of the agenda setting but coaches the client to progressively take over as part of the process of becoming their own 'counsellor', in preparation for the ending stage (Chapter 11). We will now review the main items that would normally be standard agenda items. Since these items are by now likely to be routinely included, a Session and Homework Report Form (Figure 10.2) is provided below, which the client can fill in during and following a session, and during the week in preparation for the next session. The counsellor also keeps a copy of this form.

Brief Update

This is often the first item on the agenda. The counsellor uses her person-centred counselling skills (see Task 3, Chapter 2) to invite the client to bring her up to date on any issues that he wishes. If the client brings up difficulties with the main or subsidiary problems on the problems list, or new problems, she asks if these should go down as items on their agenda for discussion in this session. If the client is not forthcoming the counsellor asks if there have been any problems. Although open ended, the 'brief' update itself is kept relatively brief. With very talkative clients, it sometimes helps to agree a time limit in advance.

Reflection on Previous Session

The counsellor asks, again in an open-ended way, what stood out for him from the previous session. This open-ended approach gives the counsellor a good idea about how the client is orienting to and able to make use of CBC. Clients vary greatly in how they remember and maintain continuity from session to session, some assiduously keeping notes, others may not have given it a thought, often because they are so caught up in obsessive rumination or worry, or too depressed to concentrate. We include this item on the Session and Homework Report Form, but a more detailed session bridging worksheet (see Beck, 1995, p. 49 for an example) can be used, and clients asked to fill it in *after* each session and bring to each new session. Key points that both counsellor and client should keep a note of are the tasks covered, progress made or not made, and any difficulties that arose in the working alliance.

Review of Homework

The counsellor will have started to introduce homework towards the end of the preparation stage or the start of the beginning stage with the first such task – the request that the client initially keeps a Daily Thought Record and then 'graduates' to the ABC Diary. The client should have recorded the assignment on the Sessions and Homework Report Form at the previous session, and briefly reported on the result on the same form, in preparation for the current session.

The counsellor will be sure to routinely include homework review on the agenda since clients are very unlikely to persist in these assignments without it. She will also make sure that she explores failures to carry out the assignments, since such failures provide 'grist to the mill' of identifying emotional/behavioural problems and dysfunctional beliefs that led to them. This rationale is pointed out to the client, a) to show him that valuable information is gained from successes or failures and b) to ensure he does not feel blamed, nor blame himself, with such 'no lose' assignments.

Main Topics

Under this heading the counsellor and client will want to concentrate on the main items which will normally provide the 'meat in the sandwich', namely work currently ongoing, including the associated homework between sessions, and problems experienced. To help with this process the counsellor may choose to review the overall progress of CBC, including tasks and steps completed, tasks that are currently being undertaken or re-visited and tasks yet to be undertaken. The following Progress Review Checklist (Figure 10.1) is designed to facilitate this review. How are the counsellor and client progressing on the items in the checklist? Items that are currently being undertaken or re-visited are then entered on the agenda as the Main Topic for the current session.

Revision of CBC Techniques

The main task in the Ending Stage (Chapter 11) will be for the client to become his own counsellor. One way of facilitating this is for the client to learn the CBC techniques as he goes along, and one way of achieving this is for him not only to carry out the steps specified in the techniques as they are reached and implemented in the checklist, but to *learn* the techniques themselves. So the counsellor invites the client to make a note of the current technique on the Session and Homework Report Form, and not only to apply it with the counsellor's guidance to overcome his problem, but also to learn it so that he can apply it if necessary after discharge. He can then revise his knowledge of the technique in session with the counsellor. This revision, therefore, will be another item on the agenda.

Preparation Stage I and II	Done ✓	Work ongoing ✓
Task 3: Establishing, maintaining, or re-establishing a strong working alliance:		
Tasks 4 to 8: Preparing for cognitive behavioural counselling (CBC): • clarifying the key aspects of the main problem in general terms (Client Preparation Steps 1, 2 and 3) • clarifying a general emotional/ behavioural goal (Step 4) • clarifying further problems and goals and drawing up a Problem List • understanding the cognitive perspective and exploring the client's unhelpful beliefs in and helpful alternatives for his initial prioritised problem (Step 5) • reaching an informed decision and commitment to CBC		
Beginning Stage I and II		
Task 9: Establishing a specific example of the client's initial prioritised problem (Client Assessment Step 1)		
Task 10: Carrying out a detailed cognitive assessment of the specific example of the client's initial prioritised problem or a new problem: • identifying the specific unhealthy emotional and behavioural consequence (C) (Step 2) • describing the specific adverse event (A) that triggered (C) (Step 3) • identifying the biased inferences that contributed to (C) (Step 4) • identifying the extreme evaluations that led to (C) (Step 5)		
Task 11: Understanding the B–C connection and vicious circles		
Task 12: Choosing a specific emotional/behavioural goal and constructing alternative functional beliefs for the specific example: • Choosing a specific emotional/behavioural goal (Assessment Step 6) • Constructing alternative unbiased inferences (Step 7) • Constructing alternative realistic evaluations (Step 8) • Imagining an alternative to the remembered adverse event (Step 9)		
Middle Stage I to IV		
Task 13: Checking the B–C connection insight		

(Continued)

(Continued)

	Done ✓	Work ongoing ✓

Task 14: If choosing the inference change option:
 	
• Weighing the evidence
   ○ Assembling evidence for the biased inference (Inference Change Step 2)
   ○ Assembling evidence for the unbiased inference (Step 3)
   ○ Questioning the quality of the evidence (Step 4)
   ○ Weighing up the evidence, rating conviction levels (Step 5)
• Testing the evidence
   ○ Designing and carrying out a behavioural experiment (Step 6)
   ○ Examining the result of the experiment and rating conviction levels (Step 7)		

Task 15: If choosing the evaluation change option:
 	
• Disputing the empirical, pragmatic and logical validity of the evaluations
   ○ Disputing the demanding v. preferring evaluations (Evaluation Change Step 2)
   ○ Disputing the awfulising v. non-awfulising evaluations (Step 3)
   ○ Disputing the discomfort intolerance and discomfort tolerance evaluations (Step 4)
   ○ Disputing the self/other/life depreciation v. self/other/life acceptance evaluations (Step 5)
   ○ Weighing up the result of the disputes and rate conviction levels (Step 6)
• Changing evaluations through REI
   ○ Learning and carrying out the Rational Emotive Imagery (REI) exercise for the first time (Steps 7 and 8)
   ○ Practising the REI exercise between sessions and keeping a record (Step 9)
• Changing evaluations through behavioural exposure
   ○ Planning and carrying out a behavioural exposure task after rehearsing with REI and implementing the same evaluation change method (Steps 10 to 13)		

	Done ✓	Work ongoing ✓
Task 16: If choosing the cognitive change option through imagery rescripting: • Identifying trauma memory hotspots through the reliving procedure • Restructuring the disturbing information and beliefs by CBC • Rescripting the trauma memory by introducing the new information into the hotspots during a repeated reliving • Playing the tape over a number of times between sessions		
Task 17: Keeping to the method of working: Routine updating, homework review and setting, agenda setting:		
Ending Stage		
Task 18: Preparing the ground for termination		
Task 19: Coaching tasks and steps for self-counselling		
Task 20: Preparing for setbacks after termination – general issues		
Task 21: The client's last minute termination problems		
Any other tasks or difficulties not so far identified		

FIGURE 10.1   *Progress Review Checklist*

Homework Assignment

A new homework assignment may emerge out of an item on the checklist. Setting up a new homework assignment can take considerable time and this must be allowed for in setting the agenda.

Clients are often reluctant to carry out assignments between sessions, and so to increase the likelihood that they are carried out, the counsellor tries to ensure the following: she fully discusses and negotiates the assignment, making sure it is clear and understood, is relevant from the client's point of view and follows from the work they have done in the session. She ensures it is challenging but not overwhelming, explains the 'no lose' concept, ensures that he has the skills and commitment to carry it out. It needs to be specified in concrete detail – where, when and how often – and any obstacles anticipated and dealt with in session. To help

Name ....   Date ....   Session ....
Brief Update
Reflection on Previous Session
Review of Homework
Main Topics for this Session
Revision of Previous Main Topic
Homework Assignment
Feedback on the Session

FIGURE 10.2   *Session and Homework Report Form*

the counsellor make sure she covers these and other points, we provide a Homework Skills Monitoring Form in Appendix 3.

The client is invited to write the assignment down on the Session and Homework Report Form (Figure 10.2).

Feedback

The client is asked for feedback on the session, and encouraged to be completely frank as this is the only way that the counsellor can get guidance as to the relevance and direction of the work, and problems that need to be addressed. This feedback can be written down on the Session and Homework Report Form. It is always important to ensure the client is not distressed when he leaves the session, or has time and a room or place to collect himself before leaving the building.

11

Ending Stage – Coaching the Client to Become his Own Counsellor

Task 18. Preparing the Ground for Termination

Briefing

A common assumption of the newly referred client and the novice counsellor is that the roles of counsellor and client are quite distinct, the counsellor being the helper, the client the recipient of the help or 'helpee', much as in the doctor–patient relationship. In this relationship the counsellor might assume they are responsible for solving the client's problems, and the client might reciprocally assume that that is indeed the counsellor's job, and that the counsellor, like a doctor, will 'cure' him or her. One of a number of problems with this assumption is the client may misinterpret the occasional setback as a relapse and will then feel help*less*, dependent on the counsellor as helper, and therefore vulnerable when counselling is terminated. The client worries, 'I might have a relapse, and I won't be able to cope'.

However, unlike physical medicine which can often 'cure' diseases, CBC, like any psychotherapy, does not eliminate negative emotions and adversities but aims to help people cope more successfully with distressing life events.

In this model, periodic setbacks are part of the course and to be expected. CBC is therefore designed as a 'giveaway' form of therapy, in that it aims to teach the client key aspects of counselling so that to an important extent he can become his own counsellor.

We recommend that the counsellor makes the client aware of the uneven course of CBC as he progresses through the stages, and clarifies the role relationship early in the process, preferably during the preparation stage. She should clarify that she will not only have the role of skilled helper but also of counselling coach, so that he can learn to become his own counsellor. In this approach, he will have reciprocal roles of course, but not only of the receptive client, but also of a role more like that of a student or trainee. This is to prepare the ground well in advance for independent self-help after termination.

One way of introducing the idea of coaching early in the counselling process is to ask the client to consider how he will manage when the time comes to be discharged. This then can lead to a discussion of the tasks and steps that need to be established throughout the counselling process.

Case Example

Counsellor:	(*during the preparation stage*) Brian, it may seem surprising but sometimes our clients have concerns about the *ending* of a course of CBC, even at the beginning of counselling, and I was wondering if you had any concerns about that?
Client:	I can't say I have thought about it. What kind of concerns?
Counsellor:	Well, for example some people are worried that if they had a setback they wouldn't be able to cope on their own.
Client:	Well, now you come to mention it, it's the sort of worry I probably will have, once we get into it.
Counsellor:	I don't want to worry you! But it may be useful for us to anticipate it and plan for it. So what do you think we could do, as part of CBC that would help to ensure you could indeed cope with a setback in the unlikely event that you had one after discharge?

Client:	I will have to think about it, but to be honest I think I would panic.
Counsellor:	You might panic if you weren't prepared for it. Often people expect or hope that they will get steadily better with CBC until they are 'cured', like if they had a physical illness and took the right medicine, and then after discharge, they would remain cured.
Client:	That was what I was hoping.
Counsellor:	Actually most clients have ups and downs on the way to overcoming their difficulties – on a graph progress is rarely a straight incline but is saw toothed like this (draws a simple graph to illustrate). So this is the first point – it's normal to have ups *and* downs in CBC.
Client:	Right, so I shouldn't panic about the down part.
Counsellor:	That's right, but the reason you shouldn't panic is because the down part is followed by an up part.
Client:	But how do I know that will happen – it could just keep going down!
Counsellor:	That's where CBC comes in. CBC is designed to ensure the average slope is upwards – it is designed specifically to overcome psychological problems like yours.
Client:	That's fine while I'm having it, but what happens when I'm discharged?
Counsellor:	That brings us back to my question: what do you think we could do, as part of CBC that would help to ensure you could indeed cope with a setback in the unlikely event that you had one after discharge?
Client:	I could help myself?
Counsellor:	Absolutely you could. You can learn to become your own counsellor. So I suggest you not only engage with the psychological treatment as a client, but at the same time you let me coach you how to become your own counsellor.

Task 19. Coaching Tasks and Steps for Self-counselling

Briefing

There are three aspects of the counsellor role that we recommend the client should acquire: knowledge of and skill in applying the methods and techniques of assessment, conceptualisation and intervention, a problem-solving and goal-oriented mindset and an attitude of care and compassion.

Learning and Remembering the Methods and Techniques

First, the client needs to acquire knowledge of and skill in using the methods and techniques of CBC. For example, at the assessment stage, he needs to learn the ABC framework and the differences between facts at A, inferences and evaluations at B, emotions and behaviours at C and the causal relations between them. He needs to understand the different kinds of bias and distortions in beliefs and how these can affect perception of events and consequent emotions and behaviours. He needs to understand the different kinds of challenge, for example between an empirical and a pragmatic challenge and the methods to put this knowledge into practice to produce emotional and behavioural change.

It cannot be assumed the client will learn *and* remember the techniques if he does not see it as his role to take on the responsibility to be his own counsellor. Certainly if the client follows the guidance of the counsellor in our guide, he will learn the methods as part of his 'treatment' and he will also have learnt the idea of emotional responsibility introduced in Chapter 4. However, in addition, the counsellor should emphasise that he will need the skills not only as client receiving help, but as a counsellor responsible for helping himself when counselling comes to an end. To try to ensure the client not only learns but remembers the methods, she proposes that he includes revision of the techniques taught in each session as part of his routine 'homework', and also sets aside a time in the session agenda for revision of the methods.

Acquiring the Problem-solving Mindset of the Counsellor

Second, the client needs to acquire the problem-solving and goal-oriented mindset of the counsellor, such that his reaction to a new problem or setback is one of 'How can I best tackle this problem?' rather than 'I don't know what to do – I need to get help'. As with the techniques, it cannot be assumed that the client will have a problem-solving mindset if he does not see it as his responsibility to become his own counsellor after termination. She will need to introduce the client to this counselling mindset if he is to take over responsibility for his own care.

Strategies to help the client acquire this mindset are built into the CBC protocol. For example, Socratic questioning is used as one of the main ways of guiding the client through the counselling process. Socratic questions enable the client to 'think for himself'. Socratic questions do not provide but seek answers, so put the client in the role of the problem-solver, and prompt him to think of possible solutions. They encourage the client to take responsibility, and the answers they come up with are more likely to be memorable and convincing.

Another aspect of CBC that encourages the problem-solving mindset is the task of goal setting and planning immediately after problem clarification. One of the goals is to generate a healthy emotional and behavioural reaction to adverse events, to replace the problematic unhealthy emotional and behavioural reaction. So, for example, instead of anxiety and the associated action tendency to avoid and escape from the problem, the client is encouraged to adopt 'healthy concern' with its associated action tendency to 'approach with caution', which is a problem-solving, as opposed to a problem-avoiding, approach.

In addition to these built-in features of CBC, the counsellor goes a step further in encouraging the problem-solving mindset. We suggest the counsellor introduces and starts to coach the client to adopt the problem-solving mindset from the commencement of the beginning stage. By this point the client should have completed the preparation stage and acquired sufficient basic familiarisation with the CBC model. She then increasingly prefaces her conduct of the session tasks with Socratic questions equivalent to the following: 'If you were your own counsellor, what would you do at this point in the session/with the problem at this stage?' The counsellor coaches him to carry out an increasing number of tasks or parts of tasks.

The counsellor continues with the coaching through to the end of the Middle Stage, gradually handing over responsibility for leading parts of the session. Then in the final sessions before termination and with the client's agreement, she 'hands over' the reins to the client as much as possible, such that by this stage the client effectively takes over both roles, e.g. setting the agenda, identifying problems *and* constructing interventions; setting up and monitoring as well as carrying out homework assignments.

Adopting the Counsellor's Attitude of Care and Compassion
The third aspect of the counsellor that we recommend should be acquired by the client is that of the attitude of care and compassion. In Chapter 2 we noted the three core conditions that are necessary to establish a bond

with the client and research has been shown to be essential for effective counselling. The one we wish to emphasise here is warmth or unconditional positive regard. Just as the client does not necessarily have the counsellor's knowledge of the techniques, nor has the counsellor's problem-solving mindset, it is certainly true that the client may not, as client, have the counsellor attitude of unconditional positive regard (or unconditional acceptance) towards *himself*.

Gilbert (2007) points out that, far from having an attitude of care and positive regard towards himself, the client frequently has an attitude of self-criticism, self-attacking, self-put-down. It is a form of self-to-self relating 'where one part of the self finds fault with, accuses, condemns or even hates the self' (Gilbert, 2007, p. 138). Such self-attacking attitudes are associated with a wide range of psychological problems.

It is clear, then that the counsellor's attitude of unconditional positive regard is an extremely important one for the client to acquire, and indeed it is hard to imagine how he could be his own counsellor without it.

One of the interventions in the Middle Stage of this Basic Guide is designed specifically to help the client as client to challenge and change from a negative core belief to an unconditional self-acceptance belief (which for current purposes we take as synonymous with Rogers's concept of unconditional positive regard). Its importance in the counselling attitude is one of the reasons why we recommend the evaluation change option as one of the first to be tackled.

However, the counsellor can introduce the idea of unconditional positive regard as one of the aspects of the counsellor role he will need in order to become his own counsellor. Making unconditional positive regard a concrete activity within a specific role like this will often be an easier task for the client to undertake than the more intellectual task of disputing core beliefs, and one which will be easier to adopt early on in the counselling process.

By the end of counselling, the counsellor should be largely 'redundant', responding only to requests from the client, or intervening only when the client is significantly on the wrong track.

Action Summary

1 The counsellor uses Socratic questioning to get the client to explore what specific aspects of the counsellor role he can think of that would help him to deal with setbacks himself, after the end of formal counselling.

2 Whatever suggestions the client makes, the counsellor aims to build on them, but to steer him in the direction of recognising the three aspects reviewed in the briefing here: learning and remembering the methods and techniques, acquiring the problem-solving mindset of the counsellor and adopting the counsellor's attitude of care and compassion.

3 The counsellor asks the client to identify how he could achieve each of the three aspects. For example, what would he need to do to learn and remember the methods and techniques, to acquire and express the problem-solving mindset, and most importantly, to acquire and express the attitude of care and compassion for himself. He and the counsellor also explore ways of resolving any problems that might get in the way of achieving the three aspects of the counsellor role and mindset.

Task 20. Preparing for Setbacks after Termination – General Issues

Briefing

Once the client has prepared as best he can to be his own counsellor, the next task is to assess how he would envisage 'life after counselling' from the point of view of himself as counsellor rather than as client. During one of the ending sessions, the main item on the agenda should be set up such that the client is invited to put himself in the role of counsellor and 'thinks through' the issues as a counsellor would rather than as a client would. As the client-as-counsellor goes through this exercise, the 'real' counsellor coaches him much as she would coach a trainee, commenting, reinforcing, correcting and suggesting alternatives as he goes through the issues. As a guide to some of the issues, we suggest the following general issues, where we compare the counsellor's view with the view of a possible at-risk client.

- Dichotomous v. continuum view of recovery. The client thinks he must remain perfectly well, because even the slightest setback will inevitably lead to a complete relapse with catastrophic consequences. His beliefs will reflect this all-or-nothing attitude: 'I absolutely must stay perfectly well. If I feel down or anxious it will be a total disaster, absolutely intolerable and I will be doomed for ever.' The client-as-counsellor anticipates there *will* be ups and downs, adversities and negative emotions are a normal part of life, and 'though bad, they are never truly awful, and though hard to bear I will be able to bear it and cope with it'.

- Unpredictable v. predictable view of recovery. The client feels relapses are completely unpredictable and inevitable. The client-as-counsellor thinks problems are usually predictable, that there are early warning signs and high-risk situations and behaviours, so that most problems can be prevented or 'nipped in the bud' by forward planning.
- View of self as helpless v. competent. The client thinks they are helpless to do anything about problems, and without the counsellor or an equivalent 'doctor' to rescue them they will fail. The client-as-counsellor knows now he has the knowledge and skills to tackle most problems.
- View of self as worthless or bad v. unconditional positive regard for self as client. The client has a very negative core belief, such as he is worthless or bad and therefore there is no point in trying or they don't deserve any better. The client-as-counsellor has unconditional positive regard (or unconditional self-acceptance) for himself as client and therefore deserves unconditional care and respect.

After reviewing these issues, the counsellor 'tests' the client with imaginary setbacks, and ask the client–as–counsellor to say how he would tackle them, using his counsellor's mind.

Action Summary

1 The counsellor invites the client to 'become the counsellor' and think through the issues that might lead the client as client into a setback.
2 The counsellor tests the client with imaginary problems, coaching him throughout the exercise.

Case Example

Joan and Brian discuss a number of issues that can lead to a setback and which the client-as-counsellor needs to be familiar with, including the four reviewed in the briefing and summarised above.

Counsellor: OK, Brian, before we bring counselling to an end we have to be sure you know how to deal with your problems if they should re-emerge – you have a lapse or even a relapse, and you are just as panicky about doing a presentation, or to generalise this more to your everyday social life, about asserting your opinion, starting a conversation and similar aspects of positive and negative assertion. In other words instead of coming back to one of us, how could you be your own counsellor?

Client: I need to know how to overcome the problem.

Counsellor: Yes, anything else?

Client: The problem-solving mindset, and an attitude of care and compassion for myself as my client.

Counsellor: Yes, so let's assume you now have acquired these qualities of the counsellor (or had most of them all along but were not using them), and let's go over what you would need to do in practice if a problem came up. So imagine you wake up one morning and the problem is as bad as ever.

Client: I will avoid thinking this will be a catastrophe, as that thought will make me depressed, do nothing, get drunk, and I'd end up creating a much worse situation. So I stick with my counsellor's mind that there are always ups and downs, its not that bad, I can bear it and I can face it. Then I'm in a better frame of mind to do something about it.

Counsellor: OK, what about sitting at home on your own, and you know you are going to duck out of the next presentation and you now know your failure at uni is inevitable.

Client: As a client I could easily let myself get into that situation. But with my counsellor's hat on, I can plan ahead, I know the signs, I know when I start feeling down and I can nip it in the bud and make sure I don't stay home those nights.

Counsellor: All right. This time you are getting very anxious, don't have your counsellor any more, and you're thinking, this is it, back to square one, I'm helpless to do anything about my panic attack.

Client: I often think that way, but as my own counsellor I am saying you know what to do, identify those biased beliefs, think realistically, rehearse in imagery using REI, practice in the mirror and with a friend without my safety behaviours, and so on – those techniques I have learned and know how to use.

Counsellor: Great. But you suddenly remember what a worthless heap of rubbish you are and aren't worth bothering with anyway.

Client:	Again, I do think like that sometimes, but as counsellor I care about this 'me', I value 'me' and just having that attitude about myself puts me back into a frame of mind where I feel motivated.
Counsellor:	Can you maintain that idea even when you have such a strong tendency to drift back into those automatic self-downing beliefs?
Client:	Thinking of myself as a counsellor makes it easier to resist that, gives me a concrete role that I can hold on to.

Task 21. The Client's Last-minute Termination Problems

Briefing

Despite thorough preparation for termination and coaching of the client-as-counsellor, clients may still present termination problems at the eleventh hour – perhaps at the penultimate or even very last session. In this task we address some of these last-minute anxieties, and recommend only agreeing to follow-up sessions specifically and sparingly for consolidating self-help, client-as-counsellor coaching. In the case of genuine crises of course the counsellor can agree to review the situation and either set new sessions or refer to colleagues or another service equipped for the type of problem being presented.

There is a variety of issues that the client may bring up as counselling approaches or reaches its ending stage. These include:

- The concern that they will not be able to cope on their own and need the counsellor to turn to for further guidance and support.
- Old problems re-emerge and the methods they have learned do not seem to be working.
- New problems emerge for which they have not yet been prepared.
- They have no-one else to turn to.
- They feel abandoned and rejected by the termination.
- They are 'stuck' and not making any progress.
- They are having a genuine crisis and are extremely anxious or depressed and possibly suicidal.

In most of these cases the problem can be addressed by means of CBC where the client-as-counsellor undertakes the tasks of assessing, conceptualising and intervening himself, and the counsellor becomes the coach to enable him to learn to adopt the counsellor mindset prior to termination. The procedure for coaching is fairly similar in most cases, so we select just two examples below to illustrate the process. In these examples the client brings a last-minute problem and appeals for a continuation of CBC where the counsellor should take control again.

The Client Avoids the Behavioural Assignments

Imagine a client who insists he needs further sessions of CBC because he is not making progress because he is still avoidant, and therefore CBC is not working for him yet. For example suppose Brian, our Case Example, is still avoiding doing a presentation in front of the examiners, or taking the initiative in social encounters.

The counsellor reminds herself not to take over *as* counsellor, *and* reminds the client of his role of client-as-counsellor and that he needs to adopt his counsellor 'mindset' with regard to this problem. In her role as coach she therefore asks him to try to explain what is causing this continued avoidance, and then to design an intervention with homework tasks that will help him overcome the problem.

In coaching the client-as-counsellor in this task, the counsellor keeps in mind her own well-founded speculations about the problem and its resolution, and uses these ideas to Socratically guide the client. Her speculations are as follows:

- She suspects that each time he tries to confront or even think about confronting the adverse situation, he becomes emotionally disturbed and avoidant again. In this state of mind the new thinking and the counsellor-as-client mindset 'fly out the window' and the negative automatic thinking and dependent-client mindset fly back in.
- She speculates that the client needs to expose himself to avoided situations without using safety behaviours, in order to disconfirm his dysfunctional inferences and to use his alternative self-accepting beliefs where they really matter. For example, the client who feels totally ashamed if rejected needs to expose himself to situations where he infers he will be rejected, in order to probably disconfirm his rejection inference, and to practice disengaging from his self-condemnatory beliefs and adopting his new self-accepting beliefs even if he is.

- She knows that it is important for the client to have the actual experiences of such cognitive restructuring in the context of the feared event. It is only in this way that he will gain emotional insight, rather than simply intellectual insight into his new beliefs: 'People are unlikely to criticise me, but even if they do, I can still accept myself.'

The counsellor uses her speculations to tentatively coach the client-as-counsellor to conceptualise and plan the interventions, such that he not only gets the 'treatment' as client but he himself designs it, in preparation for caring for himself after termination.

The Client Still Avoids the Behavioural Assignments

Imagine a client who, despite the counsellor-as-client coaching we have just outlined, complains that he still avoids the crucial feared events and cannot help himself, and is now in a 'state of crisis'. The key to this problem – and to the frustration that the counsellor may experience at this point! – lies in the difference between the Discomfort Intolerance v. Discomfort Tolerance Beliefs (also referred to in REBT as the Low Frustration Tolerance v. High Frustration Tolerance Beliefs or LFT v. HFT).

Avoiding the temptation to take over as counsellor rather than coach, the counsellor again invites the client to try to explain what is causing this persistent avoidance, and again to design an intervention with homework tasks that will help him overcome the problem.

As before her coaching strategy is informed by her well-founded speculations.

- This time she suspects that the experience of high anxiety when confronting the feared event is triggering a discomfort intolerance belief and/or a catastrophising belief, that may generate automatic thoughts like 'I cannot bear this degree of anxiety', or 'I cannot cope' or 'this is absolutely awful', all of which magnify the discomfort, and result in an automatic meta-level self-instruction not to carry out the assignment.
- The counsellor knows that, according to REBT theory, discomfort intolerance is based on the false idea: 'Life must be easy (or not this hard) and go the way I want. If not, it's awful and I can't stand it.' She knows discomfort intolerance is a further type of demanding which we referred to as one of the evaluations in Chapter 7. One consequence of discomfort intolerance thinking is that doing any task that one is anxious about becomes not just difficult but impossible: 'I can't go into that situation. I would feel anxious. I must not

feel anxious. It would be terrible. I couldn't stand it.' The belief amplifies the experienced or anticipated intensity of the emotion.
- The client-as-coach needs to identify his discomfort intolerance belief, challenge it, disengage from it, replace it with the alternative discomfort tolerance beliefs, rehearse in rational emotive imagery, and so on. This will make it easier for the client to undertake the exposure tasks.
- The counsellor also suspects that the client's discomfort intolerance and catastrophising beliefs are also being automatically triggered by the setback of the apparent intractability of the avoidance problem, and magnifying the setback into a complete relapse and a crisis. He will therefore need to apply the alternative thinking to the setback.

By remaining in her counsellor–as–coach role despite the setback, the counsellor models another feature of the effective counsellor – high discomfort tolerance!

Action Summary

1 Remind yourself not to take over *as* counsellor, *and* remind the client of his role of client-as-counsellor and that he needs to adopt his counsellor 'mindset' with regard to this problem.
2 Invite the client-as-counsellor as a task to try to explain what is causing this continued avoidance, and then to design an intervention with homework tasks that will help him overcome the problem.
3 Formulate in your own mind how you would assess, conceptualise and intervene in this problem, but use these ideas to coach the client-as-counsellor in these tasks, making sure he includes the necessary components, particularly behavioural assignments.
4 If the client presents a setback or a 'relapse', repeat Steps 1, 2 and 3, adapted for the new problem.
5 Clarify with the client what he will do after discharge if these problems came up again but he had no counsellor to fall back on.
6 If necessary offer one or two booster sessions in 3 and 6 months' time or so, but design them specifically and sparingly for consolidating self-help, client-as-counsellor coaching, and not as the re-commencement of regular counselling.

Case Example

Client: I'm ashamed to say I still can't bring myself to face the examiners, or even push myself to take more initiative when out socially. I really need further counselling. I'm just not coping.

Counsellor: Sounds like you don't want us to bring counselling to an end soon and I should take over again as your counsellor.

Client: Well, yes.

Counsellor: Would it be OK with you if we try to stay with our new relationship of me as coach and you as client-as-counsellor.

Client: Oh, yes, I had almost forgotten.

Counsellor: As coach then let me ask you how you might try to understand what is going on that is causing you to still avoid going into these situations, and what you might be able to do to overcome this problem – drawing on the sessions and steps you have already learned.

(Joan then coaches Brian as he thinks through the problem and suggests interventions that might help him overcome the problem. She draws on her own knowledge and speculations as outlined in the Briefing above.)

Counsellor: Seems to me you have a pretty good conceptualisation of the problem and know now what you need to do during the next week.

Client: Yes, I feel much more in control, the fact that I have thought through it myself and come up with my own homework – with your help of course. I have a presentation next week so I will definitely do it in the way we agreed.

Counsellor: (a week later, at the final or penultimate session) How did it go Brian?

Client: Awful. I think I am right back to square one. I don't think I can go on.

Counsellor: What's happened?

Client: Push myself as I might, I just couldn't do it, I bottled out of the presentation. They said I could postpone it and do it next week, but I know I wont.

Counsellor: Are you still up for me coaching you as your own counsellor again?

Client: If you think it will work.

Counsellor: OK, what do you think caused you to bottle it this time? To give you a clue, remember (and look at your notes) two key evaluative beliefs that may be automatically

> triggered by your panicky feelings and you probably
> haven't changed yet – your discomfort intolerance
> belief and your catastrophising belief.

Brian recognises that he has these automatic thoughts, had not previously been aware of them and their power, and is now able to re-construct the conceptualisation he developed in the previous session in a way that explains the new setback. He also proposes new homework built around restructuring these beliefs with imagery rehearsal of emotional episodes of the kind he now knows will intrude into his mind during periods of worry and rumination.

PART 2

Applying CBC to Emotional Problems

12

Anxiety

Applying CBC to the Common Emotional Problems

Having covered the Basic Guide to using the CBC model in practice, we will now address how the model can be applied to specific clinical problems. Although not exhaustive, we will address some of the more commonly presented emotional problems and demonstrate how to integrate current thinking into the CBC model. For each problem, we present the key elements for our model, an example ABC and the core treatment goals for CBC. In the following chapters we adopt the REBT approach in presenting a much wider range of emotion problems than is usual in a CBT guide, so as well as anxiety and depression we cover anger, hurt, envy, shame and guilt. Not all of these have diagnostic criteria (for example, in DSM-IV), but they are frequent presenting problems in clinical practice across the lifespan and across diagnostic categories.

Anxiety

Anxiety problems and the associated disorders are among the most frequently presented problems by clients, and are the most common of all the mental disorders according to figures from various organisations such as the World Health Organization. The nature of anxiety disorders does vary according to diagnostic schedules, with differences between phobias, panic disorder with and without agoraphobia, social anxiety, health anxiety, post traumatic stress disorder, obsessive compulsive disorder and generalised anxiety disorder. Of all the disorders, anxiety has seen the most rapid development of CBT approaches, from the first comprehensive treatment of this approach for anxiety by Beck and Emery (1985), through practitioner accounts of diagnosis-specific interventions (e.g. Wells, 1997) through to recent new developments (e.g. Butler et al., 2008) which we discuss in Chapter 18. However, in this introductory text, we are keen to establish how our integrated CBC model can be applied transdiagnostically across a range of anxiety-related problems, with the core elements of the model remaining intact.

Key Elements of the CBC Model

Anxiety at C in the ABC Model

The experience of anxiety itself is nearly always described as distinctly uncomfortable. It typically involves increased heart rate, shortness of breath, racing thoughts and changes in blood pressure. Such changes are there to trigger a fight or flight response should it be required. However, rarely do most anxiety problems require a flight solution. The experience of anxiety encapsulates a distinctive set of self-defeating action tendencies.

One of the primary action tendencies fused with anxiety is avoidance. Avoidance can take many forms, but primarily is characterised by a behavioural, cognitive and affective avoidance of and escape from the threat. Behavioural avoidance occurs when the individual actually avoids that which they are anxious about. For example, if a client is anxious about public speaking they might make every effort to avoid ever having to speak in front of an audience, irrespective of whether this impacts negatively on their education or career. Similarly, a client anxious about rejection might avoid relationships where there is a risk of this occurring. Cognitive avoidance usually occurs when the upcoming threat is difficult to actually avoid and in the period running up to the experience they endeavour not to think about it. Affective avoidance involves the individual seeking to avoid the discomfort of anxiety through various means, such as reassurance seeking, distraction, relaxation strategies, alcohol or illicit substance misuse. Affective avoidance is common in health anxiety and panic disorder, where it serves as a maintenance strategy. These different types of avoidance are often used simultaneously and thereby the individual develops a repertoire of strategies to ensure their safety from the threat. These strategies are commonly referred to as safety-seeking behaviours, though they might not all be overt actions.

There are numerous cognitive consequences associated with anxiety. These include temporary mental sticking (such as being tongue-tied, lost for words or unable to think clearly), hyper-vigilance for further threat, and a need for certainty about their safety to reduce their anxiety. Of these, the need for certainty is very closely associated with avoidance behaviours, as the individual strives to be certain that they will survive, or at least have no negative outcome to, the threat.

The counsellor should enquire not only about how the experience of anxiety feels but also the action tendencies it renders, as outlined in the basic guide. Clients may be unaware of their behavioural impulses, but in reviewing an example of anxiety, the counsellor should facilitate a discussion around how the client attempted to avoid the experience, bearing the different types of avoidance in mind.

The As of Anxiety in the ABC Model

In all forms of anxiety the primary adversity is something that could happen, no matter how small the probability, in the short- to mid-term future. The adversities of anxiety take the form of a threat to one's physical, interpersonal or emotional safety.

- Physical threats are usually evident in the description of events provided by the client, such as facing some form of real physical danger.
- Interpersonal threats are those which are likely to have an impact on our interpersonal well-being, such as the threat of being rejected by a loved one.
- Affective threats are those where the feeling of anxiety (or other emotional problem) itself is feared, such as feeling anxious about becoming anxious (or experiencing shame, anger or depression to name but a few). There are two main elements to affective threats. First, the client might make themselves anxious about future discomfort or emotional pain (anticipatory fear of the discomfort). Second, the client might engage in emotional reasoning that being anxious proves they are in danger and become more anxious in an ongoing vicious circle.

Anxiety is also a common meta-emotional problem. Frequently, we have met clients who anticipate that a course of action will lead them to feel shame, guilt, depressed, hurt or anger. This is an important distinction in CBC. Individuals can feel anxious about the possible experience of healthy or unhealthy negative emotions. Here we find an anticipated emotion (or state of being) at A. In such circumstances, the counsellor will need to address both the meta-anxiety and the emotional problem the client is anticipating.

Therefore, in determining the A for anxiety-related problems the counsellor should listen for themes or events that indicate some form of threat to the individual (or significant others). The threats may seem highly unlikely events or perhaps even not likely at all, however, at the moment of experiencing the anxiety the threats are effectively real to the client and the counsellor should be careful not to be dismissive of their fears.

The Bs of Anxiety in the ABC Model

Inferences

As we have already suggested, anxiety is nearly always about some future event that is perceived as a threat and this takes particular forms in the client's belief system. Inferences will usually involve making some form of prediction about an event that is in their immediate, short- or mid-term future. Therefore, the inferences will typically start with the stem 'I (or they or it) will be …'. These cognitions are inferential because they will be either true or false. Most of us get ourselves especially anxious about a particular aspect of an event that is considered threatening. For example, in public-speaking anxiety, the client will usually predict that the audience will discover that they do not know what they are talking about, or they themselves will fall short of some personal standard or principle.

Evaluations

The evaluations commonly made in anxiety are associated with catastrophising, not being able to bear the experience and negative self-evaluation. When most people speak about their anxiety-provoking inferences they feel compelled to know that this feared event will not occur in order for their anxiety to diminish. A male client anxious about approaching a woman to ask for a date (A), might infer or predict that any woman he approaches will reject his advances or think him stupid or unattractive. He might not be made anxious by these inferences alone, however, in order to become anxious about it he then needs to evaluate that experience as bad (although this might already be flavoured by an implicit evaluation in the inference). Here, he evaluates the prospect of being rejected as terrible, something he could not stand, and therefore proves that he is unattractive as a person. Faced with such evaluations about the inference, the client is rendered anxious and avoids approaching a woman, despite his desire for a date. The inferences and evaluations in the moment occur almost automatically and instantaneously, so the client is largely unaware of them. We often refer to this experience as a thought–feeling fusion.

Therefore, the counsellor should listen carefully for future-based inferences, in the form of forecasts, and evaluations of catastrophe, unbearability and negative self-definitions. These will require focused Socratic questions and should be noted for future questioning and disputation.

Example ABC

A	B	C
Upcoming job interview	I will perform poorly and they will think I am stupid (inference) That will be terrible (evaluation) I won't be able to stand that (evaluation) It will prove that I am stupid (evaluation)	Anxiety Trying not to think about it (and not preparing adequately) Seeking reassurance that it will go well Strong impulse not to attend and lose a chance for the job

FIGURE 12.1 *Example ABC*

Core Treatment Goals for Anxiety in CBC

There is a wealth of literature about behavioural approaches to overcoming anxiety-based problems. Typically methods are used to increase the client's exposure to the threat so that they habituate and therefore over time cease to experience anxiety. However, as effective as these methods might be, they can only be used when the client understands the rationale and is prepared to take a significant risk and face that which they fear.

The first question for the counsellor to consider is what to help the client to feel in place of anxiety. Often, clients want to feel nothing instead of their intense and uncomfortable experience of anxiety. Sometimes clients will want to feel less anxious about the threat. This is the first of many challenges for the counsellor in working with clients with anxiety problems. The feeling should be one that helps the client approach, rather than avoid, the threat. Anxiety, even in small amounts, is fused with the action tendency of avoidance. So even if the client feels only a little anxious about the threat their impulse will continue to be to avoid it. Feeling nothing will not only fail to motivate the client to approach the threat or deal with it constructively, but may also significantly disadvantage them. Imagine attending a job interview feeling nothing about the opinions others may form of you; you may come across as detached at best or arrogant at worst and neither will help you to get the job. The counsellor needs to help the client identify a healthy alternative to anxiety as their goal for counselling. Some clients prefer the terms 'worried', 'nervous' or 'concerned'. When identifying the goal, the counsellor will need to check that the affect does not lead to avoidance or other safety behaviours. Most clients are able to use the emotion of concern as a healthy goal. Concern implicitly conveys a sense of dealing with the threat more constructively. If you attend a job interview feeling concerned about what impression might be formed you are naturally more likely to try to present yourself in the best (and most accurate) light.

In setting the goal, the counsellor should help the client to recognise that their avoidance strategies (and safety behaviours) are unhelpful. For clients anxious about a negative outcome to a threat that carries with it an opportunity that they want to avail themselves of (such as asking for a date, attending a job interview, attending a physician to check on their health), it is important to highlight that their avoidance strategies are acting directly against what they want to achieve. For clients where the threat is something that has no appeal or inherent possibility of reward (or achieving a broader goal), such as phobias, the counsellor can help the client recognise the impact of the avoidance behaviours on other aspects of their life.

Having established a goal with the client, the counsellor will next want to help the client to challenge their thinking patterns that create the anxiety. Here it is often tricky, though possible, to directly question the inference or prediction. It is tricky because the future has not happened, and the client will likely remain anxious because there is a small, no matter how small, possibility that their inference will come true. Rather, the challenges are best made towards the evaluations first, before tackling the inferences. Counsellors can question the catastrophising, the low frustration tolerance and the negative self-evaluation. The client is helped to discover that even if one is rejected by a possible romantic partner, or a job-interview panel, or an audience, then this is never a catastrophe, unbearable or self-defining.

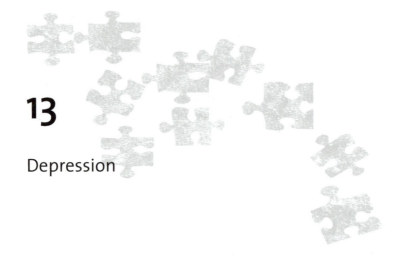

13

Depression

Depression is a psychopathological state of extreme dejection or melancholy, characterised by a mood of hopelessness. Most people will recognise this dictionary definition of depression. The various nosological systems, such as DSMIV, have of course much more comprehensive diagnostic definitions, covering the physical, motivational, cognitive, affective and behavioural features. However, we take the view that the core experience of depression is captured by the dictionary definition and is the focus of CBC – depression the unhealthy emotional problem, which we distinguish from sadness as the healthy emotional alternative.

Depression, in terms of its diagnosis, affects more people than any other single emotional disorder in the western world, with figures typically showing one person in five or six experiencing depression in the last six-month period. It is also dangerous, with a lifetime risk of suicide as high as 6 per cent for people diagnosed with major depression.

It is perhaps the best known and studied of the emotional disorders, with cognitive models having been developed as early as the 1960s (c.f. Beck, 1967) and was the first disorder to be the target of Beck's cognitive therapy approach (Beck et al., 1979), and has seen important new developments since then (Chapter 18). Up until this time, the characteristic negative thinking in depression was regarded as merely a symptom of an underlying biological disturbance and if the underlying problem was treated, then the negative thinking would disappear. Building on the work of Ellis (1963), Beck realised that the causal sequence could work the other way round, and negative thinking could cause depression and the other signs and symptoms of the syndrome, and/or maintain it over long periods of time.

Beck developed his cognitive model of depression around the core experience of loss. The model consists of three concepts. First is the cognitive triad, which consists of a negative view of self (as defective, inadequate or deprived, and because of this, as undesirable and worthless) a negative view of the world (selective attention to the negative) and the future (pessimism, hopelessness). The second is the concept of the schema, by virtue of which the individual selectively attends and interprets situations in a biased and negatively distorted way. The third is faulty information processing (arbitrary inference, selective abstraction, etc.), which are biased inferences maintained despite contradictory evidence.

Our CBC model of depression builds upon the Beck model but also draws upon concepts from REBT. For example, we suggest that it can be unproductive or even futile to help clients to become less depressed, as they will still *be* depressed and left with an urge to act in self-defeating ways. Therefore, we aim to help our clients to become sad when faced with genuine loss – the healthy variant of depression. Although at times equally uncomfortable, sadness motivates us to approach the problem we face or accept the situation if it is not changeable, rather than avoid dealing with things through withdrawal, which is implied in depression at any level.

Key Elements of the CBC Model

Depression at C in the ABC Model

The experience of depression tends to be described in terms of feelings of low mood, passivity, diminished experience of pleasure, and a tendency to withdraw from social relationships and everyday activities. Low mood may be experienced as chronic, pervasive and inescapable, as if one is being dragged down by one's emotional experiences. At other times, it may be experienced as a negation of emotion, a feeling of nothingness.

The primary action tendency associated with depression is withdrawal. In the most severe and chronic forms of depression, withdrawal commonly features a behavioural or actual withdrawal from more meaningful activities. This behavioural withdrawal is inherently self-defeating as the individual limits their exposure to other activities and experiences and are less likely to have pleasurable experiences or the opportunity to feel something other than the depression in which they are immersed. Rather, the individual then tends to remain focused on the events about which they are depressing themselves and their depressing thoughts and beliefs. Thus, trapped in behavioural withdrawal, the individual is further ensnared in a vicious circle of depressive experiences and thoughts.

Withdrawal can also occur at a cognitive and affective level. In cognitive withdrawal, the individual simply immerses themselves in their depressive thinking styles. They are then less aware of other experiences, and may see the world through a negative lens. Over time, the cognitive withdrawal will impact on their general cognitive ability, perhaps preoccupying the individual and impairing their ability to think about other topics or experiences. Cognitive withdrawal is self-defeating because the individual fails to acknowledge evidence to counter their depressive thinking style. Affective withdrawal is the withdrawal of the individual from the emotion itself. Some people describe this as an experience of 'shutting down' or 'switching off' their emotional responses. Again this is self-defeating, as it is most likely that the individual requires some degree of emotional pain or discomfort to encourage them to address the problem. Affective withdrawal simply renders the individual inert.

The main cognitive consequences associated with depression are conclusions that either one is helpless to affect change or the future is bleak and hopeless. After Ellis (1994), we would argue that these cognitive consequences stem directly from the evaluative beliefs the individual holds at B in the ABC model. For example, a common evaluation made in depression is that of 'I am a failure' (or bad, worthless). As the individual then experiences the affect of depression (at C in the ABC model), it is perhaps unsurprising that their self-condemning evaluation leads them to conclude that they are either helpless or that their immediate future is hopeless. If we were to truly believe that we were a failure, this means we could never succeed, and so the individual concludes he or she is rendered helpless and hopeless by their evaluation.

The As of Depression in the ABC Model

The adversities most often found in working with clients who depress themselves are loss and failure. Both of these can be actual experiences, memories of actual experiences, images associated with past losses or failures, or reflections on experiences in which the individual identifies a loss or failure.

When the counsellor is listening for the theme of the A in the ABC model when working with a depressed client, it is important to note that the losses do not have to be objectively great, such as the death of a loved one. Actual loss might also relate to the end of a relationship, job, ability or opportunity. Similarly, when the client reflects upon, remembers or experiences images associated with a past loss, this loss might at first not appear obvious. The fact is that for the client the loss was indeed a loss and the task is then to help the client to see how they are depressing themselves about the loss.

Not all failures are obviously problematic to the client or the counsellor. There may be times when an actual failure occurs that is clear and present, such as failing to pass an exam, failing in a relationship or job. However, there will be times when the failure (or the memory, reflection, or image of a failure) may be very subtle. We have found that often the most subtle forms of failure are associated with not achieving a personal goal. This can lead to depression, as long as the individual does not feel that they are responsible for the failure. Where the client feels they are at fault, the emotion may be called depression by the client, but it is much more likely to be associated with shame or guilt. Some clients will report feeling depressed after someone has treated them badly, such as being rejected by a loved one. Here it is important to determine whether the individual sees themself as undeserving of the rejection, as if this is so, the emotional problem might be better formulated as hurt rather than depression.

Perhaps because the main As associated with depression are loss and failure, it is not surprising how frequently depression itself can become a new A about other emotional problems. If the individual depresses themselves about having failed, they will continue to act as if they have failed. In turn, they may reflect upon this new set of failures and so depress themselves about having been depressed. Indeed, there can often be complex cycles of ABCs associated with depression as a meta-emotion.

The Bs of Depression in the ABC Model

Inferences
The inferences (or thoughts) that begin the cognitive processing that leads to depression are what Beck (1976) refers to as Negative Automatic Thoughts and Dysfunctional (or Conditional) assumptions. Negative

Automatic Thoughts, as described by Beck, are mainly negative inferences about what is observable in the experience of the individual. Unlike the inferences made in anxiety, in depression these nearly always relate to an experience in the past or present.

Given that the As of depression typically relate to experiences of loss or failure, the initial inferences made also relate to these themes. As well as going beyond the available data, these inferences skew (or filter) the individual's perception so that they primarily perceive the negative elements of an experience. These inferences will also be distorted, such as through magnification (see Chapter 5), for example 'I always fail' or 'This always happens to me'. As we have already stated, in CBC we formulate depression as occurring when the individual does not feel responsible for the loss or failure (as if they did feel they were at fault, the result is more likely to be shame or guilt). As they were not responsible the individual might then infer that they are powerless to change their experience, for example 'There's nothing I can do about it'. In self-pitying forms of depression, the individual might infer that the experience was unfair, for example 'Why me? It's not fair'.

Evaluations

The evaluations made about inferences in depression effectively trap the individual into their depressed emotional response. One of the core evaluations in depression are evaluations of self-condemnation. Here the individual concludes something about themselves in their entirety, based on an experience or series of experiences or what they have been told by significant others. For example, take the individual who depresses themselves about the loss (through rejection) of a loved one. Following on from inferences such as 'Things never go right for me; they didn't love me', the individual might further evaluate this experience in terms of their worth or lovability as a person and conclude that 'I am worthless' or 'I am unlovable'. Therefore, although they might not believe they are responsible for the loss or failure, they condemn themselves for having been a victim of the experience. This evaluation feels both powerful and compelling and firmly establishes the dysfunctional emotion of depression.

The second common evaluation made by individuals when depressing themselves is an evaluation of how intolerable their situation is. Having experienced the event and made negative inferences, the individual will then see their experience as unbearable. This is particularly common when depression is a meta-emotion. At such times, it is almost commonplace for clients to believe that not depressing themselves about their experience is 'too hard'. This is simply another way of saying that their emotional pain or the discomfort required for change is intolerable.

In all cases of depression, there is also likely to be a demand about the key inference. This demand serves to seal the inference as fact and evaluate the individual's performance in the situation in an extremely negative way. Examples of this include, 'This should never have happened to me', 'I need to be loved' or 'I must not fail'. Hence, the demand establishes the principle from which the other evaluations logically (although unhealthily) follow. Take the example of the demand about failure. If an individual believes that they must not, under any circumstances, fail, they are already denying their humanity and all their previous experiences of dealing more effectively with failure. In CBC, we would argue that the demand here also operates in the background, as a rule for life, and therefore contributes significantly to generating the inferences drawn by the individual.

Therefore the counsellor in CBC should listen out for inferences about loss and failure that readily generalise to other experiences, rules for living (or personal principles) that constitute the demand and global evaluations of the self or how intolerable their circumstances are.

Example ABC

A	B	C
Failing to get a job after an interview	They thought I was useless (inference) This always happens to me (inference) I must not fail (evaluation) That I failed proves that I am a failure (evaluation)	Depressed Withdraws and gives up Dwells on the negative aspects of the interview Concludes that it will be pointless to try to get a job again (and fails to make further efforts to improve interview performance or even find another job)

FIGURE 13.1   *Example ABC*

Core Treatment Goals for Depression in CBC

In the general CBT literature one of the key intervention strategies when working with clients who experience depression is to encourage them to become more active. The logic behind this is sound, as when any of us cease inactivity and engage more in life we, however unwillingly, stumble across pleasurable or rewarding experiences. However, it is also likely that we will run into other experiences about which we might just as easily depress ourselves. Therefore, in CBC we take a modified approach. We acknowledge that the client who depresses themselves is most likely to be engaging in behavioural withdrawal, meaning that they will find it extremely difficult to motivate themselves to act differently. In time, we would encourage the client to become more active, but this would be done when the client had realised that to achieve their goal they need to act in accordance with their new, alternative, cognitions.

Next in traditional CBT the therapist would typically help the client to challenge the evidence for their Negative Automatic Thoughts. For example, if a client inferred 'nobody likes me' after being overlooked or ignored, they would be encouraged to collect evidence that some people like them. Whilst they are likely to succeed in this and so it is definitely worth pursuing, this method is not without problems. We would argue that the inference 'nobody likes me' is too great a deduction from the experience of being overlooked or ignored on several occasions. We posit that the inference here is being driven by an underlying demand (or principle) that might take the form 'in order to be happy (or at least not depressed) I need to be, and therefore must be, liked by others'. Hence the experience of being overlooked would lead to an inference that the person or persons who failed to attend sufficiently to the individual would be viewed through the lens of the demand and this in turn would lead to inferences of the ignoring meaning that the other(s) did not like them and the subsequent inference that nobody likes them.

So, in CBC we differ from traditional CBT in preferring to guide the client challenge evaluations before inferences. If, as we have argued, the inference stems from the demand (despite the inference at the point of the experience being identified in the ABC first), then the client might only be superficially reassured by the evidence that some people like them. We use the term superficial because if they are living their life according to the principle that 'I must be liked, in order to be happy', any single experience of being disliked thwarts their chances of happiness and they will go on to depress themselves all over again. In seeking evidence of being liked, unless they are extremely fortunate, we would argue that most clients are likely to identify times when they are disliked too. In CBC we would argue that it is important to first identify and question the demand, as by weakening the conviction in this belief the individual is less likely to make the same type of inferences in the first instant and continuously recreating it in further instances.

Before we address the core technical elements of applying CBC to depression, it is worth first considering any difficulties that the counsellor will need to be watchful for. Unless they are utterly affectively withdrawn (or shut down), clients who depress themselves are likely to express high levels of negative emotion in the consulting room. This may manifest in tears or overt self-condemnation. We would consider it important to encourage and permit the expression of these feelings as this will be central to understanding the cognitions that underlie the problem. Therefore the counsellor will need to be prepared for this expression of emotion. Often, when an individual cries in front of us it is difficult not to reach out and seek to reassure them. In CBC, however, the emotional expression is important to helping the client, as not only does this enable the client to more readily identify their thoughts, beliefs and action tendencies, but also it enables the counsellor to observe how the individual reacts and is an ideal opportunity to gain access to beliefs that are otherwise difficult to access. Offering comfort, although demonstrating warmth, should be undertaken cautiously. For example, in self-pitying depression, the offer of comfort might actually collude with the client's view. Similarly, in depression where the client has concluded that everything is hopeless and they are beyond help, the counsellor will need to demonstrate that they, whilst empathic and compassionate, are not overwhelmed by the problem in the same way that the client is. In working with severely or chronically depressed clients it is helpful to remind ourselves that the client is depressing themselves. Though they might not recognise this, and it should not be offered as opening advice, the client is choosing to respond to their difficulties by depressing themselves about it. In this way, we have found that counsellors can manage not to be drawn in to the defeatist and despairing attitudes of the client.

As suggested in our basic guide, one of the early tasks in working with depression is to appropriately identify a goal. In response to the question 'how would you like to feel about this problem?' most clients might immediately respond with 'happy' or 'nothing'. In such instances, the counsellor will need to negotiate the goal with the client. We have found it helpful here to restate the problem and ask whether the client would be helped by feeling happy or nothing. For example, if a man has depressed himself about being rejected after a date, it might be helpful for him to reflect on his behaviour, his presentation, his choice of date activities, his choice of partners and so on. If he felt happy or nothing he is likely to engage in none of this reflection and might never learn from life's lessons. Similarly, if he chooses to depress himself, he is likely to enter into a cocoon of solitude and despair and ultimately find it even more difficult to enjoy a successful date.

We might use such examples with clients who are unable to generate any alternatives, as even people who excel at depressing themselves are able to help other people find their way out of depression. In some instances, we have found it necessary to tentatively suggest an emotional goal to clients, usually sadness. In some cases, we have found that clients are unable to differentiate meaningfully between sadness and depression and we have then found it helpful to teach the client the difference. This does not have to be a didactic lecture in the session, but many books and films depict individuals who experience sadness or depression and the client can begin their understanding there. However the counsellor chooses to guide the client towards an appropriate goal, it will always be important to help the client to understand that by feeling their emotional goal they will be better placed to overcome, accept or otherwise deal with the problem about which they are currently depressing themselves.

Having established a goal, the counsellor should then pursue a specific example of the problem to begin the process of Socratic questions about the thoughts and beliefs the client had about the problem. We tend to avoid questions such as 'What were you thinking when that happened?' because the client is likely to detach from their emotional experience in the here and now and conversely this makes the thoughts and beliefs more difficult to access. Staying with the emotion, we might choose to let the client simply describe their experience of the problem, and then use follow-up questions such as 'and what did you make of that?', 'and what led you to feel most depressed about that?', 'and that was so difficult for you because . . .?' and so on. In so doing the counsellor is listening out for the inferences made about loss or failure and the underlying evaluations (self-condemnation, low frustration tolerance and demand). In our experience the low frustration tolerance and self-condemnation evaluations are easily identified by the client and are often a feature of their general description of the event.

The demand, however, can be more difficult to identify. Here the importance of working within the emotion can be vital. The counsellor can ask open questions about whether the client violated any of their rules for living, but this might simply confuse the client. We have found direct questions to be particularly effective for most clients, and frequently, though always tentatively, will ask 'And how should it have been?' or 'And what shouldn't have happened?' The client's response is usually a part of their demand evaluation and the counsellor can paraphrase and clarify that this is so with the client.

In working with depression, the counsellor, having established goals and the inferences and evaluations, will need to help the client to generate some alternative thoughts and beliefs. This is important because in depression it can often be very difficult for individuals to generate alternative views of the situation. Keeping the goal in mind, the counsellor can choose whether to help the client to search for ideas, or to make tentative suggestions and seek the client's feedback on them. At this stage the client is not expected to believe the alternative cognitions, simply to accept that they are an alternative point of view. The counsellor should then discuss with the client whether the alternative views would enable them to achieve their emotional goal, which in turn might help them deal better with the problem (usually at A) that they have described.

We suggested earlier that the most common evaluations in depression are demands, low frustration tolerance and global self-rating. Working on these beliefs should follow the process we described in the Basic Guide section for questioning the beliefs (both the dysfunctional and functional) according to their pragmatism, logic and evidence. We have found that the demands and low frustration tolerance can be addressed as in any other problem. However, the tendency for global self-rating (self-condemnation) in individuals who depress themselves warrants additional attention. The counsellor can of course encourage the client to consider a more self-accepting view and use the pragmatic, empirical and logical disputation strategies, yet with some clients they find that they readily slip into global self-rating. In depression, this becomes a particularly important evaluation to address as it contributes so substantively to the cognitive consequences of helplessness and hopelessness. Furthermore, in our experience of working with clients who depress themselves, these beliefs can be amongst the most difficult to change. Therefore, we will summarise some of the techniques we have found to be successful.

Challenging Global Self-rating

Global self-rating involves redefining oneself based on some arbitrary criteria. For example, an individual might define their worth based on the outcome of a relationship, their success in a particular important task, or their general treatment by others. Having had such an experience they conclude that they are worthless, based upon their implicit criteria for human worth. Therefore, we find it helpful to draw this element out. The counsellor can help the client to establish the criteria for the judgement of worthlessness. In most clients this relates to one or two behaviours or situational outcomes. For example, after Wessler and Wessler (1980), if a client believes they are worthless because they do not have a job, we would first help the client to see that they are using the situational outcome of not having a job as evidence of their worthlessness. Next, we might ask the client whether they know other people who do not have a job. If not, we might ask them that if (the counsellor) lost our job would we suddenly become worthless. The purpose of these discussions is to help the client to see that they are accepting (when depressing themselves) as true that their worth as a person can be defined solely on the basis of not having a job. The client is unlikely to define other things in their life according to such arbitrary criteria. As humans we can define anything as good or bad, success or failure, worthy or unworthy. For example:

Counsellor:	I'm learning to play the guitar, and I want to be really good at it. It's important to me, as I've always wanted to be good at playing a musical instrument. Now if I play a bad note does that make me a failure?
Client:	No, but that's not the same as my problem.
Counsellor:	Could you explain why not?
Client:	Well, it doesn't really matter if you play a bad note.
Counsellor:	It does to me, it's really important.
Client:	Yeah, but that wouldn't make you a failure.
Counsellor:	Well, what would you think of me if I couldn't play the guitar well?
Client:	Well, maybe just that you can't play the guitar well.
Counsellor:	And if you failed at something important to you, would you also be a person who has failed, but not a failure?

We might then make use of a paradoxical approach. Here, we would take the client's belief (about being a failure or being worthless) and follow this through to its logical conclusion. We might say to the client that if they truly believed that they were a failure, why are they depressing themselves about having failed? After all, a dog does not get depressed when they act like a dog.

Finally, to bring the issue back to the client and their current problem, we would also make the point about human existence being a process. There are countless examples in history to support the fact that humans can and do change. We prefer to tailor this to the cultural context and interests of the client, but the examples are so numerous that this is relatively straightforward. For clients who believe that bad actions mean you are a bad (or worthless) person, we might talk to them about Nelson Mandela or other personalities or reformed characters who were once labelled as terrorists or murderers who subsequently became role models and heroes. For clients who believe that failing makes you a failure, we might talk about Scott of the Antarctic who has been immortalised for his courage. For clients who believe that not being romantically desired by another means that you are worthless, we might talk to them about the on and off relationship of Richard Burton and Elizabeth Taylor. The point here is that we simply cannot define our humanity based upon our past or present experiences, as we are likely to act later today, tomorrow and the next day, and none of us can know what the future holds.

After having helped the client complete the disputation process, it will be important to then engage the client in planning how they intend to feel and act differently outside the session. This might mean rehearsing their new thoughts and beliefs, engaging in imagery-based assignments, or behavioural homework experiments and tasks, as spelled out in the basic guide, particularly Chapters 8 and 9.

14

Anger

Typically, anger is considered the emotion of conflict, aggression and hostility. Yet anger is also one of the commonest emotional experiences for many people (Oatley and Duncan, 1994). In the consulting room, we encounter clients with anger problems frequently. Not all of these clients have histories of aggression and violence; in fact many clients who experience unhealthy anger seek to suppress the experience, such that they almost never act on their angry feelings. Presently, there are no diagnostic criteria for problem anger, and the emotion is often subsumed within other categories such as Intermittent Explosive Disorder and the personality disorder diagnoses in DSM-IV. Few introductory texts on CBT even address anger as a problem. Indeed, in comparison to anxiety and depression, despite its prevalence within human experience, anger remains an overlooked problem within the research literature.

The English language has few words for anger. Often anger is labelled as annoyance, frustration or rage. Traditionally, the research literature defines anger as problematic when is it too intense, experienced for too long a duration or is experienced in a severe or profound manner (Novaco, 1994). In working with clients we find these definitions of problem anger too arbitrary and of little benefit, as too often they point towards a reduction in the intensity of the emotion rather than a change to an emotion that will be more self-enhancing. The REBT position on anger has always been relatively clear and we find the distinction of healthy and unhealthy anger to be a very useful one with clients. Unhealthy anger leads to self-defeating consequences, such as violence, suppression and health problems. Healthy anger leads to self-enhancing consequences, such as acceptance, protest and assertion. In CBC, as in anxiety, we do not believe that just reducing the intensity of unhealthy anger to be all that helpful to clients, as they will still be motivated to act in self-defeating ways. This underpins the CBC model to understanding anger problems.

Key Elements of the CBC Model

Anger at C in the ABC Model

The experience of unhealthy anger is associated with significant physi-ological arousal. Individuals often feel energised by their unhealthy anger as if it is somehow preparing them for action. In fact, the physiological response to anger is very similar to that of anxiety, and therefore we can consider this in terms of the fight or flight response mechanism, where anger prepares the body for fight. Clients who express their unhealthy anger freely often report feeling powerful and unstoppable at the time, whereas those who suppress their unhealthy anger feel somehow inca-pacitated by the experience, trapped momentarily in an inner battle of wills. The feeling of unhealthy anger is common to us all, whether we express or suppress the emotion. Readers will be familiar with the notion of their blood boiling, seeing red and seething. These phrases capture the potency of the experience of unhealthy anger.

The action tendencies associated with unhealthy anger do not vary as much as the overt behaviours associated with unhealthy anger. When we feel unhealthily angry we usually have a very strong sense of being wronged or crossed, and the urges associated with this are typically retali-atory. If we feel anger towards another person we may experience an action tendency to aggress, destroy, diminish or punish. Thankfully for the social good, most people most of the time do not act impulsively and without restraint on these action tendencies, although some do.

The overt behaviours associated with unhealthy anger vary according to whether the emotion is actively or passively expressed or suppressed by the individual. When unhealthy anger is actively expressed, this might take the form of verbal or physical aggression. Some philosophical views on anger would suggest that this is motivated by a desire to dominate that which we feel angry towards, where others suggest that this is simply the venting of the emotional arousal. In our experience clients with anger problems rarely come to counselling for help in re-aligning their desire to dominate others, or to seek a mechanism for the safe release of emotional tension. We mention these perspectives here because both involve a potential means of positively reinforcing the behaviour associated with anger. Try to recall a time when you stubbed your big toe on a door, chair or sideboard. Did you immediately bend forward and inspect your toe or the object you collided with for damage? We would imagine that the vast majority of times you will have started hopping around issuing expletives in loud or hushed tones. Those readers currently nodding in agreement will also be aware that their behaviour did little to undo the pain, but the release of the anger temporarily helped them to feel better, thereby reinforcing that behaviour such that you are more likely to engage in it the next time you stub your toe.

Similarly, imagine that you are standing in a queue in a shop and someone pushes in line ahead of you. Feeling a sense of responsibility for those behind you, you might speak up and point out that the behaviour of the individual is impolite and respectfully ask them to step to the end of the line. Alternatively, you might simply attract their attention and make them aware that the end of the queue is not where they joined the line. Now, if that person then turned upon you and through snarling teeth threatened you to stop interfering or there will be trouble, how would you act? Some of us might instinctively decide that our principle that all people should observe proper queuing etiquette was not worth defending right now and simply go quiet, feel anxious or embarrassed. In this circumstance the individual who responded with anger fended off your advice, and for that brief moment of existence assumed a dominant position. This most likely produced the result they wanted, perhaps to stifle the interests of interfering busy bodies, and so their behavioural response to their emotional state will have been positively reinforced. Despite there being circumstances when our overt aggressive behaviours stemming from unhealthy anger might help us to feel temporarily good and might even be positively reinforced by the small reward that follows, the behaviour itself remains self-defeating.

Perhaps the most iconic example of this can be found in the BBC television comedy series *Fawlty Towers*. In one famous episode, hotelier Basil Fawlty, keen to impress some guests, is rushing back and forth between his hotel and a restaurant. As the journeys become more time limited and courses are forgotten he becomes more and more angry, until the fateful moment when his car breaks down. Rather than act to address his problem (such as seek to identify what is wrong with the car or summon assistance) he gets out of the vehicle, picks up a nearby fallen branch and begins to beat this down on the roof of the car whilst verbally chastising the poor vehicle. He might have felt better, but what had changed about the problem he faced? Herein is the self-defeating aspect of the actively expressed behavioural consequences of unhealthy anger.

When unhealthy anger leads to more passive forms of expression there are less obvious overt expressions of the emotion. When expressed in a passive manner, the individual who feels unhealthily angry might seek to covertly undo the reputation of the other person, towards whom they feel their anger. They might speak ill of the person to others, attempt to trick or fool the other person, or simply set about trying to make them look foolish. This passive form of expressing unhealthy anger might be characteristic of the individual, but is commonly used when a judgement that direct action is ill-advised. Many of us may have had a similar experience in a work setting with a colleague or manager. Here, any anger we feel toward the individual might not be expressed actively because we are aware that such behaviour will not be tolerated. Therefore we might engage in complaining to others about the bad behaviour of the colleague or manager, running down their character or establishing a hate campaign, seeking to recruit others to share in our negative views. Again, this passive expression is self-defeating as the initial problem with the individual or their behaviour is not addressed.

Unhealthy anger might also be suppressed. This occurs when there is no direct means of active or passive expression available. For example, if an individual feels angry towards a loved one who has died or about a past experience that they cannot change, there is little they can directly do to express the anger. The suppression leads to an extended duration of the unhealthy anger. At times, suppressed unhealthy anger might lead to indirect or displaced aggression occurring. We have noticed that some individuals seek to hide their unhealthy anger from others, thereby forcing a suppression. A common example of this is familial discord. Take for example the daughter who feels continually ordered around by her new father-in-law. Although she might feel extremely angry about this (and towards others for not siding with her), she might recognise that she is unable to express her unhealthy anger, and therefore has no apparent option other than suppressing the anger. We would argue that suppressed anger is most common when there are meta-emotional problems associated with the anticipated shame or guilt that would be felt if the anger was expressed. We will come back to this in the section on the As of anger.

The cognitive consequences of unhealthy anger are typically ones of hostility, revenge and belligerence. After experiencing unhealthy anger towards another, the individual is cognitively prepared to view the other in a more hostile manner. In some of the literature pertaining to cognitive models of anger a hostile attributional bias is seen to be one of the cognitive systems that create anger. However, in CBC we see a hostile attributional bias (a tendency to ascribe hostile intent to the other) as one of the cognitive consequences of unhealthy anger. Here, having felt unhealthy anger the individual maintains a hostile view of the other (or situation).

The As of Anger in the ABC Model

Although the emotion of anger, both healthy and unhealthy, is often labelled as frustration, it is important for the CBC counsellor to clearly understand where frustration fits into the ABC model. Within the CBC integrated model we would argue that frustration is shorthand for the events about which individuals make themselves angry.

Research has produced lists (e.g. Averill, 1982) and inventories (e.g. Novaco, 1991) of events that typically people find are provocative of anger. Although these might be helpful in assessing a client who is unsure of their emotional problem, we have found that clients who experience problems with unhealthy anger find it almost easy to describe that which they are angry about.

The sources of As of unhealthy anger for the counsellor to listen out for are not just those involving other people. Although interpersonal events are common in unhealthy anger, it is important for the counsellor to be aware that as individuals we can make ourselves angry about external and internal events, for example we can feel angry about the experience of pain.

One of the typical themes in As of unhealthy anger is that of a personal goal being thwarted. When we feel angry towards others, we are usually aware that a personal goal has been thwarted (such as being treated with respect, looking strong and courageous, indomitable, or at least not looking weak or cowardly). Here, the goal may then be thwarted by the actions, as interpreted, of another person.

However, we can just as easily make ourselves angry about conditions in which we find ourselves. Consider the example of a home-improvement task. Needing storage, we might decide upon a goal of erecting a shelf. This task is made up of multiple sub-tasks, including measurement, ensuring the appropriate tools are available and to hand, checking the holes in the wall are level and so on. Having proceeded through these tasks, you stand back to admire your handiwork. Impressed, you set about the task of placing some ornaments on the shelf and again step back to take an overview of your arrangement. As you do the shelf collapses on one side and your ornaments smash upon the floor. It is perhaps not uncommon for people in similar circumstances to feel angry at this.

The As of anger therefore can be broadly categorised into interpersonal transgressions and events that thwart our goals. We would consider these both as types of frustration, and consequently always construct the ABC with frustration at A. Occasionally, clients will find it difficult to describe their problem as anything other than 'feeling' frustrated. Usually, we will encourage the client to tell us more about what they find frustrating, listening out for an interpersonal transgression or thwarting of a goal. We will then encourage clients to reflect further on their emotional response to that frustration.

As with other emotional formulations within the ABC model, anger itself can also be an A. When this occurs we might refer to the initial ABC where anger is the C as the primary or initial problem formulation and the secondary ABC, where anger is at A, as the meta-emotional problem. When anger is at A, it is important for the counsellor to establish whether the anger at A is healthy or unhealthy. For example, some individuals have devout principles about feeling angry, and even if they are healthily angry about something, they might make themselves feel guilty or ashamed. Although in CBC we would not seek to alter the morality of the client, we would endeavour to encourage the client to accept themselves unconditionally rather than define their worth based upon an emotional experience, however unacceptable they believe that emotional experience to be. Some individuals may make themselves anxious about the experience of anger (healthy or unhealthy). Here they might have unrealistic expectations about what might happen if they experience anger. Some clients who direct unhealthy anger at themselves might then depress themselves about their inability to bring about any change. Whatever the emotional consequence when anger is at A, we would still continue to use the ABC model, simply formulating this as links in a chain. We would also want to help the client with their original anger ABC (unless the anger produced was healthy).

The Bs of Anger in the ABC Model

Inferences

The inferences that occur in anger set the ground for the later evaluations that turn up the emotional heat. In anger between individuals, where the behaviour of the other is the focus of the anger, the inferences usually have themes about the nature of the transgression and the deliberation of the other. In other words, if we think that someone has acted badly towards us, we also need to infer that they did this on purpose, that it was their fault. The attribution of blame is core to anger, as if we thought that someone treated us badly because of something we had done, that we therefore deserved to be treated badly, then anger is unlikely to result and the individual is more likely to develop evaluations that lead to shame or guilt. The next stage of inferences in interpersonal anger is associated with the inferred intent of the other. So not only have they treated us badly, on purpose, but they have also done that to disadvantage us in some way (such as by seeking dominance, making the individual look bad in front of others and so on). The penultimate inferential process then seeks to explain the motivation of the other. If someone treated you badly on purpose to make you look stupid, what do they actually think of you? In other words why would they do that? Most individuals proceeding through these inference stages (and eventually experiencing unhealthy anger) are likely to conclude that the opinion held of them by the other is very poor indeed to permit them to act in such a way. Beck (2002) describes this inferential process as projected low self-worth, where our own internalised negative view is temporarily considered to be held as true by the other. We posit that the final inferential process is a conclusion about the other's behaviour. Typically this conclusion links directly to the evaluations made that we will come to soon. This conclusion can perhaps best be summarised as 'they don't respect me'. Although this may sound a little vernacular given the modern way that the term 'respect' is often used, we have rarely worked with a client whose unhealthy anger was associated with an interpersonal encounter where the inference of not being respected has not occurred.

When individuals become angry about conditions in which they find themselves and not about an interpersonal event, the inferences made differ. For example, thinking back to the example about stubbing your toe, you are unlikely to be convinced that the object you bumped into has little or no respect for you. Similarly, if we are stuck in a traffic jam, we are unlikely to conclude that the hold-up has been caused by someone disrespecting us. The frustration remains in place, such as experiencing a pain or a delay that will make you late, but the inferences differ in content. Here the inferences involve the, albeit temporary, conclusion that conditions have conspired against you on purpose. One client described being overcome by rage because on an otherwise sunny day they found themselves in the midst of a thunderstorm. They drew inferences such as 'this always happens to me'. Curiously, the weather conditions were then personalised, with thoughts such as 'Why did you have to go and do this to me?' The core inferential process occurring here is that conditions, and at times life itself, are unfair.

Evaluations

The evaluations associated with anger are what determine whether the emotion is healthy or unhealthy. In unhealthy anger, there are demands, low frustration tolerance and the global rating (usually of other, self or conditions). In healthy anger, the evaluations are preferences, high frustration tolerance and unconditional acceptance (of self, others and conditions).

The demands made usually relate to (and actually bring forth) the final inference discussed above. In interpersonal anger, we would expect to discover a demand about how others must respect the client, for example 'I hate it when John doesn't respect me and therefore he must respect me'. Again, the word *must* can often be substituted with 'need', 'should', 'ought' and 'have to' and often prefixed with the adjective 'absolutely'. In interpersonal anger the demand is simply an assertion of the principle to which the other must abide, in order not to become the object of your anger. Thus, the desire to be treated respectfully becomes a principle or rule that others simply should observe. Most of the time, typically when people are acting respectfully and not breaking the rule, the demand lies low and is not at the forefront of the individual's thinking. However, if another acts in a way that is interpreted as disrespectful then the demand drives the inferences home.

Another way of considering this is to see the demand as a filter rule, with many conditions. Certain acts and events pass through the filter because they meet the conditions of the rule (e.g. 'She was just very polite to me' (therefore the rule is not violated)). However, some acts or events (as we call them in CBC, frustrations) do not meet the conditions of the rule and therefore require further attention (e.g. 'I must not be spat at (because that would be an example of people disrespecting me, which they must not do')). When rule violations occur, the inferences take place (driven by the demand) and the other evaluations are triggered. The counsellor is wise therefore to work on uncovering the demand and helping the client to recognise how much of a problem it is to them. Preferences, instead of demands, do not operate as a rule filter (though they do inform the rules we establish). In fact much of the time, when events occur that are in keeping with our preferences, we do not actually make inferences about them, we simply know that we prefer events like that. Consider your favourite ice cream: when you eat it you are unlikely to be inferring that there are various aspects of the ice and cream and sugar and flavouring that you enjoy; no, you simply know that you like it. The preferences associated with healthy anger in interpersonal situations assert the desire component (being respected) and negate the demanding component. For example, 'I love it when others treat me with respect, but they don't absolutely have to'.

The demands associated with anger that is not based on an interpersonal reaction, such as anger with an object or a set of conditions, follows a similar principle, although we would expect the content of the demand to differ. Typically, we do not demand respect from objects or conditions. For example, we may feel angry when a computer crashes halfway through an unsaved piece of work, but our anger is not created because we are demanding that the computer respect us. In shorthand, this is an example where conditions are not what we would want them to be. In unhealthy anger, we turn this want into a demand, a must, a should, an ought and so on. Here, the demand establishes a principle or rule about how conditions (or sometimes outcomes) must be in order for us not to feel anger. Usually, this demand is directly associated with the thwarting of our goal, and in general terms we are making demands that our goals should never be thwarted, by kith, kin, object or machine. Evidently, this is an unhelpful rule for living as life experience shows us all that conditions do not always play out as we want them to. We have found that the demand therefore relates to an insistence that frustration (at A) should not be or should not have occurred. Therefore, if we make demands about conditions, we are demanding that those conditions should not go awry. Putting this into simple terms, the demands in non-interpersonal anger generally follow the principle of the statement of the desire (e.g. 'I really didn't want that to happen …') followed by an imposed demand that creates the rule that has been broken (e.g. '... and therefore it shouldn't have happened'). This type of demand, principle or rule, perhaps more than any other, is prima facie illogical, unhelpful and inconsistent with our experience of reality.

The demands that lead to anger at self are very similar in content to the demands about conditions. In anger at the self, the condition is simply applied directly to the self. Often this relates to our knowledge, behaviour or ability to predict the future. For example, rushing to answer a telephone call we might accidentally bump into a door frame and fail to get to the call. We might feel angry with ourselves, but at that moment we are not demanding that we respect ourselves (although this would be a logical abstraction ultimately). At that point in time we might feel angry with ourselves for knowing that more haste equals less speed, yet we acted against our knowledge and hence we conclude 'I should have known better', or for our behaviour we conclude 'I should have acted differently', and so on.

After the demands come two important further evaluations that intensify the emotion of anger, low frustration tolerance and global rating. Typically both of these will occur in interpersonal anger, low frustration tolerance is more salient in conditions-based anger, and both are present in anger at self. We would consider these as being sequelae of the demands as these evaluations are effectively conditional on the demand being believed to be true. For example, if we wanted somebody's respect, but did not demand it, would we logically conclude that they were an entirely bad person for not respecting us? In CBC we would consider this unlikely.

Low frustration tolerance beliefs have been well documented (Harrington, 2006). Given that the As of anger in the ABC relate to a sense of frustration, it is perhaps unsurprising that we find this form of evaluation so common in anger. The low frustration tolerance evaluation follows the principle that we find conditions difficult to bear and then assert that therefore we cannot bear them. Take the example of a lovers' quarrel. Both are arguing, trying to prove themselves correct over some, usually, trivial matter. At some point, it is common for one or both of them to feel complete exasperation (anger) at the situation and the other person. They have a feeling that this experience cannot go on, and they throw their hands up and storm out of the room slamming the door shut behind them. The moment of that exasperation is the evaluation of low frustration tolerance. In the consulting room (or in the home, or on the road, or in the supermarket) a common phrase that informs us of the presence of low frustration tolerance is 'I can't stand it'. Ellis (1963) conceptualised this idea into the phrase I-can't-stand-it-itis and in many ways we would argue that this is central to many emotional problems but most definitely in unhealthy anger. The alternative that leads to healthy anger is high frustration tolerance. Here the evaluation is that the experience is difficult to bear, but that it is bearable (e.g. 'this is hard to bear, but I can stand it').

In unhealthy anger towards others or the self, the evaluation of global rating, of the other or self, seeks to diminish that person. The cognitive process and content is similar to that on global rating of the self that we have seen is core to depression. In interpersonal anger, however, it is the other person who is denigrated for acting in a way that is not consistent with our demands and principles. We have perhaps all experienced heated arguments with others where the global rating of the other person rolls off the tongue. Typically, the global other evaluations are paraphrased into the key elements when spoken aloud, for example 'you idiot', 'you're a pratt', 'you shit' and so on. If we reconstruct the global rating of the other, we find that there is a judgement passed about the behaviour of the other (or some other criteria, such as what the other might be thinking of us) that contradicts our principle (or demand) and we then define the whole person based on that aspect of their behaviour. So, if we take the general example, the global other evaluation is likely to take the following form: 'Because you acted disrespectfully towards me (and therefore acted against my demand/principle), you are a bad person.' Once condemned in such a way, it is perhaps no surprise that one of the cognitive consequences of anger is a hostile bias toward that other. Imagine you were convinced that somebody was bad to the bone, how else might you expect them to behave if not with disrespect towards you and therefore you maintain a hostile view of them. In anger towards the self the only difference is that it is the self that is condemned for having broken the rule. So the demand 'I should have known better' is often followed by 'and that proves what a complete fool I am'.

In conditions-based anger, global rating is perhaps less commonly explored, but might be present. We would consider them often less explored in therapy because clients are quickly able to see how illogical such beliefs are the moment they voice them. Take the example used earlier of stubbing your toe on a sideboard. Here our language used might reveal the global rating of the object or condition, such as 'f★★★ing thing'.

We might not continue life with a contemptuous regard for the sideboard or the door that once trapped our hand, or the rug we once slipped on, but nevertheless in the heat of the moment the global rating evaluation is present. It is perhaps because this evaluation is most likely so transient in nature that the need for it to be addressed in therapy is less of a priority; unless of course, like many of us and many of our clients, we feel unhealthy anger towards more than just objects, but others and ourselves too. Therefore, unless the client's only problem is an unhealthy anger towards objects, we would seek to explore the global rating evaluation as this might be of benefit later in therapy when formulating angry feelings towards others.

Example ABC

A	B	C
Disagreement with colleague at work	They don't think my views are important (inference) They don't respect me (inference) They ought to respect me (evaluation) I can't stand it when they don't (evaluation) They're an ignorant, stupid person (evaluation)	Unhealthy anger Desire to verbally aggress Passive-aggressively runs the colleague down to co-workers (fails to address the real issues)

FIGURE 14.1 *Example ABC*

Core Treatment Goals for Anger in CBC

The first stage of the treatment of anger in CBC is for the counsellor to recognise some of the potential difficulties in working with clients who experience anger problems. Usually, the therapeutic alliance is based on warmth, empathy and unconditional positive regard, yet clients with unhealthy anger problems may challenge each of these aspects.

When a client is expressing hostile views about some transgression they have experienced, it might be difficult for the counsellor to genuinely experience warmth towards them. Consider, for example, a client with sexist or racist views expressed during their anger. Empathy is also likely to be a challenge when the client may have over-reacted to a situation, such as in cases of domestic violence or physical chastisement of a child. In such circumstances, the counsellor might find it difficult to fully empathise with the client. When individuals present with hostile views, the counsellor may slip into the trap of globally rating the client, rather than practising unconditional other acceptance, where the client's behaviour and not them as a person may be rated.

In order to try to prevent some of the above pitfalls, we would recommend beginning by acknowledging the transgression to the client. At this stage we do not seek to collude with the client's A; rather we are interested in demonstrating to the client that we can understand that they made themselves unhealthily angry about the frustration they experienced. Here, we are careful not to condone the self-defeating behaviour that was part of their anger, but rather that they did seem to find the problem very hard to deal with without experiencing unhealthy anger and this in turn led them to act in ways that did not really help them to overcome the problem.

Next, we would attempt to help the client understand that their unhealthy anger led to behaviours that were not helpful to them in pursuing their goal. Although many clients are energised by anger and have a corresponding sense of righteousness, we endeavour to help the client reflect on whether their anger actually got them what they wanted. For clients whose anger leads to violence, we would help them to reflect on whether the use of violence got them the respect, and not the fear, that they wanted. Occasionally, clients will equate fear with respect, and in such circumstances we try to help them to acknowledge that their display of anger would most likely lead to them being viewed negatively by the other. This can be aided by the use of metaphors from films or other sources. For example, consider the case of the man who had significant problems with the noise and interference of his neighbours. Whenever something happened that he did not like, he took this as a message that his neighbours did not respect him. Over time he became accustomed to challenging the neighbours to violent confrontation, but the interference continued. In fact the local children would purposely throw stones at his windows just to watch him become angry and threatening. The children and neighbours had little or no respect for the man. Though they feared his violence, their troublesome behaviour only escalated and the client never attained the respect they wanted.

The counsellor should then seek to understand the client's capacity for healthy anger. Ask them for examples when they have encountered a frustration but been able to address the problem or at least accept that there is nothing they can do to affect a change. At first, some clients may find this difficult, and we might help them by directing them to some common examples when most of us may have experienced healthy anger. Most readers will have been poorly served at some point in a shop or restaurant and will have complained or asked for a refund. This is an example of healthy anger, as we are able to assert our wishes without seeking to diminish the waiting staff or shopkeeper. If the client is unable to recall the experience of healthy anger, it may be necessary to teach them about the emotion and help them to see that life could be more fulfilling if they are not controlled by unhealthy anger. At times we have used metaphors such as the client simply being a puppet with someone else pulling the strings. The counsellor should then encourage the client to consider whether healthy anger would be a suitable goal for the client in addressing their problem or at least accepting it if there is nothing they can do to affect change.

The process for anger then follows the tasks specified in our Basic Guide section. Having established the A, C and emotional goal, the counsellor should use Socratic dialogue to identify the key inferences and evaluations and commence the disputation process.

15

Shame and Guilt

Shame and guilt are not usual subjects of individual attention within introductory CBT books, although the important work of Gilbert and his introduction of the compassionate mind approach (2007, 2009) has recently brought them more to the forefront. Presently, in diagnostic schedules, shame and guilt are usually symptoms of other problems, such as depression, obsessive-compulsive disorder and social anxiety. However, in CBC we consider them to be emotional problems in their own right and to be important enough to warrant further attention. We have grouped shame and guilt together because in terms of the emotional experiences they are very similar and produce similar arousal. Both emotions revolve around the commission of a misdeed or the omission of a deed. Where they differ is that shame occurs when we fall short in the eyes of others, and guilt does not require external scrutiny. However, both emotions, unlike depression, involve the individual feeling responsible for what has gone wrong and subsequently over-estimating the degree of responsibility.

The defining feature of shame is revealing some aspect that is judged by others to indicate a failure of the whole self in the eyes of the other, and then accepting this definition of the whole self. This is what Gilbert (2007) calls external and internal shame. The failure can be anything from doing something bad, being stigmatised, or believing that one differs from a norm of some kind (for example, being too short, overweight and so on). Guilt, however, does not necessitate the witness of the other, and is always defined by doing wrong to others (even when they do not know about the wrongdoing).

Key Elements in the CBC Model

Shame and Guilt at C in the ABC Model

The emotional experience of shame and guilt at C are often described by individuals as distinctly uncomfortable. Both carry with them a sense of having made a mistake, or committed a misdeed. As such, the individual feels that they have wronged, usually others, and their own standards. They are likely to feel uneasy with themselves and will typically seek ways to make the experience disappear. Both shame and guilt are considered to stem from a more basic human emotion of disgust (Power and Dalgleish, 1997). Therefore, they are both emotions of self-disgust, shame stemming from the disapproval of others (real or imagined) and accepting this disapproval as an evaluation of the whole self and guilt from disapproval by the self.

This can be considered further by reviewing some of our basic goals as humans. One of our goals is to seek affiliation with others. In so doing we want others to desire or value us and this in turn improves our social standing (Gilbert, 1992). However, when this social status is removed by being disapproved of or stigmatised, the result is shame. Therefore, it is perhaps no surprise that shame (the loss of our social status) is one of the main things about which we get ourselves anxious. Both shame and guilt are emotions of self-blame, and may be present even if we feel that we have been treated badly by others.

The primary action tendencies associated with shame are to hide, to escape the gaze of others, or avoid contact with those in front of whom we may have fallen short of our personal standards. These are urges to hide our head in the sand, or perhaps wishing that a hole would open up so that we could jump through. When we act on these action tendencies we rarely address the problem we have faced, as we feel too uncomfortable to face up to the event we experienced. The behavioural escape is also accompanied by a cognitive escape, where the individual tries hard not to think about what it is they feel shame about. This might take the form of distraction or seeking reassurance from others, but effectively this is an effort to cognitively distance themselves from the event. Unfortunately, the distraction achieved or reassurance provided rarely makes any great impact on the experience of shame. Therefore, the behavioural and cognitive efforts to escape are self-defeating as the individual fails to address the situational problem they have faced. Furthermore, often the efforts to escape lead to a higher probability of further shaming experiences as we seek to run away from being noticed. The healthy variant of shame is disappointment, because when we feel disappointed about ourselves in the scrutiny of others, we are intrinsically motivated to address the wrongdoing or the shortfall in our self.

The action tendencies associated with guilt are different from shame. Individuals have reported a desire to punish themselves, a desire to disclaim responsibility or deny any wrongdoing. Other action tendencies include a strong desire to promise that you will never make the same error again, or to beg for forgiveness. Self-punishment may take many forms and may be the infliction of punishment or the deprivation of pleasure. Cognitively, we might seek not to think about what it is that we did wrong, thereby trying to affectively avoid the emotion of guilt. Alternatively, we may seek to ameliorate the negative feelings with substances (such as drugs or alcohol).

The cognitive consequences of shame and guilt are to over-estimate shamefulness or guiltiness of the behaviour we engaged in. We therefore convince ourselves that we were right to feel shame or guilt because of how badly we acted, and these cognitive consequences perpetuate the experience of shame and guilt.

The As of Shame and Guilt in the ABC Model

The As of Shame
The As associated with shame involve experiences where an individual does something wrong in front of others or falls very short of one's personal standards in front of others and by which the others are thought to have judged the person critically. Shame is always concerned with some failure before the other. In order to generate the inferences and evaluations that lead to shame, however, we do not need other people to literally witness our wrongdoing, as sometimes we can feel shame when

we anticipate that others will discover what we have done. The mistakes, failures and misdeeds of the As of shame are usually very personal, and what one person may make themselves feel shame about another may not. Often, the things we are most likely to feel shame about are kept secret and we do not reveal them to others. However, there are also many times when we can act, often unintentionally, in ways that court the disapproval of others.

Sartre's (1957) comments on the generation of shame can be helpful when discussing the emotion with clients and trainees alike. In his analogy, Sartre beckons the reader to imagine spying through a keyhole on an individual who is undressing. It is not until our behaviour is observed that we feel shame (or possibly guilt).

Because as humans we are surrounded by others, either in reality or in our internal referencing to relationships, many of us have become adept at making ourselves feel shame. When other people are present and we observe them noticing our shortcomings then a humiliating shame may result. However, some of us are able to feel shame by imagining that something might be revealed. Consider for a moment the things you keep very private, perhaps rarely if ever share with other people. This secret might relate to some physical anomaly, a desire for an experience that we know is unusual and may be frowned upon. Now consider walking up to a stranger or a work colleague and revealing that secret. We are able to imagine ourselves into feeling shame.

The As of Guilt

For guilt, the As often take the form of an experience in which we have not followed our moral code. This may be that we have acted against our moral code, or omitted to act in accordance with it. Imagine feeling guilty after not taking the opportunity to intervene when you saw what you thought was a robbery in the street. Most of us take no pleasure in observing others in danger or being hurt. However, most of us are also aware of times when have-a-go heroes have been badly injured. Our moral code might drive us to act in such a way as to help the victim of the robbery, perhaps by summoning aid or running in to hold off the robber. However, statistics and research experiments demonstrate that very few people would actually take such action. Rather, we might omit to act in accordance with our moral code and feel guilty afterwards.

Similarly, we might (intentionally or otherwise) act in ways that cause pain, both physical and emotional, to those people that we care about. During a disagreement with a loved one (when we might well have been feeling unhealthy anger) we may recall having made a cruel or hurtful comment. This comment does not necessarily need to be contrary to our moral code in order for us to feel guilty; it is often enough to realise, or suspect, that an action we have taken has been a source of hurt or pain to another. As we reflect on what was said or done we might begin to feel guilt.

So far we have described As in guilt where it is probable that many people might concur with the moral code that has been broken or the act that has been omitted. However, this is not necessary for us to feel guilt. Take the example of the newly married husband who loves his wife dearly. It is possible that he may feel guilt if he notices himself having intentional or unintentional thoughts about another woman, perhaps as he passes one in the street. Therefore, internal events themselves may also be As for guilt.

The Bs of Shame and Guilt in the ABC Model

So far we have argued that shame and guilt are sufficiently similar that we can consider them together. However, it is when we come to consider the Bs of shame and guilt that we notice some significant, though subtle, differences. Most of these are differences in the type of inferences drawn in order to feel shame or guilt. The subsequent evaluations then follow a relatively similar pattern.

The Bs of Shame

We will start with considering the inferences associated with shame. The inferences all refer to the awareness of the behaviour or event that has been made public, or is imagined to have been made public. If we were unaware that the behaviour was in some way unacceptable or posed a threat to our social status we would not then proceed to draw inferences in that it would lead to shame. Therefore, the initial thoughts relate to the inferred impact or meaning of the behaviour on those who have seen it occur. For example, if you were making a presentation and could see people shaking their heads when you stumbled over a word or idea, the first set of inferences would be about what the audience thinks of your mistake. For example, 'They think I don't know what I'm talking about' or 'They think I'm terrible at public speaking' or 'They think I'm nervous'. The next inference stage is to make a conclusion about the thoughts of others. For example, 'They are right, I can't even present my ideas without stumbling and making mistakes'. Therefore at this stage of inferences, the perceived conclusion of the other is internalised and applied to the self. The final stage of inferences in shame is to tie this into one's personal standard and conclude that we have fallen short of it. For example, 'it is important for me that others don't see me make mistakes'. It is this combination of scrutiny (real, imagined or inferred) and the attribution of this being the responsibility of the individual that lead to the core evaluations that produce shame.

Alternatively, images can occur at B that can engender a shame response. Usually this relates to the previous example of others discovering a secret that we would not want them to know. Imagining this revelation, or the image of otherwise falling short of some personal standard, is often sufficient to activate the evaluations, and therefore it might be that no specific inferences are evident.

The inferences of shame usually stem from the evaluations. As we have said before, in therapy we would place the inferences before the evaluation, as the inferences effectively filter the experience of A. However, the inferences are driven by the evaluations and so they are heavily influenced by them. For example, if, as above, you were left feeling shame after making a mistake during a presentation that you observed was noticed and reacted badly to by the audience, your inferences about that experience will directly relate to the personal standard that you should not fall short of. Without the dogmatic assertion of this personal standard you are not likely to make the same inferential leaps. The personal standard is prototypically the same as the principle or rule that makes up a demand based evaluation. In general terms, the demand (should or must) associated with shame often follows the template of being found out or exposed as weak. For example, 'I hate it when people notice my flaws (whatever the flaw might be) and therefore I have to ensure that they never find them out'.

Two other evaluations are important in shame. The first is to catastrophise about falling short of the personal standard (which is usually the demand or should statement). This might take the form of 'it's terrible that people have found out X about me'. These evaluations simply magnify the harm done by the demand evaluation, suddenly making it all the more important never to be found out again. The final evaluation at B in shame is that of global self-rating. As in depression, this evaluation is nearly always present in shame. Typically, given that the individual sees themselves at fault for revealing their secret or falling short of their personal standard, global self-rating in shame takes the form of defining the self as weak, unlikeable or bad.

The Bs of Guilt

Inferences in guilt are linked to the behaviour undertaken at A. The inferences serve to begin the process of judgement of the individual about their behaviour. They do this by guiding the recognition that the deed was in fact wrong or bad in some way. Hence, the first stage of inference is the behaviour (or desire, wish, or thought) at A is not consistent with our social or moral code. Without this inference it is difficult to feel guilt. These inferences may take the form of 'I did a terrible thing', 'I know I was wrong to do that' and so on. The next stage of inferences relates to fault, responsibility and blame. If we thought that we had hurt somebody by our words or actions, we would not feel guilt unless we considered ourselves, and not the other person or some environment, responsible for that action. These are the inferences of self-blame. For example, 'I did that on purpose', 'That was my fault', 'I'm responsible for how they feel or what they did'. Remember, in these inferences the examination of the individual is internal; we do not need the scrutiny of others in order to feel guilt as this is a conclusion we reach all by ourselves.

The evaluations of guilt are similar to those of shame, albeit with some subtle differences. To begin with we have the assertion of the moral code. Typically this is expressed as an ought, but might also take the usual form of demands (musts, shoulds, have tos). We find that demanding oughts are more common because these relate to morality. When we think about our moral codes, we think about how we ought to act. These moral codes may at times be at odds with how we want to act, however, and that is often how we end up with feelings of guilt. Examples of oughts as demands include 'I ought to be kind to other people and therefore I have to be', 'I ought to be proper in my behaviour and therefore I have to be', 'I ought to honour my convictions and therefore I have to'. As with shame, these oughts form moral principles, and these moral principles drive the inferences that serve to judge our behaviour. Indeed, the moral principles filter our views of the world and our interactions with others.

The next evaluation follows logically from the ought. Here we tend to exaggerate how bad it was of us to compromise our moral code (our ought). This takes the form of seeing our actions at A as terrible, awful and catastrophic. The final evaluation again then follows on from there; if we have broken our moral code (which we ought, absolutely never to have done) and the result is so terrible, what does that tell us about the kind of person we are? Hence, the final evaluation is one of global self-rating. The global self-rating is a condemnation of the self for having acted so poorly. For example, 'I'm bad', 'I'm a horrible person', 'I'm no good'. It is these evaluations, rather than the inferences alone, that set up the emotional, behavioural and cognitive consequences of guilt.

Example ABCs of Shame and Guilt

Shame

A	B	C
Making an obvious mistake whilst giving a presentation	They (the audience) noticed that (inference) They think I don't know what I'm talking about (inference) They think I'm a complete fraud (inference) Maybe they're right, I never wanted to be revealed like that and I should have performed better (to my personal standard) (irrational evaluation) It's terrible that I made such a stupid mistake (irrational evaluation) It just proves I'm totally stupid/a fraud (irrational evaluation)	Shame (emotion) Desire to run out of the room (action tendency) Exaggerates the impact of the mistake (cognitive consequence)

FIGURE 15.1

Guilt

A	B	C
Saying harsh words during an argument with a loved one	She (or society) might think that was a horrible thing to say (inference) I have hurt their feelings, and that's my fault (inference) I absolutely ought to be caring towards those I love (irrational evaluation) It's awful that I acted like that (against my moral code) (irrational evaluation) It just proves I'm a bad person (irrational evaluation)	Guilt (emotion) Desire to beg for forgiveness (action tendency) Exaggerates the impact of the harsh words (cognitive consequence)

FIGURE 15.2

Core Treatment Goals for Shame and Guilt in CBC

In CBC we would consider shame and guilt to be central to many of the other types of emotional problems. Within the network of emotional problems (vicious cycles) we often find the presence of shame or guilt. We would argue that this is because the emotions of shame and guilt relate to how we should act and be in the eyes of ourselves and others. The problem is that as humans we are prone to making mistakes, misjudging situations, or being overwhelmed by other emotions that lead to us acting poorly (for example, anxiety and shame, and anger and guilt). Therefore, one of the core treatment goals for CBC is to acknowledge the likely presence of problems associated with shame and guilt in our clients. This is rather unusual in the CBT approach because shame and guilt are usually subsumed under other syndromes or diagnoses. We would again assert the importance of prioritising explicit work on these as emotional problems, as in the important recent developments by Gilbert (2007).

When considering how clients with shame or guilt problems present, it is important for the counsellor to recognise that these emotions generate distinctly uncomfortable experiences for the individual. In shame the action tendency and often the overt behavioural consequence is to hide away, become invisible or unnoticed. Therefore, in the counselling session, if these emotions are present the client will want to move quickly away from them. This might take the form of introducing other problems to deflect attention from the shame or guilt. It might also take the form of the individual berating themselves openly and this then leading to the counsellor also feeling stuck and not aware of where to go next in helping the client.

Once again, the first step in working with shame and guilt in CBC is to help the client to consider how else they might feel about the event at A. When working with shame we have found that clients readily agree to alternative emotional goals of embarrassment (which might simply be a less intense form of shame) or more appropriately, disappointment. This is because the experience of shame is inherently self-defeating. Imagine finding yourself in the scrutiny of others, feeling shame, and then being paralysed by the emotion, simply crumbling before them, the shame simply becomes a self-fulfilling prophecy. Therefore, clients readily accept the importance of establishing a means to helping them to feel differently about whatever they have ashamed themselves. Guilt, however, can be more difficult. As one of the cognitive consequences of guilt is to exaggerate the consequences of breaching our moral code, many clients who experience problems with guilt often conclude that there is no realistic alternative emotional response to having done such a bad deed (which itself is an inference and therefore open to disputation). Indeed, some clients believe that feeling guilt will help them to behave better in the future. Furthermore, guilt as an emotion is often described in rather positive terms, as it is seen to draw our attention to an error or bad deed. However, this is problematic as clients, and some researchers, fail to recognise that guilt leads to self-defeating behaviour and the healthy variant, remorse is what actually leads us to attend to the wrongs we may have committed. As such it becomes very important for the counsellor to help the client to understand how their guilt is self-defeating for them. In turn the counsellor can then help the client to consider how their healthy remorse might enable them to approach the problem better.

Once the inferences and evaluations have been assessed and the client is helped to see that by changing these cognitions, particularly the evaluations, they can help themselves to feel differently and therefore act in a less self-defeating way, the counsellor can begin the process of questioning the cognitions at B. There are numerous options here, as with other emotional problems, but we would recommend one strategy for shame and another for guilt.

In preparing to dispute the thoughts and beliefs in shame, it is worth considering how easily the client makes themselves feel ashamed. In our experience, most humans, and therefore clients, excel at making themselves feel ashamed. Therefore, they experience shame about many things. As a consequence, it might be rather time consuming and inelegant to address each inference that leads to shame. Rather, we would suggest beginning with a dispute of the evaluations that lead to shame. This becomes particularly relevant when we consider our previous point about the inferences stemming from the evaluations. Thus, if we change the evaluations, the inferences will simply dissipate. Although this is our preferred strategy in shame, we would also adjust this if we felt that the client was unable to grasp the role of the evaluations at first and so would focus on a specific example of shame and work on the inferences.

We might approach the cognitions of guilt in a different way. We have found that clients often make themselves feel guilty about specific events (though we accept that some clients are capable of generalising their guilt). We have also found that some counsellors, when beginning in CBC, tend to make an attempt to dispute the moral code of the client. We would see this as a grave error, not only because we are likely to lose the client's confidence, but also because CBC is not about changing the client's morality. Therefore, we would commence with helping the client to review and question their inferences. Here we want the client to reflect on whether their behaviour at A was wrong as they had previously concluded. In one of his famous demonstration sessions, Albert Ellis was working with a woman whose husband had committed suicide in front of her. She had tried to persuade him otherwise for over eight hours, until exhausted she told him to go ahead. He then hanged himself and she could not prevent it. She was feeling guilty because she blamed herself for his final act. Ellis carefully helped the client to consider whether her husband's suicide was her fault, or whether some other cause may have been responsible. In so doing, he helped her to alter the inferences that had been leading to her guilt.

Of course, there might be occasions when the client's inference that they did a bad thing was indeed correct. We need only to think of clients who feel guilty for having committed a criminal offence. In these circumstances, we would want to leave the conclusion about having done a bad thing relatively intact, as this would be appropriate in helping the client inhibit future bad behaviours, but we would still want to help them with their feelings of guilt as this will not help them in the future. Therefore, in such circumstances we would seek to address the evaluations in guilt first, disputing them as covered in the basic guide.

Evidently, in working with guilt, the counsellor will find themselves having to dispute the moral ought or principle of the client. Here we would promote caution. We do not want to help the client to fundamentally alter their morality, but we do want to help them become less distressed about having broken their moral code. In CBC, we would encourage the client to identify their moral rule (usually expressed as an ought). For example, 'I ought not hurt those I love'. Now, if we helped the client to accept a preferential belief at this stage, this might take the form 'I don't like hurting those I love, but I don't not have to'. In addition to being clumsy language that might be difficult for someone to grasp, we are also asking them to care less about hurting others. We do not see this as the point of counselling. Rather, we would help the client to uncover the hidden demand about their moral rule. This is complicated because in effect this represents a demand about a demand. So, if we have a client whose moral rule is 'I ought not hurt those I love', the hidden demand here is 'and I must always do as I ought (or else I'm a totally wicked person)'. It is this demand that leaves them trapped in guilt. Therefore it is this second demand that we would encourage them to change. This would then take the form of 'I ought not to hurt those I love and I really want to, but don't absolutely have to, do as I ought'. This preference maintains their moral rule but removes the demand that it always has to be observed. This allows the client to once again accept their humanity. After all, nearly all religious faiths assert moral rules, and anyone observing those faiths would want to follow those rules. However, humans being humans, we would argue that not one religious moral rule has been always observed all the time by everyone. Therefore, it is important for the client to accept the limits of their humanity, that they will make mistakes and only in this acceptance will they find the courage to learn from, rather than be paralysed by, their mistakes.

The next task for the counsellor in working with clients experiencing shame and guilt is to dispute the magnification beliefs (awful, terrible) and global self-rating. Of utmost importance here are the global self-rating beliefs. This is because in both shame and guilt, if we conclude that we are weak or bad (for having been seen to make a mistake, or having broken our moral code) we are more likely to continue to act in weak or bad ways. Therefore, the client needs to accept themselves despite their disapproval or bad behaviour.

Finally, we have found that there is a very powerful homework in working with shame. In CBT this homework might be found in books on behavioural experiments (Bennett-Levy et al., 2004), and in REBT this homework is called 'shame attacking' (see Chapter 7). The purpose of the behavioural homework for shame is to help the client act against their shame-based beliefs. We would only suggest this after the client has worked on disputing their beliefs, as to do so beforehand might only lead them to make themselves feel even more ashamed. There are countless examples of shame-attacking exercises, but it is best to tie this closely to their shame-based inferences and beliefs. Rather than having debilitating results, nearly everyone who engages in this finds it a liberating and rewarding experience, and above all learns they can accept disapproval.

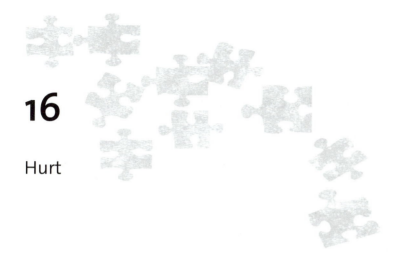

16

Hurt

Hurt has been characterised as the neglected emotion (Leary and Springer, 2000) and little is written about it within the cognitive behavioural literature outside of REBT. We believe this is because feelings of hurt are often subsumed within depression. We find this too inelegant when working with clients where their emotional problem is clearly one of hurt rather than depression. In CBC we consider the behavioural and cognitive consequences of hurt to be very different to those of pure depression and this is another reason why we have dealt with this emotion separately.

The hurt to which we refer is emotional, rather than physical, although it can be as acute and aversive as the physical pain of bodily injury, and it sometimes lasts far longer. It is an interpersonal emotion, in that our feelings rarely feel hurt by the actions of inanimate objects. Most of the academic work on hurt has been carried out by social psychologists, and research findings support the central role of perceived 'relational devaluation' and disassociation in hurt feelings (Hareli and Hess, 2008). For example, Leary et al. (1998) found that the magnitude of victims' hurt feelings correlated highly with the degree to which they felt that the perpetrator accepted versus rejected them. The types of hurtful events identified all appeared to involve real, implied or imagined social disassociation. Some of the hurtful episodes involved events that conveyed that the perpetrator desired to ignore, avoid or exclude the victim. Similarly, episodes classified as betrayal involved disassociation in which the victim was rejected for another person.

One of the few commentaries in the CBT literature is that of Dryden (2007) who provides a summary of hurt from the REBT perspective, and which is consistent with the social psychological research literature.

Key Elements in the CBC Model

Hurt at C in the ABC Model

Although many clients will often say they are 'upset' when usually they mean hurt, we have observed hurt to be one of the most painful emotions experienced by clients. It is frequently accompanied by a sense of being overwhelmed by the emotion, and often manifests in tears and sobbing. We have also noticed from training other therapists, that when clients begin to describe their experience of hurt the emotional arousal is almost immediate. In session they will become tearful and act as if they are wounded.

One of the primary-action tendencies and behaviours associated with hurt is sulking. Sulking is a form of withdrawal, where the individual becomes more silent and aloof. This process is effectively a withdrawal from that which has hurt them. However, the sulking behaviour is self-defeating. Whilst withdrawn in this manner, the individual is dependent on the other person making the first move to affect reparation. Therefore, the withdrawal into sulking serves to disconnect communication with the other person. Dryden (2007) notes that sulking also has the purpose of regaining a sense of power, as if by sulking the hurt individual seeks to gain the moral or actual high ground. We also concur with Dryden in that sulking is an overt punishment of the other, to demonstrate just how badly they have treated you and that sulking can be used to attempt to evoke a more caring response or apology from the other.

The primary cognitive consequence of hurt is to exaggerate how unfairly you have been treated. As such this tends to lead to further feelings of hurt at a meta-emotional level, whereby having seen just how badly someone has treated us, we simply amplify the feelings of hurt. Because, having been hurt, we exaggerate the unfairness of the behaviour of the other, we become even less motivated to approach the other in conciliation without losing further face. If we do approach it, it might be to accuse the other of acting so unfairly (which will no doubt also lead to further emotional problems of anger). Such an act, when hurt, is one of illusory protection and self-defence because if we do this when we feel hurt we are likely to be hurt all over again if the other stands their ground. There is also a common side-effect of sulking, in that other people do not enjoy spending time in the company of one who is sulking. Thus, we might notice others distancing themselves from us, which only then confirms how unfairly we are being treated and the hurt cycle is perpetuated.

The healthy alternative of hurt is sorrow. Sorrow remains a negative emotion, in keeping with having been treated badly by another, but does not lead to self-defeating behaviours in the same way as hurt does. Rather, when we feel sorrow we are able to consider the behaviour of the other person and think about how best to accept what has happened or act in ways that will reduce future exposure to such bad behaviour. If we feel sorrow after being treated badly by another we are more likely to be willing to make the first move, rather than punish the other by passive resentment and sulking. Also, a striking difference between hurt and sorrow is the preparedness we feel to consider our own role in how others have treated us. In hurt we are subdued by our exaggeration of the unfairness of it all, too immersed in this to reflect on whether our behaviour was a contributing factor. Whereas when we feel sorrow, this is not the case.

The As of Hurt in the ABC Model

The events that eventually lead to hurt are usually either in the past or present. Although it is possible to imagine ourselves feeling hurt at some point in the future, rarely is this sufficient to bring about the full emotional experience of hurt. Hurt about past events suggests that the hurt has been maintained by the individual (most probably by the cognitive consequence of exaggerating the unfairness of the behaviour).

The events that lead to hurt tend to be associated with our interpersonal relationships. Usually, we are most hurt by those we care most for, although it remains possible for us to feel hurt after interacting with a complete stranger. What is far less likely is that we feel hurt outside of human interaction. If a shelf suddenly collapses, or a computer crashes, or a car does not start, we are highly unlikely to make ourselves feel hurt in response.

The interpersonal events about which we usually feel hurt include:

*   Being criticised by another person
*   Being used or abused by another person

- Being rejected by another person
- Being betrayed by another person
- Being excluded or ignored by another person

As can be seen from this list, all the As of hurt relate to our interaction with others. We would posit that the above adverse events are notable for humans because of one or two of our basic goals in life. Social interaction and remaining cohesive with our social domain are crucial to us in our daily lives. Hence, our goals are about maintaining these social relationships. However, when a person, to whom we are relating, acts badly towards us, this threatens the safety of our goal and therefore threatens our safety. Thus, the goal of maintaining a healthy relationship with that other person is interrupted.

The Bs of Hurt in the ABC Model

Inferences

The first set of inferences in hurt relate to how the other person has behaved. We might be able to readily observe behaviours and hear the comments made by others, but in order to feel hurt, we need to categorise the behaviours or comments as negative. For example, if a loved one reveals that they have betrayed us, our first inference relates to the categorisation of the behaviour as betrayal. The same paradigm applies to criticism, use, abuse and so on. Until we define the behaviour as harmful to us we do not establish a process that leads to hurt. The categories suggested by Dryden (2007) include being neglected, being under-appreciated, being excluded and being deprived. We might also add to this list inferences about being used by the other person or abused.

Second, we need to determine whether or not we deserved to be treated in the way that we were. For hurt to occur, the inference that the other's unfair treatment (inference 1) was undeserved or uncalled for is necessary. Here we are filtering out our responsibility. Where we have no sense of deserving how the other has treated us, we are not responsible, and this sets us up to react with hurt. Commonly with clients, it is possible to use this inference to help understand the emotional response. For example, a colleague who was overlooked by their supervisor at work, by not being asked to apply for a job working directly with them, described feeling upset by this. When asked whether they had done anything wrong to suggest why the supervisor had overlooked them, they responded vehemently that they did not deserve to be treated in the way that they were (with the kind permission of our colleague, we have expanded on this as the example ABC below). Therefore, we have found the question 'Did you deserve to be treated like this?' a direct and effective method of establishing that the emotional problem is hurt.

Evaluations

In the REBT literature, there is a distinction drawn between ego hurt and non-ego hurt (the former involving an evaluation of global self-rating, and the latter involving low frustration tolerance). In our experience, however, such a distinction is usually theoretical rather than reflective of many clients' actual experience. In CBC we note that there are three evaluations that are central to the experience of hurt.

The first evaluation is a demand. Like the demands in other unhealthy emotions, the demand in hurt entails a reciprocal relationship with the inferences about the event. By establishing the rule about how one should be treated by others the demand simply forces the dichotomous thinking that is not sufficiently deduced from the inference alone. Therefore, the demands relate to the inferences about the actions of the other. These might be relatively simple in their form, such as 'You must not betray me' or 'You must not criticise me'. Yet the more the powerful demand lies just below these more superficial ones, and takes the form 'You must not treat me in ways that I don't deserve'. This is more powerful because it further drives the individual towards hurt after their two inferences (being treated unfairly and not deserving it).

The second evaluation common to hurt is low frustration tolerance. Because most of the events at A are inferred to be unfair as they are not deserved, the common form of low frustration tolerance (i.e. 'its not fair') is often present. Here, the evaluation is that the experience (the undeserved maltreatment) was so unfair that it was not bearable.

The third and final evaluation in hurt is global self-rating (see also Hareli and Hess, 2008). If someone treats us badly even though we did not deserve being treated that way what does that tells us about us as a person? We strongly feel that this element of defining the self in the eyes of others has crept into the cognitive tradition from an existential perspective and we find this existential aspect compelling when attempting to understand the cognitive processes in hurt. We arrive a global self-rating in hurt by concluding that to the other person we must be less than human, insignificant, bad and of no value (otherwise they would not have so readily excluded or denigrated us). We then determine that they are right, that in fact we are no good, subhuman and undeserving of better treatment.

Example ABC

A	B	C
Not being invited to apply for a position working alongside supervisor	They are overlooking me (inference) I don't deserve to be overlooked (inference) I should not be treated in this way (evaluation) I can't stand being treated so unfairly (evaluation) They must think I'm useless and they are right (evaluation)	Hurt (emotion) Sulking withdrawal, waiting for the supervisor to make the first move (action tendency) Exaggerates the unfairness of being overlooked (cognitive consequence)

FIGURE 16.1

Core Treatment Goals for Hurt in CBC

In our introduction to this chapter, we described hurt as a very painful emotional experience. Therefore, it is of utmost importance to recognise this and communicate this understanding to the client. Without this recognition, clients might seek to protect themselves against feeling hurt and express the problem in terms of anger or some other emotional difficulty. This is not because they are wilfully evasive, but rather because they do not wish to re-experience the pain associated with the hurt. Also clients may view their experience of hurt as a weakness, and fearing the disapproval of the counsellor they became anxious about the prospect of revealing themselves and then feeling ashamed about feeling hurt. Unfortunately, in order to effectively uncover their thinking process the counsellor will need the client to experience the feelings of hurt, as only then will the core evaluations be accessible. In the absence of the emotion the client might simply rationalise their experience, appear to have accepted their lot and leave counselling without any real benefit. By acknowledging the presence of the painful experience to the client, the counsellor is making it safer for the client to fully express their feelings of hurt.

Associated with the overt use of empathy as described above (and see Basic Guide), we would caution the counsellor to follow the client's experience and description of that experience. No matter how trivial the event might seem to the counsellor, the client is hurting themselves about it and the counsellor should not betray their own efforts to help the client by seeking to minimise or explain away the behaviour of the other in the client's problem.

One of the major goals for CBC in hurt is to help the client recognise that their hurt feelings lead them to further self-defeating behaviours and thoughts. These in turn prolong the experience of hurt and therefore only elongate the misery of the client. In doing this, the counsellor is attempting to motivate the client to identify a healthy alternative emotion. Dryden (2007) uses the term sorrow as the healthy variant of hurt, and we have adopted that term here. However, we also recognise that many clients might view this as a superficial effort to replace one word with another. Indeed, in many individual lexicons, the phrases hurt and sorrow might be interchangeable. Therefore, when negotiating the emotional goal with the client, we are always keen to express that sorrow is healthy because it can help us to accept what cannot be changed and to recover or to set about change in a more active way. As a shorthand, therefore, and to prevent the confusion of the client, we might preface hurt and sorrow with 'healthy' and 'unhealthy' respectively.

Clients often find it difficult to generalise from one experience of hurt or sorrow to another. Therefore, whilst they might be able to experience and act on sorrow in one set of circumstances, we cannot expect them to simply conjure this information to mind when attempting to resolve another specific set of difficulties. Here, therefore, we often find helpful to teach the client about the self-defeating nature of hurt and the more self-enhancing (and relationship-enhancing) sorrow. At this point we also avoid phrases such as accepting what has happened, and prefer terms such as recovery. In recovering we are able to live a more fulfilling life no matter what impairments we carry with us.

The disputation of beliefs in hurt follows the processes defined in our Basic Guide section. However, we would seek to emphasise to core outcomes of the disputation process. First, is whether the unfair behaviour of the other is bearable and worth bearing. Here we might negotiate with the client that by learning how to bear the unfair behaviour of others we are left in a more courageous and resolute position than if we assert that we cannot bear it. Our subsequent courage might then affect protest or further introspection to deal more effectively with the problem behaviour of the other. Second, following on from the existential nature of global self-rating in hurt, we would encourage the client to consider what actually changed about them as a person when the other person treated them badly. Here we are seeking to construct a barrier between being defined as a person by the views of others. In actual fact, when others treat us badly, we do not change, we feel different, but our self is not altered. We are simply choosing to redefine ourselves according to this new set of (arbitrary) criteria.

17

Envy

In CBC practice we have noticed that many clients seem stuck and unable to address some of their other problems because of a hidden envy and therefore we find envy often presenting as a meta-emotional problem. However, we have worked with numerous clients where envy has been a particular, primary, problem, though it is often disguised as anger or depression, we believe because people find it difficult to acknowledge their envy. However, there are few if any CBT models of envy and it is not generally covered in introductory texts. We will therefore seek to introduce the reader to how envy can be formulated and worked with from the CBC position.

Envy that is healthy is a relatively common human emotion and possibly is used by advertisers to encourage us to buy products in a 'you too could have a life like this' subtly underpinning messages to buy lifestyle products, cars, houses, and so on. Healthy envy therefore encapsulates our desire to have what others already have and motivates us to work hard towards achieving what we desire. This is not the envy we would choose to address in CBC.

There is an English proverb about envy that we feel summarises the CBC position well: 'Envy shoots at others but wounds itself.' In the following sections we elaborate on the application of the CBC model of envy and when to consider this problem with clients.

Key Elements in the CBC Model

Envy at C in the ABC Model

The emotional experience of envy has received considerable attention within the philosophical literature – indeed as far back as Aristotle – and is also a feature of other psychological models (such as Bowlby's attachment theory, 1969). However, much of the previous discourse focuses on how we come to feel envy (usually a combination of As and Bs) rather than what envy actually feels like. This is rather peculiar as we are aware not only from our own experiences but also based on the frequency with which clients describe the experience of envy, that many of us will automatically be familiar with the feelings associated with envy. When envy is healthy and benign we are motivated to strive to better ourselves or achieve some coveted object or good. However, when envy is unhealthy and invidious we are frequently paralysed by it, feel miserable, unhappy and bereft. We might also pity ourselves at our lack of good fortune. In this sense, we posit that unhealthy, invidious envy renders us passive and undermines our basic goals in life, or lead to a desire to maliciously bring down the individual we envy (van de Ven et al., 2009). Furthermore, unhealthy envy may circulate in our psychological backdrop, undermining our efforts to help or better ourselves.

As well as undermining our other efforts, envy can also be experienced as a real emotional pain. This might take the form that something profound is missing from us, and consequently there is a sense of emptiness and hollowness where the thing we covet belongs. This psychological pain may often be misrepresented as or subsumed by depression, particularly given the likelihood of a passive and embittered response. However, rather than feeling as if we are nothing, empty and hollow, which is the core emotional process of pure depression, envy has with it a strong sense of what is missing, that we are not hollow, just that we are not whole.

When we envy something that we feel is integral to our sense of self, our future prospects and status, or our general well-being, the emotion rarely dissipates. In clients we find that envy is almost parasitic, clinging to other emotional problems and weakening their resolution for effort and a commitment to change. This is often represented in sessions by questions such as 'Why should I always have to work so hard when others have it so much easier than me?' This 'poor me undeservedly lucky them' position is often chronic. As the Greek philosopher Heraclitus (540–480 BC) put it, 'Our envy always lasts longer than the happiness of those we envy'.

The action tendencies and behaviours associated with envy are perhaps what classified it as a sin in the Christian faith. In unhealthy, invidious envy it is not enough that we do not have what we covet but we are motivated to spoil or reduce the pleasure this brings to our rival. Therefore, our primary action tendencies might include efforts to undo the good fortune of the other (van de Ven et al., 2009). Here, we use the term good fortune as a euphemism for the As of envy. These action tendencies might lead to verbal put-downs of the other's success or luck, a denigration of the other for only having what they have because of some morally inferior reason, or direct efforts to outdo the other just to achieve a sense of craved superiority.

The cognitive consequences of envy are conclusions about the value of the goods that the other has and we do not (the goods may be actual, such as possessions, or based on lifestyle and status, such as good fortune). Imagine you envied a colleague at work who had just been promoted. Prior to the promotion you may have thought of your colleague as an equal, and as such they have bested you. If your envy was healthy and benign you might be motivated to draw attention to your strengths and seek a promotion for yourself. However, if you experience an unhealthy and invidious envy, you may feel that there is little that can be actually done to outdo your colleague and might therefore conclude that their promotion was more a curse than a blessing for them. This process reveals the cognitive consequences of envy as we seek to put down, diminish, belittle and knock their achievement and their future role. An alternative type of cognitive consequence is a conclusion that the other only achieved their good fortune because of some morally inferior reason. In other words we might conclude that had they been compared point for point to you they would not have deserved it, and therefore there must be some other reason for their promotion over you. Here we might further conclude that they may have used flirtation, bribery, blackmail or some other deviant means to get one over on you. Therefore, the cognitive consequences are either a denigration of what others have or a smear campaign about how they got it. Neither of these are likely to increase your own chance of promotion.

The As of Envy in the ABC Model

The fundamental A of envy is the observation that others have something which you desire. They might possess some object, relationship or apparent good fortune, or may at the very least not experience the difficulties you have. These may take the form of specific events, such as the example of the promotion of a work colleague above, or maybe something more general about the lifestyles and status afforded by those we consider well-off. What is fundamental about the As of envy is that the other possesses goods (be they objects, relationships, some trait or characteristic, or status) which the client lacks, and this lack conflicts with the basic goal of the individual to experience happiness, or not to experience misery. Consider the child who hankers for the toy of another child. They might tell their parents that without the toy they will be miserable and bored. It is this combination of the coveted object, whether that is a possession or experience, together with the sense that life is somehow lesser without it that establish the theme of As of envy in the ABC model.

Where the As of envy are a little more complex is when we perceive that others do not have the difficulties that we face. A depressed or angry client might be paralysed further by their envy that others do not have to work as hard to get on in life. Therefore, one of the other common forms of A in envy is another emotional problem and in this sense envy would be considered a meta-emotional problem.

The Bs of Envy in the ABC Model

Inferences

The inferences made in envy are closely associated with the observations made at A. The first stage of the inferences is the conclusion that someone else has something good that the individual lacks. This might simply be a fitting statement of the desire for the object, trait, relationship or status. But it then goes on to infer that we lack this object. This is usually an inference that is comparative or competitive in its construction, for example 'They have a better life *than* me'. This is more than observation, because we cannot possibly know everything about the life of the other.

The next construction of our inferences is that our own life would be better if we were to have the coveted object. This inference might take the form 'If only I had that [object] my life would be better/easier/more fulfilling'. This inference goes beyond the available data because we truly have no way of knowing what impact the possession of the object might have, other than perhaps resolving our envy in the short term. Hence, this second stage of inference relates to a prediction of how our life would be improved if we had what our rival possessed.

Evaluations

The first of the irrational evaluations of envy follows on from the inference about the difference in possession and the prediction that life would be better if the difference were to be resolved. Thus the individual establishes a rule about this difference. The rule, as in other emotions, takes the form of a rigid demand. When spoken aloud, this might emerge as 'I shouldn't have to go without that which I want'. Obviously, this might take a more specific form dependent on what is being coveted, but that structure suffices to explain the rigid rules that lead to envy.

The second evaluation is an extreme negative appraisal of the difference. This follows a form of low frustration tolerance. Fundamentally, if, as we have argued, envy is based upon the inferred difference between one and others, and this difference flouts the rigid rule about having to have what one desires or covets (or one would never be able to be happy or get better), then it follows that the continued absence of the coveted object would not be bearable. This evaluation serves to reinforce the rigidity of the demand rule, because if we cannot bear being without that which we covet, the demand that we absolutely should have it is magnified.

The final evaluation of envy is the appraisal of the self given the absence of the object. Here our sense of self is enveloped by the superiority of the other for having the object we covet. As we see them as so better-off for the difference, we evaluated our lacking of the object as intrinsic to our sense of self-worth. Therefore, in CBC terms we globally rate ourselves for being lesser by the absence of the object. So, if an individual covets the trait of another (for example, being physically attractive), they demand that they should have what they covet, that life is too hard without it, and that they are ugly, worthless or wholly depreciated without it. Alternatively, at times we have worked with clients who merge their sense of self into existing only in the shadow of that which they desire. As such, when they observe the absence of the object they desire, they conclude that they are effectively nothing, or a non-being, without it.

The evaluations explained above are those associated with unhealthy envy. The evaluations that lead to healthy, benign envy are more rational and helpful to the individual. The demand is replaced by a preference, for example 'I would love to have what I desire, but I don't need it'; the evaluation of low frustration tolerance by one of high frustration tolerance: 'Life might be more difficult without that which I want, but I will be able to bear that life and it would be worth bearing.' The global self-rating is replaced by unconditional acceptance of the self: 'My immediate comfort might be detracted from by not having what I want, but this does not define me as a person, my worth is not dependent on having what I want.'

Example ABC

A	B	C
Colleague at work gets promoted ahead of me	They have been luckier than me (inference) If only I had their good fortune my life would be easier (inference) I deserve and therefore absolutely should have as much luck as them (evaluation) I can't stand not having the luck I want (evaluation) Without good fortune I'm forever stuck and worthless (evaluation)	Envy (emotion) Desire to undermine the achievement of the other (action tendency) They only got lucky because the boss fancies them (cognitive consequence)

FIGURE 17.1

Core Treatment Goals for Envy in CBC

As we stated at the beginning of the problem of invidious, unhealthy envy may be more prevalent in counselling and therapy than might be immediately apparent. We have occasionally found that clients who seem stuck, seemingly unable to affect any changes in other emotional problems despite understanding what to do and why to do it. At such times, clients' might reveal that their lack of change is due to not working hard enough because of problems associated with envy. Therefore, when considering envy in CBC we recognise that envy might be rare as the initial presenting problem, but may undermine progress on other emotional problems, and so it is important to give this attention, particularly when clients seem to be making slower than expected progress. In particular, this might be manifest when the client repeatedly fails to do homework assignments that they accept would be helpful to them. At such times the counsellor should be mindful of the role envy might play. For example, a client might not expend the required effort because they envy those people who do not have problems like them or have an apparently easier life.

Once envy is identified as a problem, one of the counsellor's first tasks will be to consider whether the envy is healthy or unhealthy. We have found that clients benefit from reflecting on whether their envy leads them to act in self-defeating ways. If they do, we recommend inviting the client to name this emotion as invidious envy. If, however, their envy leads to self-enhancing behaviours that do not impinge on the lives of others, we recommend inviting clients to call this healthy negative emotion, benign envy. Most clients are readily able to identify past experiences of benign envy, where they have coveted some object, trait, skill or status that they have worked hard towards achieving. A common example is learning to drive. Clients will be able to recall a time when they could not drive and perhaps benignly envied those who could. At such times we might ask the client to recall how they acted. Did they diminish the driving skill of others? Did they conclude that people only passed their test out of good fortune? Mostly clients will state that they took driving lessons and worked hard to pass their test. This helps establish the difference between invidious envy, which never helps the individual, and benign envy, which helps them work hard towards a specific goal.

The next task for the counsellor and client is then to identify the object that is envied. In our ABC model, this is the process of identifying the A. This can be rather obvious, particularly if it relates to a possession, as clients are able to readily name the object. However, when the invidious envy is associated with some trait, or aspect of another person's life, the object that is envied can be more difficult to identify. Here it is helpful to make use of model-driven hypotheses about the A, accessed through the inferences and evaluations. For example, if the client is finding it difficult to describe the envied object, which might be a trait or something subtle, then questions such as 'And what is it you are finding is so unfair?' might enable the counsellor to tentatively guide the client towards the identification of the A.

Once the C, the emotional goal, and the A have been established the counsellor should then begin the Socratic questioning process to help the client elicit the thoughts and beliefs, at B, that led to the envy. If the inferences, as is quite typical, take the form of Negative Automatic Thoughts, these should be readily accessible to the client. From here the counsellor can then use an inference chain, or downward ladder, technique to identify the further inferences and evaluations. We find it helpful to use the emotion to drive this process. Hence, questions such as 'And what about that do you feel envious?' might be useful. By driving the process using the emotion, the evaluations should be more readily identified.

Once the inferences and evaluations leading to envy have been identified, the process of considering alternatives can begin. Here, the counsellor is aiming to help the client establish more rational, functional thoughts and beliefs that might help them to feel benign rather than invidious envy. In envy we might give equal weight to the disputation of inferences and evaluations, as the inferences are often quite general. In example ABC above, the inference 'they have been luckier than me' usually relates to the luck of the other in a domain seen as highly pertinent to the client. However, this domain is yet another example of an arbitrary criterion that the client has focused on. Here, we might help the client to be more specific about the precise nature of the good fortune. For example, the colleague might have been fortunate in their promotion, but they might not be so lucky in other areas of their life. Indeed, their luck itself has attracted negative views about them as a person from the individual. We might then encourage the client to develop alternative hypotheses about how the promotion might have been achieved; for example, it might have come about because of the colleague's efforts at work, or their ability to have their good work noticed. This process is important because it also shines a light on behavioural consequences the client might be able to adopt when they can begin to experience benign envy and work towards achieving their own goal, such as being promoted. The global self-rating, low frustration tolerance and demanding rule can be readily disputed as suggested in the Basic Guide section.

Finally, if envy exists as a meta-emotional problem to other emotional difficulties, it will be worth the counsellor frequently checking on their progress in working towards benign envy over invidious envy. This is important because the self-defeating nature of invidious envy makes it rather easy to slip back in to. This can happen if the rival or object suddenly changes. For example, a client who realises that they need to work hard on changing their attitude to achieve benign rather than invidious envy, might develop a new rival, the counsellor, which could start a new problem with envy. One client revealed this by remarking, 'This all seems to come so easily to you; maybe you don't have it as hard as I do'. This could lead to ruptures in the therapeutic alliance and the counsellor will need to be ready to notice and address this.

18

Concluding Remarks

In writing this second edition, we have had to maintain a disciplined focus – on the tasks that the counsellor needs in order to maximise his or her effectiveness in delivering CBC for a range of mild-to-moderate psychological problems. This has meant excluding much that we would have liked to have included, but which would have turned this slim practitioner guide into a mammoth tome that would probably stay on the shelf rather than in the counsellor's bag!

For example, before even beginning CBC with a new client, there are many issues to be considered beyond the basics that we have covered, and for which the counsellor needs to consult elsewhere for guidance – from colleagues, from resources and guidelines within the service the counsellor may work or provide input, and from publications. There are the complex issues concerning suicide risks to the clients themselves or risk of harm to others, including the counsellor; issues concerning personality disorders or litigation complications where the problem presented may not be the genuine one that the person is seeking help for; issues concerning physical health problems, and other complex problems which require the involvement of a medical or psychiatric team or home-treatment team and would be hazardous or inappropriate for an individual counsellor to take on alone.

Third Wave CBT and Recent Developments

Another major area of interest that we have had to exclude is the newer developments in CBT. Even 'standard' or basic CBT has evolved with such stunning rapidity since our first edition that it has been challenging enough to cover some of the key areas in our integrative CBC, where we have confined ourselves to the inspirational models of the founding fathers, Beck and Ellis, and the developments that have come out of but are largely encompassed within these models.

The newer, 'third wave' approaches and other recent developments move beyond our remit, but are also well provided for by their own practitioner guides. Although beyond the remit of our book to be included in any depth, we nonetheless have drawn upon them where they facilitate our integrative CBC model, and believe our guide provides the fundamental building blocks necessary for more fully engaging some of these exciting newer applications and for undergoing training in them.

Some of the third wave approaches can be grouped together as advocating a move from mainly targeting the content of dysfunctional cognitions to changing the relationship with them. This key idea was already being advocated by Beck in his early formulations. For example, Beck (1976) described *decentring* as the ability of a person to examine his automatic thoughts as psychological phenomena rather than as identical to reality. Decentring involves being able to make the distinction between 'I believe' and 'I know'. 'The ability to make this distinction is of critical importance in modifying those sectors of the patient's reactions that are subject to distortion' (Beck, 1976, pp. 243).

Many psychologists recognise the concept of decentring as key to the third wave approach. Indeed, although emerging from different theoretical frameworks, the third wave therapies tend to follow a final common pathway, of which decentring is a key concept and the first step in the process.

Mindfulness Based Cognitive Therapy (MBCT)

Segal et al. (2002) point out that the traditional cognitive therapy approach to depression had its effects through changing the *content* of depressive thinking, but '... we realised that it was equally possible that when successful, this treatment led implicitly to changes in patients' *relationships* to their negative thoughts and feelings' (Segal et al., 2002, p. 38). They noticed patients switched to a perspective within which thoughts and feelings could be seen as passing events in the mind. This insight led to a fundamental shift in approach. Rather than seeing decentring as one of a number of things going on in cognitive therapy, it was now seen as central. This shift could protect people with a history of depressive relapse from future depression.

Prevention of recurrent depression can be achieved by teaching 'mind management' skills that enable the person to disengage from depressive thought patterns. This approach led to the development of mindfulness-based cognitive therapy (MBCT; Segal et al., 2002). It was adopted from a method developed by Kabat-Zinn (1990) as the method by which patients would be taught how to decentre from their negative thoughts, to see them simply as just thoughts, freeing them from the distorted reality they created and which led to depressive relapse. MBCT enables the individual to radically change the relationship with, rather than content of, negative thoughts and feelings. The non-judgemental, present moment, focus of mindfulness enables disengagement from dysfunctional mind states.

Metacognitive Therapy (MCT)

Like MBCT, Metacognitive Therapy (MCT; Wells, 2009) does not advocate challenging the content of negative automatic thoughts or traditional schemas. In contrast, the metacognitive approach focuses on mental processes of thinking style, attending and controlling cognition. Adrian Wells, the founder of MCT states '... in CBT disorder is caused by the content of cognition but in MCT disorder is caused by the way thinking processes are controlled and the style they take. Content *is* important in MCT but it is the content of metacognition rather than the content of cognition that counts' (Wells, 2009, p. 651).

Treatment is focused at the metacognitive level without the need to challenge the content of negative automatic thoughts or schemas. Patients are helped to know both what to do in response to threat and negative thoughts; and also how best to do it. Metacognitive programmes or 'how-to' knowledge are shaped through experiencing different types of relationships with cognition and through manipulating cognitive processes such as the control of attention and worry. MCT therefore incorporates techniques such as attention training, which is one type of detached and situational attentional refocusing to modify and develop the necessary procedural or 'how to' (i.e. experiential) metacognitions (Wells, 2009).

Acceptance and Commitment Therapy (ACT)

Acceptance and Commitment Therapy (ACT; Hayes et al., 1999) follows a similar final common pathway to the others, particularly the employment of mindful acceptance. However, ACT is derived from a fundamentally different and earlier heritage than the other third wave therapies, namely radical behaviourism.

ACT differs from traditional CBT in that rather than trying to teach people to control their thoughts, feelings, sensations, memories and other private events, people are taught to 'just notice', accept, and embrace their private events, especially previously unwanted ones. ACT helps the individual get in contact with a transcendent sense of self known as 'self-as-context' or the conceptual 'I' – the 'I' that is always there observing and experiencing and yet distinct from one's thoughts, feelings, sensations and memories. ACT commonly employs six core principles to help clients develop psychological flexibility:

1 Cognitive defusion: Learning to perceive thoughts, images, emotions and memories as what they are, not what they appear to be.
2 Acceptance: Allowing them to come and go without struggling with them.
3 Contact with the present moment: Awareness of the here and now, experienced with openness, interest and receptiveness.
4 Observing the self: Accessing a transcendent sense of self, a continuity of consciousness which is changing.
5 Values: Discovering what is most important to one's true self.
6 Committed action: Setting goals according to values and carrying them out responsibly.

Dual Representation Approach

Brewin (1989) and Brewin et al. (1996) proposed dual representations in memory of emotional experiences as the minimum cognitive architecture within which the complex relationship between emotion and cognition could be understood. One was knowledge gained through the unconscious parallel processing of their responses to aversive situations, stored in situationally accessible memories SAMs, the other knowledge is gained through the more limited conscious experience of such situations, and stored in verbally accessible memories SAMs. Whereas verbally accessible knowledge can in principle be deliberately interrogated and retrieved, situationally accessible knowledge can only be retrieved automatically when environmental input matches features of the stored memories. In this dual representation theory, both kinds of knowledge can give rise to maladaptive emotions and behavior.

Dual representation theory and the other multi-level theories of this type (e.g. SPAARS, ICS) have been influential in *integrating* conditioning-based approaches to learning and therapy (as in flashbacks in PTSD) and cognitive-based approaches (as in cognitive restructuring of 'hotspots' in flashbacks in PTSD), in the conduct of CBT interventions. Trauma and trauma-type images encoded in SAMs are accessed via re-experiencing and then modified by and re-introduced following conventional cognitive therapy. This approach, first developed for PTSD, is now being widely applied to other anxiety disorders and depression and is one of the most vigorous growth areas of CBT currently (e.g. Butler et al., 2008; Grey, 2009; Stopa, 2009).

Compassionate Mind Training

From his evolutionary psychology-based 'social mentality theory' Paul Gilbert has developed a form of cognitive intervention called Compassionate Mind Training (CMT; Gilbert, 2007), which is aimed at helping depressed clients overcome particular types of negative automatic thoughts that were resistant to basic CBT. These were self-attacking thoughts that produced enduring shame and associated patterns of dysfunctional behaviour. CMT aims to help those with internal shame, self-criticism and self-condemnation, develop compassion towards themselves and thus reduce or eliminate their feelings of shame.

Schema Therapy

Schema Therapy (Young et al., 2003) draws on a wide range of therapy schools as well as cognitive therapy, and was originally developed for personality disorder problems, particularly borderline personality disorder, but has been applied to other problems such as depression. Schema Therapy ultimately seeks to replace maladaptive schemas by more healthy schemas. Maladaptive schemas, according to Young, are defined as and relate mainly to the lack of basic emotional needs in childhood and a lack of appropriate relationships, bonds, and behaviours of the parents, caretakers and others involved in the life of a growing child. One of the experiential techniques involves helping the client relive a traumatic interaction from childhood in order to activate a key maladaptive schema. The therapist then enters the childhood scene, bonds with the child through partial reparenting, and then helps the client as adult to take over the reparenting and modify the schema by meeting needs previously unmet.

The above summary of more recent developments is selective and not exhaustive, the key to our selection being those models that we have drawn upon, implicitly or explicitly, in our CBC approach.

And finally

Irrespective of our exclusion of many of the developments, we feel that the CBC model updated in this second edition will facilitate an integration of recent developments. For anyone making use of this approach we would recommend reference to the Cognitive Therapy Rating Scale (revised: Blackburn et al., 2001) and the REBT Competency Scale (Dryden et al., in press). This is based on our use of the ABC model, which can be readily adapted to include the new developments in CBT. We hope that you and your clients will have found this second edition a helpful addition to your counselling library.

APPENDICES

Client's Guides and Worksheets for CBC

These guides and worksheets are provided to help the client carry out his or her tasks, to keep a record and track his steps through the stages of CBC. There are three guides, namely Preparation Guide, Assessment and Goal Planning Guide and Options for Change Guide.

Suggestions as to how and when the counsellor can introduce the guides to the client are provided in the Task Briefings, Action Summaries and Case Examples.

Appendix 1

Preparation Guide

Dear ....

You can use this Preparation Guide and Worksheet to start to unravel a problem you might be experiencing and for which you are seeking help. These steps will help you and your counsellor to understand the problem better, help you decide if CBC is an approach which could help, and start to prepare you for it. Try to describe this problem in *general* terms – the kind of thing that typically happens. Use the steps to help you fill in the Preparation Worksheet.

After you have completed the Preparation Worksheet, your counsellor will invite you to put it to the test as a between session experiment, to help you discover for yourself whether you have negative automatic thoughts (NATs) and beliefs whenever you have a disturbed feeling. For this experiment you can use the Daily Thought Record (DTR) to record your feelings and thoughts.

Preparation Steps

- Step 1. On the Preparation Worksheet, write down an account of the main problem in general terms, in your own words and in your own way.
- Step 2. Write down the disturbed feeling you typically have when you are faced with this type of problem, and the probably unhelpful way you typically behave or want to behave when so faced.

- Step 3. Write down the kind of adverse event that typically happens when you experience this problem.
- Step 4. Write down how you would like to feel and behave when faced with this type of problem.
- Step 5. Write down the negative thoughts you might typically have when faced with this problem and which probably makes you feel and behave worse. Then write down an alternative way of thinking that would likely lead to how you want to feel and behave.

Step 1

Box A1.1

Account of the Problem in General Terms
This is my account of the problem I am experiencing, in general terms

Step 2

Box A1.2

Key Aspects of the Problem and Goal		
		Problem Emotion/ Behaviour This is how I feel and behave when faced with this type of problem

Step 3

Box A1.3

Key Aspects of the Problem and Goal		
Adverse Event This is the kind of thing that happens or might happen when I experience this problem		

Step 4

Box A1.4

Key Aspects of the Problem and Goal		
		Emotional/ Behavioural Goal This is how I would like to feel and behave when facing this type of problem

Step 5

Box A1.5

Key Aspects of the Problem and Goal		
	Biased Belief This is what I usually think about this kind of event that probably makes me feel and behave worse	
	Alternative Belief This is an alternative way of thinking that should lead to how I would like to feel and behave	

Your completed Preparation Worksheet should have all the boxes filled in as shown below. Notice the connection between the beliefs and the consequent emotions and behaviours – the b–c (belief–consequent emotion) connection.

Completed Preparation Worksheet (Steps 1 to 5 review and summary)

Box A1.6

Account of the Problem in General Terms		
Step 1: This is my account of the problem I am experiencing, in general terms		
Key Aspects of the Problem and Goal		
Step 3: Adverse Event This is the kind of thing that happens or might happen when I experience this problem	Step 5: Biased Belief This is what I usually think about this kind of event that probably makes me feel and behave worse	Step 2: Emotional/ Behavioural Problem This is how I feel and behave when faced with this type of problem
	Step 5: Alternative Belief This is an alternative way of thinking that should lead to how I would like to feel and behave	Step 4: Emotional/ Behavioural Goal This is how I would like to feel and behave when facing this type of problem

Preparation Worksheet

Name............................

Date...............................

Account of the Problem in General Terms		
Key Aspects of the Problem and Goal		
Adverse Event	Biased Beliefs	Problem Emotion/ Behaviour
	Alternative Beliefs	Emotional/Behavioural Goal

Thought-monitoring Steps

- Step 6. Between counselling sessions, try to notice each time you experience that typical disturbed feeling you wrote down on the Preparation Worksheet. This feeling may be triggered by a real event, a physical sensation, or simply during a period of worry or rumination. You can also set a time to bring the disturbed feeling to mind on purpose, in order to practise this thought-monitoring exercise.
- Step 7. While you are noticing the disturbed feeling, try to notice any negative, disturbing thoughts you might be having at the same time.
- Step 8. On the Daily Thought Record (DTR), write down the feeling in box 1, and the thoughts in box 2. Also rate the intensity of the feeling on a scale 0 to 10 where 0 = neutral and 10 = the worst ever experienced. Also note the date and time in box 3.
- Step 9. You can if you wish also make a brief note of the adverse event you had in mind (box 3), choose an alternative feeling and behaviour you would prefer (box 4) and an alternative way of thinking that would lead to your preference.

Daily Thought Record (DTR)

Adverse Event	Beliefs/NATs	Emotional Problem
3	2	1
	Alternative Belief	Emotional Goal
	5	4

Appendix 2

Assessment and Goal Planning Guide

Dear ....

Thank you for completing the Preparation Worksheet. You can now go on to use this Assessment and Goal Planning Guide and Worksheet to carry out more detailed assessment and goal planning. The worksheet is divided into a section for carrying out an ABC assessment of the problem, where A stands for your description of the adverse event, B for your beliefs about the event and C for your consequent reaction, and a section for planning the goals for counselling. Finally, you can later record the extent to which you achieve your goals.

In the Preparation Worksheet we asked you to describe the *type* of problem you wanted help with in general terms. This time try to give a *specific* example of the problem in Step 1, *and then hold this example in your mind while you complete the other steps with your counsellor's help.* As with the Preparation Guide, use these steps to help you fill in the Assessment and Goal Planning Worksheet. Use a separate worksheet for each specific problem.

Assessment Steps

- Step 1. On the Assessment and Goal Planning Worksheet (p. 258), write down a *specific* example of the problem

- Step 2. In the box headed C: Consequent Emotional/Behavioural Problem, write down the disturbed way you felt and unhelpful way you acted or had a tendency to act in the problem situation. Rate the strength or intensity of your feeling on a 0–10 scale, where 0 means you didn't feel it strongly at all, and 10 means the most intense you can imagine.
- Step 3. In the box headed A: Specific Adverse Event, describe the adverse event, namely what actually happened or you imagined might happen specifically.
- Step 4. In the box headed B^1: Probably Biased Inferences about A, write down at least one very negative and biased inference that you might have been drawing about the adverse event. Rate the extent to which you believe this inference to be true (conviction level) on a 0–10 scale where 0 means you don't think its true and 10 means you are completely convinced it is true, and 5 is a half way mark where you are evenly balanced.
- Step 5. In the box headed B^2: Extreme Evaluations about B^1, write down two or more of the listed extreme evaluations you might have made about the event, given what you were inferring about it. Rate your conviction level in this evaluation on a 0–10 scale, as above.

Goal Planning Steps

- Step 6. In the box headed Emotional/Behavioural Goal, write down how you would *like* to feel and behave, that is, not disturbed but still a negative feeling but a 'healthy' negative one and a more effective way of behaving.
- Step 7. In the box headed B^1: Alternative Unbiased Inferences, write down one or more unbiased alternatives to the biased inferences, which might contribute to your emotional/behavioural goal. Rate your conviction level as above.
- Step 8. In the box headed B^2: Realistic Evaluations, write two or more alternative evaluations under the headings listed, which might help you achieve your emotional/behavioural goal. Rate your conviction level in these evaluations.
- Step 9. Finally in the box headed A: Adverse Event Rescripted, write down how you would prefer the event to have happened, or might have happened if you had misremembered it in an unduly negative way. Rate your conviction level in this alternative description.

Goals Achievement Step

- Step 10. During the Middle Stage of Counselling, return to this worksheet and record in percentage terms the degree to which you feel you have achieved each of the goals as you work through them.

These steps are repeated below, showing where in the worksheet you need to put the answers. A fictitious case example is also provided to illustrate how to fill it in.

Step 1

Box A2.1

Specific Example of the Problem
This is my account of a *specific* example of my problem

Step 2

Box A2.2

ABC Assessment of the Specific Example			
A:	B¹:	B²:	C: Consequent Emotional/ Behavioural Problem **This is the disturbed way I felt and acted when this happened, or would feel and act if this happened**

Step 3

Box A2.3

ABC Assessment of the Specific Example			
A: Specific Adverse Event **This is what actually happened or I imagine might happen**	B¹:	B²:	C:

Step 4

Box A2.4

ABC Assessment of the Specific Example			
A:	B^1: Probably Biased Inferences about A: **These were the very negative and biased inferences I had which contributed to my disturbance** ? Biases:	B^2:	C:

Step 5

Box A2.5

ABC Assessment of the Specific Example			
A:	B^1:	B^2: Extreme Evaluations about B^2: **These were my extreme evaluations, which resulted in my disturbance:** Demand: Awfulising: LDT: Self/Other/Life downing:	C:

Step 6

Box A2.6

ABC Goals			
A:	B^1:	B^2:	C: Emotional/ Behavioural Goal **This is how I would have liked to have felt and acted when this happened**

Step 7

Box A2.7

ABC Goals			
A:	B¹Alternative: Unbiased Inferences **These are more positive and unbiased inferences that will contribute to my emotional goal**	B²:	C:

Step 8

Box A2.8

ABC Goals			
A:	B¹:	B²: Realistic Evaluations **These are more realistic evaluations that will result in my emotional goal**	C:

Step 9

Box A2.9

ABC Goals			
A: Adverse Event Rescripted **This is how I would prefer to remember or imagine the event**	B¹:	B²:	C:

Step 10

This is my record in percentage terms of the degree to which I achieved each goal.

Box A2.10

ABC Goals			
A: Adverse Event Rescripted This is how I would prefer to remember or imagine the event	B[1] Alternative: Unbiased Inferences These are more positive and unbiased inferences that will contribute to my emotional goal	B[2]: Realistic Evaluations These are more realistic evaluations that will result in my emotional goal	C: Emotional/ Behavioural Goal This is how I would have liked to have felt and acted when this happened
% Achieved:	**% Achieved:**	**% Achieved:**	**% Achieved:**

Summary of the Steps to Complete the Assessment and Goal Planning Worksheet

Box A2.11

Specific Example of the Problem			
This is my account of a *specific* example of my problem			

ABC Assessment of the Specific Example			
A: Specific Adverse Event This is what I remember actually happened or I imagine might happen specifically	B^1: Biased Inferences about A These were my very negative and probably biased inferences that contributed to my emotional and behavioural disturbance ?Biases	B^2: Extreme Evaluations about B^1 These were my rigid and extreme evaluations that directly resulted in my emotional disturbance: Demanding: Awfulising: LDT: Self/Other/Life Downing:	C: Consequent Emotional/ Behavioural Problem This is the disturbed way I felt and acted when this happened, or would feel and act if this happened

ABC Goals			
A: Adverse Event Rescripted This is how I would prefer to remember or imagine the event	B^1: Alternative Inferences These are more positive and accurate inferences that will contribute to my emotional goal	B^2: Realistic Evaluations These are realistic evaluations that will result in my emotional goal: Preferring: Non-awfulising: HDT: Self/Other/Life Acceptance:	C: Consequent Emotional/ Behavioural Goal This is how I would have liked to have felt and acted when this happened
% Achieved:	**% Achieved:**	**% Achieved:**	**% Achieved:**

Brian's Specific Example

Box A2.12

Specific Example of the Problem
Just after Christmas, in one of the small seminar rooms, I made a complete mess of a presentation I had to give as part of my course work at university. I felt absolutely awful

ABC Assessment of the Specific Example			
A: Specific Adverse Event	B[1]: Probably Biased Inferences about A	B[2]: Extreme Evaluations about B[1]	C: Consequent Emotional/ Behavioural Problem
While feeling very anxious gave a presentation to a critical and unfriendly audience of tutors and fellow students and tried to hide my anxiety symptoms	1) I'm convinced that, without safety behaviour, they would all stare at me visibly shaking, going red in the face, heart racing, and really screw up 10/10 ?Biases: Magnification, Mental Filter 2) I'm convinced that, because of 1) they all think I am a complete idiot. 10/10 ?Biases: Mind reading	Demanding: Awfulising: This is absolutely terrible LDT: I just cant bear it Self/Other/Life Downing: I really am an idiot	Feeling very anxious 9/10 Not looking at the audience, reading word for word from my script

ABC Goals			
A: Adverse Event Rescripted	B[1]: Alternative Inferences	B[2]: Realistic Evaluation	C: Consequent Emotional/ Behavioural Goal
I'd like to be able to change how I remember or imagine the event, that I didn't do too badly and the audience were reasonably understanding	1) My symptoms aren't that visible, so people may not notice so much 3/10 2) People will vary, some negative, some neutral, some even positive. 4/10	**Preferring:** I really don't want this to happen, but it might (I can't stop it by demanding) **Non-awfulising:** It's not actually awful, but is very bad **HDT:** It is hard to bear but I can just about bear it **Self/other/Life Acceptance:** I can accept being fallible like this	Healthy concern Looking at the audience, coping despite symptoms
% Achieved:	**% Achieved:**	**% Achieved:**	**% Achieved:**

Assessment and Goal Planning Worksheet

Name.......................................

Date..

Specific Example of the Problem			

ABC Assessment of the Specific Example			
A: Specific Adverse Event	B[1]: Probably Biased Inferences about A	B[2]: Extreme Evaluations about B[1] Demanding: Awfulising: LDT: Self/Other/Life Downing:	C: Consequent Emotional/ Behavioural Problem

ABC Goals			
A: Adverse Event Rescripted	B[1]: Alternative Unbiased Inferences	B[2]: Realistic Evaluations: Preferring: Non-awfulising: HDT: Self/Other/Life Acceptance:	Emotional/ Behavioural Goals

ABC Diary Steps

After your session on ABC Assessment, your counsellor will suggest you start to use this ABC Diary, instead of the DTR, to monitor your thoughts in between sessions. As you and your counsellor work through the CBC tasks, you will be invited to add these tasks to your homework, so not only monitoring your thoughts, feelings and behaviour, but changing them, as you progress towards achieving your goals.

- Step 1. Each day between counselling sessions, again try to notice each time you experience the disturbed feeling you wrote down on the Assessment Worksheet. This feeling may be triggered by a real event, a physical sensation, or simply during a period of worry or rumination. You can also set a time to bring the disturbed feeling to mind on purpose, in order to practice this thought monitoring exercise.
- Step 2. While you are noticing the disturbed feeling, try to notice any negative inferences and evaluations you might be having at the same time.
- Step 3. On the ABC Diary, write down the feeling in the C box, and any inferences and evaluations you became aware of in the B box. Also rate the intensity of the feeling on a scale 0 to 10 where 0 = neutral and 10 = the worst ever experienced. Also rate the level of conviction you have in each belief on a similar scale where 0 = you don't believe it at all and 10 = you are completely convinced.
- Step 4. Make a brief note of the adverse event you had in mind (or was happening) in the A box.
- Step 5. *Carry out this step only after your session with your counsellor on how to construct ABC goals.* When you are carrying out your thought monitoring (steps 1 to 4), also choose and note down a healthy emotion and helpful behaviour that you would prefer, and an alternative inference and evaluation that would help you feel and act that way.
- Step 6. *Carry out this step only after your session on challenging and changing inferences.* When you carry out your thought monitoring and notice a negative biased inference comes to mind, and you choose an alternative unbiased inference, weigh the evidence for each, and also look for an opportunity to put them to the test. Your counsellor will help you choose a test to try. Mark down any percentage change in level of conviction.
- Step 7. *Carry out this step only after your session on challenging and changing your extreme evaluations.* When you carry out your thought monitoring, and notice an extreme evaluation comes to mind, and you choose an alternative realistic evaluation, try one or more of the following: dispute and

compare the two beliefs for validity, practice REI using the two beliefs, carry out a shame attacking exercise. Your counsellor will guide you in these tasks. Mark down any percentage change in level of conviction.

- Step 8. *Carry out this step only after your session on changing distressing memories.* When you carry out your thought monitoring, and notice a distressing image comes to mind, try to bring to mind the rescripted image that you practiced in session with your counsellor. Write down the rescripted image, and also any change in conviction.

ABC Diary

ABC Assessment		
A: Specific Adverse Event	B^1 and B^2 Beliefs: Dysfunctional, Probably Biased Inferences and Extreme Evaluations	C: Consequent Emotional/ Behavioural Problem
ABC Goals		
A: Adverse Event Rescripted	B^1 and B^2 Beliefs: Functional Unbiased Alternative Inferences and Realistic Evaluations)	C: Emotional/Behavioural Goal
% Achieved:	% B^{1}Achieved: % B^2 Achieved:	% Achieved:

Appendix 3

Options for Change Guide

Dear ....

Thank you for completing the Assessment and Goal Planning Guide, in which you carried out a detailed assessment of the As, Bs and Cs of your prioritised problem, and the A, B and C goals for change.

Now that you have identified your beliefs (B) and the consequent way you feel and react (C) to the adverse event (A), and the goals for change, you can now move on to putting the change options into practice, which should result in new and better ways of responding to your problem.

We describe first the Inference Change Option, which has two parts, Weigh the Evidence (Steps 1 to 5), and Test your Inferences in a Behavioural Experiment (Steps 6 and 7). Next we describe the Evaluations Change Option, and finally the Imagery Change Option. We provide worksheets where needed, together with guidance steps. You and your counsellor may not consider it necessary to complete all of the options and steps, nor to undertake them in the order presented here.

Inference Change Option Steps

Weigh the Evidence

- Step 1. Take the Inference Change Worksheet and copy across your answers from the Assessment Worksheet all the information asked for in the boxes. This will include the A (Adverse Event), B^1 (Probably Biased Inference) and

Alternative Inference, the C Problem and C Goal. Box A3.1 (p. 263) shows an example of the Inference Change Worksheet as you should fill it in.

- Step 2. Try to think of all the evidence you can that would support your Probably Biased Inference (B^1) and write the list in the column alongside B^1. Box A3.2 (p. 264) shows an example of the Inference Change Worksheet as you should fill it in.
- Step 3. Try to think of all the evidence you can that would support the Unbiased Inference (B^1 Alternative), and write the list in the column alongside the alternative inference.
- Step 4. Look at the two lists and, with the counsellor's help, question the quality of the evidence. Is it reliable evidence? Would it stand up in a court of law? If the evidence doesn't stand up to scrutiny, cross it out.
- Step 5. Weigh up the two lots of evidence carefully and consider which of the two inferences has the strongest support. Re-rate your level of conviction in each inference and re-rate the intensity of your feelings in the C boxes. Has there been a real change? Box A3.3 (p. 265) shows an example of the Inference Change Worksheet as you should fill it in.

Testing the Evidence

- Step 6. If your conviction hasn't changed substantially as a result of weighing the evidence, you may choose to go on to test the evidence in a real-life behavioural experiment. With your counsellor's help, you design and carry out an experiment in which you will experience *dis*confirmation of your inference (B^1) and confirmation of the alternative. Write down the result of the experiment.
- Step 7. After your experience following the experiment, again rate your level of conviction in each inference and re-rate the intensity of your feelings. Has there been a change this time? Box A3.4 (p. 266) shows an example of the Inference Change Worksheet as you should fill it in.
- Step 8. When you think you have achieved your inference change goal and, partly because of that, your emotional/behavioural goal, record this on your Assessment and Goal Planning Worksheet.

Box A3.1   Step 1

	AB[1]C Assessment of the Specific Example	
A: Specific Adverse Event **This is what I remember actually happened or might happen**	B[1]: Probably Biased Inferences about A **This is one of my probably biased inferences about the adverse event which contributes to my disturbed feeling and behaviour**	C: Consequent Emotional/ Behavioural Problem **This is the disturbed way I felt and acted when the adverse event happened, or would feel and act if this happened**
	ABC Goals	
	B[1] Alternative: Unbiased Inference **This is an alternative unbiased inference**	C: Consequent Emotional/ Behavioural Goal **This is how I would have liked to have felt and acted when this happened**

Box A3.2 Step 2

AB¹C Assessment of the Specific Example		
A: Specific Adverse Event This is what I remember actually happened or might happen	B¹ Probably Biased Inferences about A This is one of my probably biased inferences about the adverse event which contributes to my disturbed feeling and behaviour	Evidence for B¹ **This is the list of evidence that convinces me that my inference (B¹) is true**	C: Consequent Emotional/Behavioural Problem This is the disturbed way I felt and acted when the adverse event happened, or would feel and act if this happened
ABC Goals		
	B¹ Alternative: Unbiased Inferences This is an alternative unbiased inference		C: Consequent Emotional/Behavioural Goal This is how I would have liked to have felt and acted when this happened

Box A3.3   Steps 3–5

AB¹C Assessment of the Specific Example		
A: Specific Adverse Event This is what I remember actually happened or might happen	B¹: Probably Biased Inference about A This is one of my probably biased inferences about the adverse event which contributes to my disturbed feeling and behaviour	Evidence for B¹: This is the list of evidence that convinces me that my inference (B¹) is true	C: Consequent Emotional/ Behavioural Problem This is the disturbed way I felt and acted when the adverse event happened, or would feel and act if this happened
ABC Goals		
	B¹ Alternative: Unbiased Inferences This is an alternative unbiased inference	**Evidence for Alternative:** **This is the list of evidence for the alternative and against my probably biased inference**	C: Consequent Emotional/ Behavioural Goal This is how I would have liked to have felt and acted when this happened

Box A3.4 Steps 6–7

AB¹C Assessment of the Specific Example		
A: Specific Adverse Event This is what I remember actually happened or might happen	B¹: Probably Biased Inferences about A This is one of my probably biased inferences about the adverse event which contributes to my disturbed feeling and behaviour	Evidence for B¹: This is the list of evidence that convinces me that my inference (B¹) is true	C: Consequent Emotional/Behavioural Problem This is the disturbed way I felt and acted when the adverse event happened, or would feel and act if this happened
ABC Goals		
	B¹ Alternative: Unbiased Inferences This is an alternative unbiased inference	Evidence for Alternative: This is the list of evidence for the alternative and against my probably biased belief	**Behavioural Test of Inference and Result:** **This is the result of the behavioural experiment designed to show the alternative unbiased inference is true and the B¹ inference is false**
			C: Consequent Emotional/Behavioural Goal This is how I would have liked to have felt and acted when this happened

Box A3.5 Case Example 1: John

A: Specific Adverse Event	B¹: Probably Biased Inferences	Evidence for B¹	C: Consequent Emotional/Behavioural Problem
Got dizzy and light headed when in supermarket yesterday	Feeling dizzy and light headed means I have heart disease and might die	I get dizzy and light headed sometimes Dizziness and light headedness is evidence for heart disease They have made a mistake in health check	Panicked and had to sit down

ABC Goals			
	B¹ Alternative: Unbiased Inferences	Evidence for Alternative:	Behavioural Test of Inferences Result:	C: Consequent Emotional/Behavioural Problem
	Feeling dizzy and light headed does not mean I have heart disease	Dizziness and light headedness are not evidence for heart disease but for over breathing, which is harmless A mistake is very unlikely because I have had it done several times	Breathed rapidly for several minutes to show this is the cause of my dizziness and light headedness and not heart disease	Remain calm, just carry on

Box A3.6   Case Example 2: Brian

A: Specific Adverse Event	B¹: Probably Biased Inferences	Evidence for B¹:	C: Consequent Emotional/Behavioural Problem
While feeling very anxious gave a presentation to a critical audience of tutors and fellow students and tried to hide my anxiety	1) I'm convinced they are all staring at me shaking like a leaf, going bright red in the face, heart racing fit to burst 2) I'm convinced that because of (1) they all think I am a complete idiot	1) If I feel anxious I just know it's a dead give-away, and everybody will be looking at that 2) I know that's how they think They keep asking me to speak up and talking among themselves I can feel their eyes boring into me	Feeling very anxious, not looking at the audience, reading word for word from my script
	Unbiased inferences	Evidence for Alternative:	C: Consequent Emotional/Behavioural Goal
	1) If my symptoms aren't that bad, people may not notice so much 2) If people notice they are probably sympathetic and interested	1) I have no evidence that they notice. I never look at them 2) I cannot read their minds Their behaviour means I am speaking too quietly and want to hear what I have to say	Feel healthy concern, look at and engage audience, ad lib from memory
		Behavioural Test of Inferences Result:	
		1) Looked at the audience and 2) didn't use 'safety behaviours' to hide anxiety Showed my biased inferences were untrue and the alternative inferences were true	

Inference Change Worksheet

	AB¹C Assessment of the Specific Example	
A: Specific Adverse Event	B¹: Probably Biased Inferences about A	C: Consequent Emotional/Behavioural Problem
	Evidence for B¹:	

ABC Goals		
	B¹ Alternative: Unbiased Inferences	C: Consequent Emotional/Behavioural Goal
	Evidence for Alternative:	Behavioural Test of Inferences Result:

Evaluation Change through Disputing Steps

Although your very negative evaluations are distressing, they probably seem very valid to you and so you may think you don't have much choice but to go on believing them. In this task we show you how you can challenge them and change them and make a fundamental difference to how you feel.

- Step 1. Take the Evaluation Change Worksheet and copy across your answers from the Assessment Worksheet all the information asked for in the boxes. This will include the A (Adverse event), B^1 (Probably Biased Inference) and Alternative Unbiased Inference, B2 (Extreme Evaluations) and Non-extreme Alternative Evaluations, and the C Problem and C Goal.
- Step 2. With the counsellor's help, dispute your *demanding* and your *preferring* evaluations together.

  ○ First, ask yourself: which of these two beliefs is more *realistically* true? Place a tick against the one that you consider more true, and a cross against the other one, plus any brief comments.
  ○ Second, ask yourself: which of these two beliefs is more *useful* or *helpful* to me? Again place a tick against the one that is and a cross against the one that isn't.
  ○ Third, ask yourself: which of these two beliefs makes most *logical sense* to me? Again place a tick next to the one that does, and a cross next to the one that doesn't.

- Step 3. With the counsellor's help dispute your *awfulising* and your *non-awfulising* evaluations together, using the same three disputing questions above. Place ticks and crosses against your choices.
- Step 4. Again with the counsellor's help, dispute your *low discomfort tolerance* (LDT) and your *high discomfort tolerance* (HDT) evaluations together, using the three disputing questions. Place ticks and crosses as before against your choices.
- Step 5. Finally with the counsellor's help dispute your 'self' or 'other' or 'life' *depreciation* and your 'self' or 'other' or 'life' *acceptance* evaluations, again using the three questions. Place a tick and a cross as before against your choice.
- Step 6. Weigh up the effect of all your disputes on the validity of your extreme evaluations compared with the alternative evaluations. Rate your overall conviction in each set of evaluations on a 0–10 scale (where 0 = totally unconvinced and 10 = totally convinced), and compare this with the rating you gave originally. Has there been a change?
- Step 7. When you think you have achieved to some degree your evaluation change goal, and because of that your emotional/behavioural goal, record this on your Assessment and Goal Planning Worksheet as a percentage where 100% is totally achieved, 50% half-way achieved and so on.

Step 1

On page 272 (Box A3.7) is an example of the Evaluation Change Worksheet as you should fill it in Step 1, namely the emboldened sections.

Step 2 to 6

On page 273 (Box A3.8) is an example of the Evaluation Change Worksheet as you should fill it in Steps 2 to 6, namely the emboldened sections.

Evaluation Change through Imagery Steps

By now you may be able to doubt your unhelpful evaluations in your head by disputing them, but you don't feel any different, so what good is it just to doubt them? This time we show you how you can experience how switching to the alternative evaluations will change how you feel.

- Step 7. Bring to mind as vividly as you can the adverse event A, and your unhealthy negative emotion (e.g. anxiety) and behaviour (e.g. avoidance) C. Your unhelpful beliefs (B^2) should automatically come into your mind without even trying.
- Step 8. Change your negative emotion from unhealthy to healthy, e.g. anxiety to healthy concern. Try to do this not by changing the situation A in your mind, but by changing your irrational beliefs (B^2) to the rational alternatives. Tell your counsellor any difficulties you had in doing this, and your counsellor will coach you in how to make this exercise realistic and effective.
- Step 9. Practise this exercise three times a day at home between counselling sessions and keep a record of how you get on with each part:

  - whether you can bring the situation (A) vividly to mind,
  - whether you can really feel the unhealthy emotion (C),
  - whether the irrational beliefs (B) automatically come into your mind,
  - whether you manage to change the emotion, e.g. from anxiety to concern,
  - whether you changed it by changing from irrational beliefs (B^2) to the rational alternatives, e.g. from 'I would feel completely useless if I failed at this' to 'I would completely accept myself even if I failed'.

Box A3.7

	AB²C Assessment of the Specific Example					
A: Specific Adverse Event

This is what I remember actually happened or might happen | B¹: Probably Biased Inferences about A

This is one of my probably biased inferences about the adverse event which contributes to my disturbed feeling and behaviour | B²: Extreme Evaluations

These were my rigid and extreme evaluations that directly resulted in my emotional disturbance:

Demand:

Awfulising:

LDT:

Self/Other/Life Downing: | True?
✓ ✗ | Useful?
✓ ✗ | Logical?
✓ ✗ | C: Consequent Emotional/ Behavioural Problem

This is the disturbed way I felt and acted when the adverse event happened, or would feel and act if this happened |
| | | ABC Goals | | | | |
| | B¹ Alternative: Unbiased Inferences

This is my/the counsellor's alternative unbiased inference | B² Flexible Alternative

These are realistic evaluations that will result in my emotional goal:

Preference:

Non-awfulising:

HDT:

Self/Other/Life Acceptance | True?
✓ ✗ | Useful?
✓ ✗ | Logical?
✓ ✗ | C: Consequent Emotional/ Behavioural Goal

This is how I would have liked to have felt and acted when this happened |

Box A3.8

	AB²C Assessment of the Specific Example					
A: Specific Adverse Event This is what I remember actually happened or might happen	B¹: Probably Biased Inferences about A This is one of my probably biased inferences about the adverse event which contributes to my disturbed feeling and behaviour	B²: Extreme Evaluations These were my rigid and extreme evaluations that directly resulted in my emotional disturbance: Demand: Awfulising: LDT: Self/Other/Life Downing:	**True?** ✓ x ✓ or x ✓ or x ✓ or x ✓ or x	**Useful?** ✓ x ✓ or x ✓ or x ✓ or x ✓ or x	**Logical?** ✓ x ✓ or x ✓ or x ✓ or x ✓ or x	C: Consequent Emotional/Behavioural Problem This is the disturbed way I felt and acted when the adverse event happened, or would feel and act if this happened
		ABC Goals				
	B¹ Alternative: Unbiased Inferences This is my alternative unbiased inference	B² Flexible Alternative These are realistic evaluations that will result in my emotional goal: Preference: Non-awfulising: HDT: Self/Other/Life Acceptance:	**True?** ✓ x ✓ or x ✓ or x ✓ or x ✓ or x	**Useful?** ✓ x ✓ or x ✓ or x ✓ or x ✓ or x	**Logical?** ✓ x ✓ or x ✓ or x ✓ or x ✓ or x	C: Consequent Emotional/Behavioural Goal This is how I would have liked to have felt and acted when this happened

Evaluation Change Worksheet

A: Specific Adverse Event	B¹: Probably Biased Inferences about A	B²: Extreme Evaluations	True? ✓✗	Useful? ✓✗	Logical? ✓✗	C: Consequent Emotional/ Behavioural Problem

AB²C Assessment of the Specific Example

Demand:

Awfulising:

LDT:

Self/Other/Life Downing:

ABC Goals

B¹ Alternative: Unbiased Inferences	B² Flexible Alternative evaluations	True? ✓✗	Useful? ✓✗	Logical? ✓✗	C: Consequent Emotional/ Behavioural Goal

Preference:

Non-awfulising:

HDT:

Self/Other/Life Acceptance:

Evaluation Change through Behavioural Exposure Steps

You have hopefully now made good progress in changing your beliefs and your feelings for the better. Now we look at how to bring these changes more into your ordinary life.

- Step 10. Plan as a homework task to face the problem situation you brought for counselling help.
- Step 11. Go through a rehearsal in your mind like you did in steps 7 to 9, of entering the event and being mindfully aware of your irrational beliefs and feelings. Then go into the actual situation and do the same thing – be mindfully aware of your irrational beliefs and feelings and action tendencies.
- Step 12. Just as you did in steps 7 to 9, change your feeling from the unhealthy to the healthy, e.g. anxiety to concern. Remember to do this by changing your beliefs, from the irrational to the rational.
- Step 13. Even if you can't change the emotion very easily, keep rehearsing at least one of the rational beliefs, e.g. 'I completely accept myself despite … feeling anxious, etc.', and also act according to this self-acceptance, so staying in the situation, standing tall, looking at people rather than hiding away.
- Step 14. When you think you have achieved to some degree your evaluation change goal and your consequent emotional/behavioural goal, record this on your Assessment and Goal Planning Worksheet as a percentage, where 100% is totally achieved, 50% half achieved and so on.

Steps for Cognitive Change Option through Imagery Rescripting

Despite all the work you have done on changing the beliefs that cause you to be distressed in your problem situation, you still get so distressed when it comes to facing the situation that you still don't face it. This may be because the traumatic event and toxic beliefs are actually locked up inside your memory of the event. There is a way of unlocking it and changing it called imagery rescripting, and through this method you may be able to achieve your goal of rescripting your memory of the adverse event in the preferred way you recorded on the Assessment and Goal Planning Worksheet. The following are the steps for carrying out one version of imagery rescripting:

- Step 1. With the counsellor's close guidance and support, try as best you can to go back and 'relive' the specific adverse event from beginning to end, and give an account as if you are actually there.
- Step 2. When you come to the worst, most distressing bits, or 'hotspots', try to slow down and report what you are feeling and seeing, as well as your probably very negative beliefs about it.
- Step 3. Once out of reliving, work on these hotspots with your counsellor just as you have now learned to do in CBC – get the ABCs, challenge and change the Bs and make a note of your new, helpful, unbiased benign beliefs. Also make a note of any inaccuracies and new information that was absent from the memory image.
- Step 4. Rehearse the new information and beliefs so that you are thoroughly familiar with them, then again go back into reliving and with your counsellor's guidance, pause at the hotspots and introduce the new information and beliefs.
- Step 5. Make sure your narrative is tape or digitally recorded, and then play the tape a number of times as homework, in order to consolidate the changes, each time rating the intensity of affect on the 0–10 on a subjective units of distress (SUDS) scale.
- Step 6. When you think you have achieved your goal of 'rescripting' your memory of the adverse event (A) and your consequent emotional/behavioural goal (C), record these on your Assessment and Goal Planning Worksheet, and also compare your rescripted memory with the one you previously wrote down as your goal.

Homework Skills Monitoring Form for the Counsellor

Listen to the recording of your therapy session and circle 'Yes', 'No' or 'N/A' (Not Appropriate) for each item. For every item circled 'No', write down in the space provided what you would have done differently given hindsight and what you would have needed to change in order to have circled the item 'Yes'.

1. Did I use a term for homework assignments that was acceptable to the client?

   Yes   No   N/A

2. Did I properly negotiate the homework assignment with the client (as opposed to telling him/her what to do or accepting uncritically his/her suggestion)?

   Yes   No   N/A

3. Was the homework assignment expressed clearly?

   Yes   No   N/A

4. Did I ensure that the client understood the homework assignment?

   Yes   No   N/A

5. Was the homework assignment relevant to my client's therapy goals?

   Yes   No   N/A

6. Did I help the client understand the relevance of the homework assignment to his/her therapy goals?

   Yes   No   N/A

7. Did the homework assignment follow logically from the work I did with the client in the session?

   Yes   No   N/A

8. Was the type of homework assignment I negotiated with the client relevant to the stage reached by the two of us on his/her target problem?

   Yes   No   N/A

9. Did I employ the 'challenging, but not overwhelming' principle in negotiating the homework assignment?

   Yes   No   N/A

10. Did I introduce and explain the 'no lose' concept of homework assignments?

   Yes   No   N/A

11. Did I ensure that the client had the necessary skills to carry out the homework assignment?

   Yes   No   N/A

12. Did I ensure that the client believed that he/she could do the homework assignment?

    Yes   No   N/A

13. Did I allow sufficient time in the session to negotiate the homework assignment properly?

    Yes   No   N/A

14. Did I elicit a firm commitment from the client that he/she would carry out the homework assignment?

    Yes   No   N/A

15. Did I help the client to specify when, where and how often he/she would carry out the homework assignment?

    Yes   No   N/A

16. Did I encourage my client to make a written note of the homework assignment and its relevant details?

    Yes   No   N/A

17. Did the client and I both retain a copy of this written note?

    Yes   No   N/A

18. Did I elicit from the client potential obstacles to homework completion?

    Yes   No   N/A

19. Did I help the client to deal in advance with any potential obstacles that he/she disclosed?

    Yes   No   N/A

20. Did I help the client to rehearse the homework assignment in the session?

    Yes   No   N/A

21. Did I use the principle of rewards and penalties with the client?

    Yes   No   N/A

References

American Psychiatric Association (APA) (1994). *Diagnostic and Statistical Manual of Mental Disorders*, 4th edn. Washington, DC: American Psychiatric Association.

Averill, J.R. (1982). *Anger and Aggression: An Essay on Emotion*. New York: Springer.

Beck, A.T. (1967). *Depression: Clinical, Experimental and Theoretical Aspects*. New York: Harper and Row.

Beck, A.T. (1976). *Cognitive Therapy and the Emotional Disorders*. London: Penguin.

Beck, A.T. (1999). *Prisoners of Hate: The Cognitive Basis of Anger, Hostility And Violence*. New York: HarperCollins.

Beck, A.T. and Emery, G. (1985). *Anxiety Disorders and Phobias*. New York: Basic Books.

Beck, A.T., Brown, G. and Steer, R.A. (1996). *Beck Depression Inventory II manual*. San Antonio, TX: The Psychological Corporation.

Beck, A.T., Epstein, N., Brown, G. and Steer, R.A. (1988). An inventory for measuring clinical anxiety: psychometric properties. *Journal of Consulting and Clinical Psychology*, 56, 893–7.

Beck, A.T., Rush, A.J., Shaw, B.F. and Emery, G. (1979). *Cognitive Therapy of Depression*. New York: Guilford.

Beck, J. (1995). *Cognitive Therapy: Basics and Beyond*. New York: Guilford.

Bennett-Levy, J., Butler, G., Fennell, M. and Hackman, A. (2004). *Oxford Guide to Behavioural Experiments in Cognitive Therapy*. Oxford: Oxford University Press.

Blackburn, I., James, I.A., Milne, D.L., Baker, C., Standant, S., Garland, A. and Reichelt, F.K. (2001). The revised Cognitive Therapy Scale (CTS-R): psychometric properties. *Behavioural and Cognitive Psychotherapy*, 29, 431–46.

Bordin, E.S. (1979). The generalisation of the psychoanalytic concept of the working alliance. *Psychotherapy*, 16, 252–60.

Bowlby, J. (1969/1982). *Attachment and Loss, Vol. 1: Attachment*. New York: Basic Books.

Brewin, C.R. (1989). Cognitive change processes in psychotherapy. *Psychological Review*, 96, 379–94.

Brewin, C.R., Dalgleish, T. and Joseph, S.A. (1996). Dual representation theory of posttraumatic stress disorder. *Psychological Review*, 103(4): 670–86.

Burns, D. (1999). *The Feeling Good Handbook*. New York: Plume.

Butler, G., Fennell, M. and Hackmann, A. (2008). *Cognitive Behavioral Therapy for Anxiety Disorders*. New York: Guilford Press.

Byrne, S., Birchwood, M., Trower, P. and Meaden, A. (2006). *Cognitive Behaviour Therapy for Command Hallucinations*. London: Routledge.

Chadwick, P. (2006). *Person-Based Cognitive Therapy for Distressing Psychosis*. Chichester: Wiley.

Chadwick, P., Birchwood, M. and Trower, P. (1996). *Cognitive Therapy for Delusions, Voices and Paranoia*. Chichester: Wiley.

Clark, D.M. (1986). A cognitive approach to panic. *Behaviour Research and Therapy*, 24, 461–70.

Clark, D.M. and Wells, A. (1995). A cognitive model of social phobia. In R. Heimberg, M. Liebowitz, D.A. Hope and F.R. Schneider (eds) *Social Phobia: Diagnosis, Assessment and Treatment*. New York: Guilford Press.

DiGiuseppe, R. and Tafrate, R. (2007). *Understanding Anger Disorders*. Oxford: Oxford University Press.

Dryden, W. (2006). *Getting Started with REBT*. London: Sage.

Dryden, W. (2007). *Overcoming Hurt*. London: Sheldon Press.

Dryden, W. (2008). *Rational Emotive Behaviour Therapy, Distinctive Features*. London: Routledge.

Dryden, W. (2009). *Understanding Emotional Problems: The REBT Perspective*. London: Routledge.

Dryden, W. and Neenan, M. (2004). *Rational Emotive Behavioural Counselling in Action*, 3rd edn. London: Sage.

Dryden, W., Beal, D., Jones, J. and Trower, P. (in press). The REBT Competency Scale for clinical and research applications. *Journal of Rational-Emotive and Cognitive-Behavioural Therapy*.

Ellis, A. (1963). *Reason and Emotion in Psychotherapy*. Secaucus, NJ: Lyle Stuart.

Ellis, A. (1994). *Reason and Emotion in Psycho-therapy*, revised and updated. New York: Birch Lane.

Frijda, N.H. (1986). *The Emotions*. London: Cambridge University Press.

Gilbert, P. (2007). *Psychotherapy and Counselling for Depression*, 3rd edn. London: Sage.

Gilbert, P. (2009). *The Compassionate Mind*. London: Constable.

Grey, N. (ed.) (2009). *A Casebook of Cognitive Therapy for Traumatic Stress Reactions*. Hove: Routledge.

Grey, N., Young, K. and Holmes, E. (2002). Cognitive restructuring within reliving: A treatment for peritraumatic emotional 'hotspots' in post-traumatic stress disorder. *Behavioural and Cognitive Psychotherapy*, 30, 37–56.

Hareli, S. and Hess, U. (2008). The role of causal attribution in related social emotions elicited in reaction to others' feedback about failure. *Cognition and Emotion*, 22, 862–80.

Harrington, N. (2006). Frustration intolerance beliefs: their relationship with depression, anxiety, and anger, in a clinical population. *Cognitive Therapy and Research*, 30, 699–709.

Harrop, C. and Trower, P. (2003). *Why Does Schizophrenia Develop at Late Adolescence?* Chichester: Wiley.

Hayes, S.C., Strosahl, K. and Wilson, K.G. (1999). *Acceptance and Commitment Therapy*. New York: Guilford.

Jahoda, A., Dagnan, D., Stenfert Kroese, B., Pert, C. and Trower, P. (2009). Cognitive behavioural therapy: from face to face interaction to a broader contextual understanding of change. *Journal of Intellectual Disability Research*, 53, 759–71.

James, W. (1890). *The Principles of Psychology*. New York: Henry Holt and Company.

Kabat-Zinn, J. (1990). *Full Castrophe Living: Using the Wisdom of your Body and Mind to Face Stress, Pain, and Illness*. New York: Dell.

Kuyken, W., Padesky, C.A. and Dudley, R. (2009). *Collaborative Case Conceptualization*. New York: Guilford Press.

Leahy, R.L. (2003). *Cognitive Therapy Techniques: A Practitioner's Guide*. New York: Guilford.

Leary, M.R., Springer, C., Negel, L., Ansell, E. and Evans, K. (1998). The causes, phenomenology, and consequences of hurt feelings. *Journal of Personality and Social Psychology*, 74, 1225–37.

Leary, M.R. and Springer, C. (2000). Hurt feelings: The neglected emotion. In R.M. Kowalski (ed.) *Behaving Badly: Aversive Behaviors in Interpersonal Relationships* (pp. 151–75). Washington, DC: American Psychological Association.

Mansell, W. (2008a). The seven c's of cbt: a consideration of the future challenges for cognitive behaviour therapy. *Behavioural and Cognitive Psychotherapy*, 36, 641–9.

Mansell, W. (2008b). Keep it simple – the transdiagnostic approach to CBT. *International Journal of Cognitive Therapy* – Special Issue on Transdiagnostic Approaches to CBT, 1, 179–80.

Mearns, D. and Thorne, R. (2007). *Person-centred Counselling in Action*, 3rd edn. London: Sage.

Moorey, S. (2010). The six cycles maintenance model: growing a 'vicious flower' for depression. *Behavioural and Cognitive Psychotherapy*, 38, 173–84.

Novaco, R.W. (1994). Anger as a risk factor for violence among the mentally disordered. In J. Monahan and H. Steadman (eds) *Violence and Mental Disorder: Developments in Risk Assessment*. Chicago: University of Chicago Press.

Oatley, K. and Duncan, E. (1994). The experience of emotions in everyday life. *Cognition and Emotion*, 8(4), 369–81.

Power, M. and Dalgleish, T. (1997). *Cognition and Emotion: From Order to Disorder*. Hove: Psychology Press.

Prochaska, J. and DiClemente, C. (1984). *The Trans-theoretical Approach: Crossing the Traditional Boundaries*. Homewood, IL: Dow Jones Irwen.

Rogers, C. (1951). *Client Centered Therapy*. Boston: Houghton Mifflin.

Rogers, C. (1961). *On Becoming a Person*. London: Constable.

Salkovskis, P.M. (1991). The importance of behaviour in the maintenance of anxiety and panic: a cognitive account. *Behavioural Psychotherapy*, 19, 6–19.

Sartre, J.-P. (1957). *Being and Nothingness*: London: Methuen.

Scherer, K. (2009). The dynamic architecture of emotion: Evidence for the component process model. *Cognition and Emotion*, 23, 1307–51.

Scott, M.J. (2009). *Simply Effective Cognitive Behaviour Therapy*. Hove: Routledge.

Segal, Z.V., Williams, J.M.G. and Teasdale, J.D. (2002). *Mindfulness-based Cognitive Therapy for Depression*. New York: Guilford.

Stopa, L. (ed.) (2009). *Imagery and the Threatened Self*. Hove: Routledge.

Trower, P. (in press). Cognitive behaviour therapy theory. In W. Dryden et al. (eds) *Handbook of Cognitive Behaviour Therapy*. London: Sage.

Trower, P., Casey, A. and Dryden, W. (1988). *Cognitive-Behavioural Counselling in Action*. London: Sage.

van de Ven, N., Zeelenberg, M. and Pieters, R. (2009). Levelling up and down: The experiences of benign and malicious envy. *Emotion*, 9(3), 419–29.

Wells, A. (1997). *Cognitive Therapy of Anxiety Disorders*. Chichester: Wiley.

Wells, A. (2009). *Metacognitive Therapy for Anxiety and Depression*. New York: Guilford.

Wessler, R.A. and Wessler, R.L. (1980). *The Principles and Practice of Rational-Emotive Therapy*. San Francisco: Jossey–Bass.

Williams, M., Teasale, J., Segal, Z. and Kabat-Zinn, J. (2007). *The Mindful Way Through Depression*. New York: Guilford.

Young, J.E., Klosko, J.S. and Weishaar, M.E. (2003). *Schema Therapy: A Practitioner's Guide*. New York: Guilford.

Index

Preparation Guide 38, *243–8*
  preparation (steps 1–5) *243–6*
    worksheet 62, *247*
  thought-monitoring steps
    (6–10) *248*
preparation stage
  overview of 25, 30, 34, 151
  see also Preparation Guide; problems
problems, client *243–6*
  clarifying first presenting problem
    50–1, **52–3**
    A–C thinking and nature of
      problem 51–2
    case example 53–5
  further problems 58, *59*
    case example 59
  specific problem assessed *see* cognitive
    assessment

questionnaires 37–8
questions
  disputing 126–7, **133–4**
  open and closed 47

rational emotive imagery 128–30,
  132, **134**
  case example 137–9
REBT Competency Scale 240
referral *see* screening
reflection of feeling 47
relapse *see* setbacks
review and revision 149–50
rules of living, extreme 81
  alternatives to 99–100
  and depression 185, 189

safety-seeking behaviour 75, 114
  and behavioural experiments 115–16
Schema Therapy 239–40
screening and referral 35, **39**
  case example 39–40
  questionnaires and biographical
    information 37–8
  screening criteria 35–7
self-acceptance 100
self-blame 207, 212

self-counselling, client 158–61, **161–2**
self-depreciation 81, 182
self-help book 79
self-monitoring 63–4, 67, 83–4, *248*
self-rating, global 189, 190–2
Session and Homework Report Form
  150, 154
sessions
  frequency and length of 68
  initial *see* first meeting
  session report form 154
  structure and routine *see* working through
setbacks, post-termination 162–3, **163**
  case example 163–5
shame and guilt 13, 206–18
  core treatments 214–18
  key elements 213–14
    activating event/adversity 208–10
    beliefs/inferences and evulations
      210–13
    consequences/action tendencies
      207–8
shame-attacking exercise 131–2, **134**,
  139–40
SMART criteria 70
sorrow 221
stages of CBC, overview of 25–6, 28–30
sulking 220
summarising 47–8

tasks *see* counsellor tasks
termination, preparation for 156–7
  case example 157–8
  coaching for self-counselling 158–61,
    161–2
  last minute problems 165–8, **168**
    case example 168–70
  setbacks 162–3, **163**
    case example 163–5
therapeutic relationship
  and anger 203–4
  clarifying 40–1
  establishing a bond 44–8, **46–8**
    accurate empathy 44–5
    genuineness 45–6
    unconditional positive regard 45